RISE

RISE

Surviving and Thriving after Trauma

SIAN WILLIAMS

First published in Great Britain in 2016
by Weidenfeld & Nicolson

3 5 7 9 10 8 6 4

A CIP catalogue record for this book
is available from the British Library.

HB ISBN 978 1 474 60268 6
TPB 978 1 474 60269 3

Typeset by Input Data Services Ltd, Bridgwater, Somerset

Printed and bound by CPI Group (UK) Ltd, Croydon, CR0 4YY

Weidenfeld & Nicolson
The Orion Publishing Group Ltd
Carmelite House, 50 Victoria Embankment
London, EC4Y 0DZ

An Hachette UK Company

www.orionbooks.co.uk

To Paul and the children:
Joss, Alex, Emily, Seth and Eve

CONTENTS

PREFACE

A week after celebrating my fiftieth birthday and just before we were due to move house, I was diagnosed with cancer. A regular runner, green tea drinker and the daughter of a no-nonsense medic who was rarely allowed to be ill, the news seemed both nonsensical and a very poor piece of timing. Disease suddenly pitched me into a hospital theatre, where two surgeons took away my breasts, along with any naïve belief in healthy infallibility.

As the tissue and lymph nodes were examined under microscopes, I peered into what seemed like a maelstrom of emotion. Fearful, hopeful, numb, baffled – it often felt like a grinding, whirling vortex of confusion, sucking me under without warning before spitting me out, gasping for breath.

I began writing. Not for me or for anyone else to read, but just to maintain sanity during some switchback times. I didn't visit my thoughts on those I loved, because my family was already in a state of heightened anxiety and exasperated impotence. Spewing them onto paper seemed safest. My diaries were where I could scream, or laugh, or simply observe.

Despite the shock, I consider myself very lucky. I was told from the beginning that my cancer would be 'breast-threatening, rather than life-threatening'. That's a very different place to many other people. Wherever we are on the spectrum of disease, though, whatever loss we are suffering, our world can suddenly feel distorted, twisted and unsafe. In those first few weeks after the double mastectomy, I kept thinking about my Aunty Sue and my close friend Alison, who had both died of breast cancer, leaving their small children behind. I questioned my surgeons' reassurances that they'd cut as much from me as they could.

Recovery was a struggle, but one that I thought I was well equipped to navigate. I was a trained trauma assessor, helping journalist colleagues deal with the impact of covering harrowing news stories, and had just spent two years studying for an MSc in Psychology, much of which focused on growth after adversity. For my thesis, I heard from more than a hundred people and many spoke about damaging life events – how they'd coped and been changed by them. Despite all the science and investigation, though, even while knowing there could be a path out of trauma, I just couldn't find it myself. I thought I wasn't trying hard enough, that I was failing, falling, going under. I read some self-help books but they all seemed to be written by those who were healed, not still hurting. They were looking back from a place where they felt stronger. I was – and am – still finding my way.

My hospital diaries are not written with that hindsight. They're in real time and show what it's like to go through a difficult life experience with all the contradictions that come with it – perpetual frustration, volcanic anger, hideous self-pity – together with glimpses of clarity, hilarious absurdity, even pure joy. Inner thinking is here, with the visceral details as uncomfortable as they sometimes are, because I want to use my experience to show that it's OK to have fear, bewilderment and rage when life challenges you. In fact, more than OK, it's an important part of recovering.

In that spirit of painful honesty, I'll also admit I'm frightened of you reading it. Ever since my diagnosis, I've been wary of anyone knowing. I thought that it would be picked over like carrion and wanted to protect my family, so we all turned in, rather than out.

Very few people were told and even those who saw me sitting in NHS cancer waiting rooms, hearing my name being called and maybe putting two and two together, even they didn't tell.

A few television presenters were treated for cancer as I was trying to manage mine and they chose to make it public – something I was urged to do, to issue a statement and talk to the press. I realized when others did, it wasn't like birds picking at flesh; it was more like the deification of wounded martyrs, sudden social media flurries with messages of sympathy from those who had been there, those who hadn't, those in high places. Front pages, full disclosure, a bearing of scars to the world. I hunkered down further.

Why publish now, then? Because I hope that the diaries may help you, or someone you love, through a rough time. I've spent the past year between diagnosis, surgery and reconstruction speaking to many people who seem to brim with life and positivity despite going through sometimes quite unimaginable horror. I wanted to understand how they did it, to hear where they had found optimism and inspiration in the darkness. They share their stories with honesty and generosity and want you to read them too, in case they offer some practical support. Their words are backed up by the latest scientific research into how our brain responds when we're grieving or frightened, and how to rewire it, to become more resilient, so we're not in a permanent state of heightened anxiety.

Often we struggle to get back to anything resembling normality when we've suffered a loss of some kind.

In psychology, 'traumatic events' are defined as those experiences that go beyond the usual; potentially shattering our previous assumptions of life and causing emotional, psychological or physical distress. Our sleeping and eating habits may be affected and we might start to question ourselves, our relationships and our place in the world. The remarkable men and women who reveal themselves here were challenged by all those doubts and questions. Yet they didn't just pull themselves through it and survive, didn't simply 'bounce back' – they've gone beyond that. They are thriving. They rise.

Adversity means different things to different people. We are complex, nuanced individuals and not everyone will see their loss as traumatic. For those that do, the experiences of others who've been there can help. There's no one-size-fits-all, though. I know that if you're feeling fragile, you can't deal with a manual that sets out what you 'should' be doing to get yourself back on track. This is, instead, a series of reflections, tips and tools; strategies you can choose from, to work into your day. One of those extraordinary individuals I met along the way told me about the number of 'outstretched hands' that pulled her up. Think of this book as your outstretched hand. Use their advice to help you navigate a path through. Not all of it will be relevant now, but bits of it may support you at different stages.

Their words are practical, truthful, tender, inspiring and, above all, they carry hope. Never lose hope, however dark it seems. You already have courage, otherwise you wouldn't be reading this. The power of resilience and growth exists in all of us too. My eldest son, Joss, once said to me, 'A ship is safest in the harbour, but that's not where it's meant to be.' The ocean can be a lonely and unpredictable place, though, when the rough seas hit. Use us as your crew – together, we have the strength to sail through some of the toughest storms.

‘Hang on to your hat. Hang on to your hope. And wind the clock, for tomorrow is another day’

E. B. White

1

Cancer? Really? Now?

'Enjoy when you can, endure when you must'

Attributed to Johann Wolfgang von Goethe

Friday, 5th December

I'm lying on my side in a hospital bed with my right breast compressed between two glass plates and a nurse's hand firmly pressed on my head to keep me still. A consultant pricks the skin to guide a hollow needle in. 'Not much to work with, I'm afraid,' I mumble. 'Breast-fed four children.' The nurse snorts with laughter. 'Yes, we prefer 36Bs here,' she says. We all smile. This scene is surreal for me, commonplace for them.

The mood changes as a vacuum pump starts sucking suspicious tissue away. 'Sorry, I've given you loads of local anaesthetic – shout if you feel anything.' The needle works its way around the breast, pulling, tugging out cells. I begin to shake involuntarily, and tears wet my arm. The nurse's hand continues to stroke my hair, trying to settle me so the consultant can get what he wants. 'Almost over,' she says.

The consultant hasn't got it. 'This is rather more complicated than we thought,' he says. 'And brutal,' I reply. 'Yes, but I'd like to go in again,' he says, apologetically. I sit up and the nurse gives me hot, sweet tea and three custard creams. The wounds are bleeding – she calls it 'oozing' – and I wince. Sipping tea, grateful for the respite, I look to the consultant. 'Before you started, you said nine out of ten lumps are benign—' He interrupts me: 'Yes, but I'm concerned. There are more areas, more than before, and the one we were monitoring initially has grown. I'll need to discuss with the team what we do. Let's not talk through options like surgery now.' I blanch. Surgery. I don't eat meat or smoke. I run, I feel healthy. These lumps, this mass is benign, surely? I begin a relentless volley of questions, excusing them by saying all journalists are like this, bothering away until we get the facts. 'Who do you work for?' asks the nurse. The consultant laughs; 'She's famous, she's on the telly.' Ah, he recognizes the bright and breezy TV presenter. How strange for him to see me naked, vulnerable, oozing. I lie down again for Round Two; more tugging, more vacuuming, more pressing.

The following day, I'm bandaged up. That night, my husband throws me a surprise birthday party. I celebrate with friends, get tipsy, dance to Seventies disco. When I get home, I've bled through the dressings onto my sparkly gold dress.

We read the appointment letter together, my husband and me. It says I may meet a member of the consultant's team. As that means it can't be serious, I say I'll go alone. That night, in the depths of a dream, I turn to Paul and say, 'I don't know how to live with cancer.' Just nerves, I tell him in the morning – psychology tells you that fear can be exorcised through sleep.

Friday, 12th December

9 a.m.

The day of the appointment and I'm chatting with a different nurse, in a different hospital. She leads me into a room to face another consultant with a kind face and I'm not sure who she is, or why it takes two of them to tell me I'm fine. Then, I don't hear sentences. I hear 'sorry' and 'procedure' and am confused, thinking they are being overly cautious, to suggest operating on something so small and innocuous. I listen and take notes, trying to get the facts, process it like a news story, retain control. I ask what I should do to prepare for the interview. She corrects me: 'You mean surgery?'

Then I hear 'breast cancer' and all the words whoosh out, bouncing off the walls, coming back like daggers. 'We think it's early', 'low to intermediate', 'double mastectomy'. Nothing connects, everything wounds.

I look at the nurse and she looks back at me with sad eyes and sympathy.

When I'm asked if I want to keep my nipples, I wake. 'We can make you new ones.' 'Who can?' 'The nurse, she tattoos them – she's very good and you can choose the colour.' What? I laugh with the absurdity of it all. OK, take the breast with cancer, take the other one that may have it, take both, they've done their job. Recreate them, that'll be interesting. Radiotherapy? Maybe. More tests, MRI scans, appointments. A different life starts now, a different person to the one who walked into this office. Scared, scarred.

11 a.m.

Swept up and onto the cancer conveyor belt. Over the road to the other hospital, second floor, imaging. Paul's coming. I need to compose myself. Gowned up, needle in, face down, ready for the MRI scan. Breasts exposed to be photographed and analysed. Paul arrives. They don't want him in the room but he argues and demands to come in. I sit up. Brave face. Two brave faces. He's bright and brittle. 'So the nurse says it's early and it'll all be OK. You OK? Sure? I'm here. I'm just waiting outside. It'll be fine.'

Lights off, dye coursing through my veins to light up the bad cells, noises begin. Still, still, so they can take their pictures, more cold liquid shooting into my arm, more noises, whirring, banging, trapped.

After half an hour, I'm pulled out and then it's gown off and normal clothes back on. The clothes I chose this morning to go to a work party tonight. Everything has shifted, but we must go to the party, it's important for Paul to see his colleagues.

8 p.m.

So, we go to the party and I am light and chatty, asking them about their work, blunting the day with cheap fizz. We stay for an hour and go for a meal. More wine, more dazed expressions, Paul and me, not quite knowing which bits of life to start to unravel – the move, the kids' new school, the offer of a full-time job for me, Christmas . . . when do we tell, who do we tell, how do we tell?

Thursday, 18th December

I work at the language. 'Just to tell you I'm having some surgery in January. I'm fine. It's very early stage breast cancer but they think that they'll get it all and I won't need radiotherapy or chemotherapy. I know it's a shock and I'm sorry . . .' etc.

I prepare to tell my two biggest boys, Alex and Joss; they're in their twenties, adults now, men. Joss, blond and slight, dressed smartly for his new job in advertising, cracking jokes as usual, teasing his younger brother, Alex, about how easy his life must be as a medical student, feigning surprise that he made it into the college football team. They bat insults back and forth with good humour, pleased to be together again, looking forward to a family Christmas back at home. I try to ease the news into the conversation. I keep my face bright and open but it's a grinding, crunching gear change as I start the set speech. 'You know that test I had? Well, just to tell you . . .' Alex crumples a bit, like a small child. Joss comes over and hugs me. Then they both do, really tightly, as I explain it's not life-threatening, I'll be OK, I love them.

They both want to come to the MRI results tomorrow. Then, when Paul comes home, we're in the farcical position where everyone wants to come and they're arguing, almost, about precedence. So, while I'm saying 'No, no, I'll be fine on my own', I mean: I'll be better alone because then I'm managing my own worry and not yours as well. It's decided Joss and Al will come. Paul sulks for the rest of the evening.

Friday, 19th December

8.30 a.m.

We travel in by tube, talking about Christmas, work, nonsense. When we arrive at the hospital, they sit as I wait to be called. We have a Keystone Cops moment, not knowing what floor the consultation is, shuttling around the hospital for a while, other patients eyeing me up with half-recognition. When I'm at the right place, the breast cancer nurse, Shirley, calls me in. I'm surprised not to see the consultant. Must be good news. Then she starts asking how I feel and talking through practicalities. I've left the boys in the waiting area, headphones on, duffel bags at their feet scattering books, clothes; where are they going afterwards?

This is the appointment where they tell you what they do, where they cut, how they reconstruct. I'm handed leaflets and drawings of breasts with dotted lines where the incisions go. In my case, from both armpits, across to the nipples, which are being taken off.

As the gruesome part ends, I call in Joss and Alex. I haven't been told it's spread, so that's positive. They shake hands with Shirley, pull chairs closer, lean in.

She turns on the computer – 'I want to show you women who've had what you're having.' She reveals an endless rogues' gallery of evil-looking scars. It looks alien – all these brutalized torsos. Some women with one full breast and a flat second, with the scar traversing it, like a No Entry sign. Some women have scars on both breasts and they're angry, visceral, wrong-looking, going right across each breast. No woman's body is like mine. The photographs start looking better as we move towards six months, a year, two years. Shirley says, 'Let me reassure you: here are some before and after pictures.' The 'before' is a huge, black, pendulous breast with a black nipple. Next to it, the breast has been removed and the chest is flat. 'Six months later,' she says proudly, 'and she looks like this!' Two big, black, pendulous breasts with enormous black nipples. She looks triumphantly at me. 'You can look like that!' I laugh. This is so far removed from anything that is me – this essential womanhood of the anonymous, cut, taken away, sewn up, replaced – I can't imagine myself there. Even looking at the felt-tip marks on the before-surgery pictures seems bizarre, like children drawing on themselves. Most women have larger canvases than I can offer.

I'm embarrassed for the boys, who seem fascinated rather than uncomfortable – do they need to see this? To imagine their mother having it done? Do a twenty-one-year-old and a twenty-three-year-old really want to be thinking about their mum's breasts? It must make them shudder. They say they're fine, interested, pleased they've come. They ask questions about recovery time and Joss writes everything down in his phone while I write everything down in a notebook. When I pause the scribble, the nurse wants to know why I've stopped. 'What's the mortality rate?' I ask. She laughs. 'No one has died on my table.'

The consultant, Jo Franks, gusts in, shakes hands, in a rush, others to see. 'Right. So it's January fifth, I've got another surgeon working with me, Rob Carpenter, we'll do a breast each.'

'I hope you're competitive,' I say. 'I'll be comparing sides.'

'Well, you won't be symmetrical – no woman is,' she answers.

She talks with confidence, throwing out facts and schedules, and then turns to leave. I stand up, shake her hand. 'I'll see you on the fifth. Good luck,' I say.

'I don't need luck,' she shoots back. 'It'll be fine – I'll sort you out in no time.' As she walks towards the door, she turns. 'Any questions?'

I have lots, but just ask, 'Should I give up alcohol? Dairy? Put on weight? Exercise?' She smiles and tells me there's nothing I can do in the next two weeks that'll make the cancer better or worse. 'It's Christmas. Eat, drink and be merry.'

We all leave knowing a little more. The MRI scan showed cancer in the right breast, as discussed the previous week (was it only then that I knew? Feels like I've been immersed in it for months). I look back at my notes:

> Several different DCIS areas (ductal carcinoma in situ), multifocal, dispersed over at least a 6 cm area, with many microcalcifications of around 5 mm in size. In the left breast, benign changes. Lymph nodes show no cancer but we won't know until 13 January when we get the results back. Double mastectomy the only appropriate treatment. Reconstruction – a pocket put under each side, beneath the chest muscle, inflated gradually with a mixture of saline and silicone over six months. Tubes, which exit the breast, can be in place for up to two years. Can inflate as much or as little as I want (within reason!) and whatever the skin will allow.

I'm told to expect a two-and-a-half- to three-hour operation and to be in hospital for two to three nights. After I'm sent home, we can discuss further treatment based on the results of the breast tissue they take out. They'll take between one and four lymph nodes (we all have around forty) which they'll locate using a radioactive dye, which stains the most active ones, carrying the lymph from the breast and therefore, if the cancer's invasive, around the body. Clever. I have an assessment on 31 December – New Year's Eve. Neither the consultant nor the nurse will be there because they're off on their Christmas break.

When I ask about work, Shirley says don't do anything in January. I'm doing a rather nice little job with a business forum ten days after the operation. She looks at me with a half smile that says, Like hell you are! You'll probably have drain bottles attached to you, collecting your bodily fluid, clanking about. You won't be able to lift your arms above elbow height. You won't be able to wash your own hair. You are not going to be Mrs Sparkle. She warns me that, psychologically, it'll take longer than the six weeks of initial physical recovery. I say I shall see that as a project, and I will. After the fifth, I'll be different, so I'll have to retrain my mind as well as my body. Mindfulness, yoga, eating well, no sweets, less stress, more joy. In fact, everything I promise myself every year and never do. Perhaps this time, if I look at it as a survival package, it'll work; I'll stick with it.

My fiftieth year will be characterized, or at least remembered by me, as the one where I had breast cancer. It's also the year when I've been the happiest and most secure. Strange, life.

10.30 a.m.

Hotfoot from the hospital to home. I'm keeping one of my best friends, Liz, waiting. She's organized a girly weekend to celebrate my birthday and has no idea what's going on. We check into a hotel and then head off to a shopping centre, where we have a glass of bubbles and I tell her. We cry and order another. Buy some cushions, go back to the hotel, have treatments, off in a cab to her favourite Italian restaurant and then tipsily back to the hotel where I eat the chocolate cake left by the hotel staff to say Happy Birthday and go straight to sleep. Morning – and we sit in bed talking for two hours. It's the best way to handle news. Easier sometimes, to tell a friend, than your family. The perfect way to celebrate life and talk about 'what ifs', veering between raucous laughter and a few tears.

I dream when I sleep, of walking through crowded places with bloodied bandages.

I draw up a hospital checklist:

Earphones and eye mask
Radio and books
Baby wipes and cleansing wipes
Moisturizer
Hand cream and sanitizer
Camisole tops
Mobile and charger
Cheap pants

Sunday, 21st December

I need to tell other friends and extended family and I can't bear to do it on the phone, so this evening I compose an email. The subject heading reads, 'It'll all be fine':

> Hi there, I wanted to let you know about something that's happening in January because I love you and it's important to me that you hear it first (and if I tell you on the phone, Seth and Eve will hear – or you'll be kind and I'll get soppy).

I've got breast cancer and I'm going to have surgery in a couple of weeks. The surgeons think it's non-invasive and that the surgery might be the only treatment I'll need. I'm having a double mastectomy so they won't know for sure until mid-January.

I'm sorry to tell you like this – I wanted to see you first but it's happened quite quickly.

I'll be in University College Hospital early Jan and then – with all luck – back to full strength in Feb/March.

Call any time. I feel fit and healthy and have full confidence in the oncology team when they tell me they'll get it sorted. New breasts and a pixie cut for 2015. It's not all bad.

Love you – hope we catch up soon – sorry about this so close to Christmas – big hugs and kisses,

Sian xx

I send it to my uncle and aunty, to my closest friends, turn off the computer and phone and head for bed.

Monday, 22nd December

I've organized play dates for the children for the next few days before Christmas. We're moving from North London to Sussex the day after surgery so they can start their new school, and before we go, I want them to spend time with the friends they've known since nursery. I don't tell the other mums what's happening to me, no one need know. I fear if I mention it to anyone, the news will spread along each of the terraced houses on our road and through every classroom in their crowded primary school. Before I know it, there'll be gossip at the gates and murmurings at coffee mornings. Best stay shtum, for now at least. Then we can escape to a different life, in the middle of nowhere, so secrets stay safe. Paul and I talk endlessly about whether it's the right thing to do, to uproot everyone just after this huge disease has come thudding into our lives. We've decided to go, but not to sell our house. We'll try to rent it out while we look for where we want to settle. It'll mean lots of short-term holidays lets and living out of suitcases. I've booked a place already for our first few weeks; it's a little two-bed cottage in the grounds of a castle. They'll love it. The new home, the new school, the new friends – it'll be a distraction. No one need think about what's happening to me and I can just get on with things.

Wednesday, 24th December

Christmas Eve and we invite the neighbours round for drinks and some heated-up supermarket canapés. The snacks are oily but the fizz seems to work and we laugh and chat about everything other than that which remains unsaid. After they leave, Paul and I keep the Christmas music on and we start wrapping presents for five children, making sure they all have stockings at the end of their beds before we head for ours.

Thursday, 25th December

In the middle of organizing the move and in my haste to get presents sorted for family and friends, I get Paul's gift spectacularly wrong, buying him a black winter waterproof jacket which strains over his chest. Alex tries it on and it fits perfectly. 'Have it,' Paul says. 'It's your birthday in January, that can be your early present.' He takes lots of pictures, is quiet, heads into the kitchen to start preparing lunch. When we sit down together to our huge meal, we pull crackers and toast the future. Paul cries, wordlessly. It's harder for him than me.

I'm now on the cancer track, packing bags for surgery while organizing temporary homes, buying new uniforms. I'm keeping busy before I have to give myself up to this hospital operation. He's watching from the sidelines, slightly derailed by it all, not quite knowing what it means, how bad it is, how best to manage the children.

Friday, 26th December

Off to Worthing to visit Paul's vast family. He's one of six children, and these Boxing Day occasions are the stuff of legend: noisy, chaotic, siblings teasing one another, Secret Santa presents handed out, whoops of delight and laughter. I know I have to say something but don't want to spoil the day, so wait until the end. As we leave, I gather Paul's brothers and sisters together and say the same words I've been practising for a week. There are hugs, tears, stoic faces, promises of support and home-made soup when I come out of hospital.

Later, I turn on the computer and see some replies to my email. The one from Dad's brother, Uncle David, makes me laugh out loud. He applauds me for being 'very forthright. An excellent start.' He goes on: 'We wish you all the very best for the operation and trust that's the end of the whole thing.' It's a typical Williams response. We don't need any emotion clouding all this, get on with it, get it sorted, get back to normal. They grew up in South Wales, the sons of a Presbyterian minister and his disabled wife, spending much of their childhood in a freezing manse. They were toughened by a life with few home comforts; it could be hard and cold but you just dealt with it. That philosophy, at least as far as my father is concerned, extends to emotion too. We've been taught not to indulge our feelings. Practical, sensible, sometimes austere. No room for wallowing.

There's plenty of emotion in the replies of friends. Alice, with her mad curly hair, her vibrancy, her exuberance, emails: 'I am ALWAYS proud of you, my beautiful friend. You are full of grace.' Bill Turnbull, *my ex co-presenter on 'BBC Breakfast' and friend of twenty-five years, writes: 'I know you don't believe, but I do and I will be praying for you to be safe and healthy again.'*

Tuesday, 30th December

Back in London and some friends are coming to stay, bringing their children. We start cleaning the house, pulling down decorations and packing things away. If we're putting our home up for rent, it needs to look like somewhere that potential tenants might want to live. We clear all the rooms of personality, put our lives away in boxes and shove them in the loft, pack two cases that'll come with us to Sussex and set aside another with my things for the surgery in a week's time. In that bag are two sets of posh pyjamas that Paul got me for my Christmas present, together with a nice dressing gown from Joss and Alex, so I don't have to wear the hospital-issue surgical one.

Wednesday, 31st December

It's New Year's Eve and we're staying with my brother Dave, his wife Louisa and my nephew and niece. After we put all the kids to bed, we watch a television show that I'm appearing on. It's a party that was pre-recorded the night before I was diagnosed with cancer. I'm there, among the crowds, in that same gold dress that I wore for my birthday, dancing fearlessly and shamelessly with Joss and Alex. We look very happy.

Tomorrow it'll be four days to go. I'm going to power down, stop writing, focus on holding everyone close. Re-engage, reassure. It'll all be fine.

Monday, 5th January

6.30 a.m.

The day of surgery and we're late. The taxi doesn't arrive so Paul and I are haring up our road to get the bus to the nearest London underground station. I'm cross that having said all along that the tube was the best idea, he'd ordered a cab that didn't come and now I'm marching up the street, muttering furiously under my breath.

The past few days have been lovely, catching up with more friends, this time Jane and Brian in Herefordshire, following doctor's orders to eat, drink and be merry. Then having a spectacular damson gin melt-down in the evening of our last night with them, where I railed against the unfairness of it all and cried hot tears of anger and self-pity.

I tried to describe what it felt like, waiting for this operation. There's a famous Japanese print by an artist called Hokusai with a tiny rowing boat in the curve of a wave on a stormy sea. You don't know whether the boat will ride the wave, moving with the tide, buffeted yet upright – or whether it'll get tossed onto the rocks, splintering into thousands of pieces, destroyed and worthless.

I'm in the boat.

I ran through a list of things you shouldn't say to someone with cancer and Brian, a writer with the 'Daily Mail', said, 'One day, you should write something for the paper about this.' The idea that no one knows quite what to say, what's right or wrong. Because we are all so anxious to make things better, we are unremittingly positive, using examples of triumphant and beautiful breast cancer sufferers. If I hear Angelina Jolie's name one more time, I will scream.

All you want is for someone to listen, without judgement, without thinking you're weak, or wobbly. To be someone you can cry with, laugh with. Who keeps in touch but doesn't fret if you don't reply.

Who nurtures – in Jane's case, cooking big, wholesome meals like kedgeree and aubergine and mozzarella bake with plenty of homemade chocolate cake and red wine.

I have a handful of very close friends and they're calling, just to say they're there. Last night, it was Brett who rang to say that when I get home on Thursday, he'll have supper ready. He said he'd come and see me too, when I'm out of surgery. Although, he said, 'You'll be off your tits on morphine.' Then laughed and gasped, 'What a horrible faux pas! You're having your tits off – so you'll be off your tits, with no tits!' We cried with laughter. After all, he is, as he says, 'lopsided' following testicular cancer. If anyone can make me laugh about the lunacy of all this, it's him.

The goodbyes to the little ones this morning were hard. No amount of fake excitement over play dates can mask their unhappiness about me being away for four days. I went in at 6 a.m. to say goodbye. Seth, milky breath and hugs, worrying about who's looking after him and when Daddy is coming home. Eve, pulling me towards her bed, hair all over the place, giving me lazy kisses. She spontaneously burst into tears last night when I told her I'd be in hospital for three nights. They can't really understand it. It's right in the middle of moving them to a new home, too. Terrible timing. The plan was that we would all leave our London home tomorrow for the rented cottage in Sussex, finally having a go at the 'good life', after talking about it for so many years. Term begins in a couple of days and the kids will be starting at a new school. Now, while I'm in hospital, Paul will be settling them in alone. Well, it'll give him something to focus on that isn't whether I'm going to die. I know that's his fear – he really believes I may go into surgery and not come out again.

We do get to the hospital in time.

At 7 a.m. I meet one half of the surgical team. With brisk efficiency, he marches into the room, hand outstretched and with a Welsh lilt to his voice suggests I call him 'Rob'. Under these circumstances, 'Mr Carpenter' seems more appropriate. He talks about the 'bilateral mastectomy and reconstruction' and, as he speaks, his eyes wander over my clothed breasts. The workman giving his latest project the once-over. Just like my hairdresser often talks to my hair, he's speaking to my breasts.

I strip down, sit on the edge of the bed, and he draws a huge ring around each breast. Then, rather menacingly, around each nipple. 'Are they going for ever?' I say.

'Yes. But you'll get new ones,' he replies. 'At first your breasts will look flat and wrinkly . . .'

'Just like my real ones,' I say. Attempting a laugh. Wanting him to feel comfortable.

His surgical partner Jo arrives. I'm already on first-name terms with her, she's the one that told me I have cancer, she's the one reassuring me that they'll try to get it all out. Paul asks if he can stay until I go into theatre, which won't be until midday. Hours away. Before that, it's a foray into nuclear medicine where they'll inject me with that radioactive dye to spot the most active lymph glands. Those are the ones they'll take during surgery to see if the cancer has spread. If they find it there, there'll be more operations. It felt strange, hearing that. I'd imagined that everything would be whipped out and that would be the end of it. A bit of radiotherapy maybe, but otherwise, straightforward. Hearing about the possibility of further procedures suggests a longer journey, one I'm not prepared for.

The consultant says Paul can stay. 'See?' Paul says, looking at me and then addressing the doctor. 'She keeps telling me she doesn't need me here.' Not quite true. Although I'd rather he was back in Sussex looking after the children. I can manage this myself; it sounds like a lot of waiting, then lots of injections, surgery then recovery.

The anaesthetist, Georges, is from Florence. He talks about pain relief and asks for my consent. He mentions blocks: injections in the back that act like an epidural (complications, possible infections, lung damage, etc. etc.), to see whether I'm happy that he use them. I'm ignorant, as I tell him. Just do what you think best. He tells me about pain relief when I wake up. I'll be hooked to a morphine drip, which is attached to a button that I get to press. How thrilling, to be able to administer my own morphine.

It's 8.40 a.m. and I've met the 'United Nations' of NHS staff, according to Mr Carpenter, and shaken hands with each member of the team. Two surgeons, one anaesthetist, three nurses. The next time they will all be together, they'll be huddled over me, carving and slicing and sucking away blood and tissue. They will see my naked torso, breasts drawn on and a tube down my throat, using their knives to cut away cancer.

Just before he leaves the room, Georges says, 'I hear you are very famous across the country.'

'Yes,' I say. Usually I'd do a deferential and self-deprecating thing where I tell them I'm not famous at all, just a bit well-known from TV, which is true, and that they aren't expected to know who I am because I've been off air for a bit – also true. But I didn't have the energy.

'I'll look out for you after this,' he says. 'I don't usually watch TV.'

And I won't be on it any more, I think. This heralds something different, a new start, a different me. I'm not sure what, yet.

Three hours to go. One of Paul's sisters, Marianne, who lives in Holland, is very spiritual and before I came here, she promised to help from hundreds of miles away, by 'preparing the room for surgery'. She also says I've got a huge angel who'll be standing on my left-hand side. Who am I to question? I need all the help I can get at the moment. I need that angel – not just by my bedside, but by me always – or at least, while I get through this.

I'm marked up, injected, and surgery will come soon. First, there's more waiting. I sit with Paul, holding my hospital notes, a fat file of papers held together with paper clips and elastic bands. The curiosity is too much. I open it.

28th July 2009 – that's when I was first admitted with a lump in my breast. Then a follow-up in August and another needle aspiration. I'd been breast-feeding Eve, who was born in March, so the thought was that it was calcification, which needed monitoring and would go away. The results were inconclusive.

I'm sent for a mammogram on 10 December. The results will come at a later date and a note says that 'both breasts were unremarkable'. Although, comically, that remark is preceded by 'clinically'.

I read it to Paul and he laughs. Rather too much.

The next follow-up was not for another four years, so the mammogram must have come back negative. There's another a year and then the notes speed up:

> Cancer in 3 areas, 9 o'clock low-grade ductal carcinoma in situ (LGDCIS) – no calcium, 11 o'clock intermediate-grade ductal carcinoma in situ (IGDCIS), no invasion, calcium seen. MRI – anything in left? Bruising. MRI results – right breast 6 cm of enhancement in keeping with mammo and biopsy (Bx) results. Left – nil suspicious. No lymphadenopathy. Discussions with multi-disciplinary team (MDT). Right mastectomy (MX) and reconstruction. Left mastectomy and reconstruction. Consent. Date: 5th January.

And here we are.

We are sitting in a very crowded nuclear medicine department. Every seat is taken and in every one is a story. The skinny man with grey hair and a beard, who's reading a gruesome thriller. The mum, face etched with worry, sitting with her young daughter who's dressed in a pink jumper and holding a stuffed rabbit. The woman, probably a similar age to me, with . . . got to go.

9.33 a.m. Nuclear Medicine Department

Gowned up, lying down on a table, knees up, large machine hovering overhead. They inject the radioactive dye through a needle just by my nipple. I ask Paul for my mobile phone and headphones. I get to the meditation app I've loaded on it, hit play and a voice says, 'You've hit the stress SOS button – take a deep breath in and then exhale.' The needle goes in, I concentrate on breathing – in, out, in, out – and the bed moves slowly until my body is inside the machine. In, out, in, out, beep, beep, the radiation moves from my breast down my arm, towards my fingers. I feel it moving, my fingers twitching, in, out, in, out. Think of positive things – I remember Jane offering me a glass of red wine – I said I wasn't going to touch alcohol before the operation and then remembered my body was about to be flooded with poisons and toxins. Fill the glass.

Paul's sending emails to work, watching a film he's meant to be producing, sending texts to friends to let them know when I'm going into theatre.

Back in a waiting room, with a woman talking loudly about how far she's travelled, how many procedures she's had, how long she waits to be seen. I put on some headphones and listen to '50 Ultimate Chillout Classics' but her voice still breaks in, reminding me that I can't escape from all this, however hard I try to distract myself.

Back into surgical reception, I'm seen by a first-year doctor: Jas, first name Jascharindpeeta – I know that because he writes it out. He can make an anagram of 'carpenter' from it, he tells me. Which is interesting because his forefathers were carpenters in Punjab. I can't unless you use one 'r' twice. Should have come into surgery with my glasses on. We chat away. He is sweet and thoughtful, empathetic and careful. He'll be in the operating theatre, observing.

'I grew up with you,' he says, 'watching you on 'BBC Breakfast.'

'And now you're seeing me in a way that neither you or I ever dreamt of,' I say. He laughs. This will be strange. Someone who watched me on TV every day, now seeing me on an operating table, being cut into by surgeons, being there as my breasts are removed. The thought quietens my cheerful chatter about his family, his dreams of going into general practice, how humble he feels about doing his job. All I see now is a viewer, who'll be looking at me at my most vulnerable, judging, observing, a ghost at the feast. There is nowhere to go for privacy. I hope it won't be a story he wants to tell others – 'Guess who I had on the table this morning? You'll never believe what they had to do to her . . .'

All this analysis isn't helpful. We have fifteen minutes to go before I head towards the theatre; I need to think positively. Warm, yellow light flooding through my body, protecting me. An angel at my side. The love of family and friends filling the room. All will be well. My stomach is flipping every time someone's name is called, though. Any minute now, it'll be mine. I'm scared. Think positive, think warm light, think love. I'll just fall asleep and when I wake, I'll be cleaner, lighter, stronger; marked and scarred, but less fragile, disease-free. I'll wake up different – physically and psychologically. Stay strong. Here we go . . .

2

Morphine Musings

'One must have chaos within to enable one to give birth to a dancing star'

Friedrich Nietzsche, *Thus Spake Zarathustra*

Monday, 5th January

9.20 p.m.

I am in bed, legs wrapped in a heated blanket, which inflates and deflates to stop clotting and promote healing. There's another heated blanket over my chest. Nose tubes are delivering oxygen, there's a drip connecting me to morphine, and I've just realized I have a catheter. I also have a new and annoying inability to reach for a pen (so it was passed to me and I'm writing almost lying down – very little of this will be legible).

The last thing I remember before surgery was the anaesthetist putting two blocks – pain relief – into my back, in the gap between my shoulders. His eyes were connecting with me (until I had to turn my back on him) and it was immensely reassuring, having those big brown eyes locked on mine.

The next thing I know, I'm waking, groggy, in a bed, curtains drawn, on a ward, with a lovely nurse from the Philippines, who then hands over to a cross one who talks over me and is irritated by everything. The fact she's starting her shift, the fact the consultant has asked for an electric warming blanket to make my 'skin flaps' (yuck) heal faster, the fact that she's moving me to another part of the hospital. So, once we're on our own, I say, 'You seem frustrated. Is there anything I can do to make your job easier?' And she softens. I ask her about where she grew up, how long she's been nursing, what parts of my care are proving administratively difficult for her.

Once she takes me out of recovery and into my room, I'm her 'little friend'. God, it must be tiring working here. I remember my mum, Kathy, coming back from night shifts on intensive care and she was wrung out. In fact, pretty much all her nursing taxed her both emotionally and physically. Lifting all those patients certainly seemed to have buggered her back (I was lifted onto the bed by four people, one of them a male nurse, who I correctly assessed was twenty-three. Same age as Joss).

The consultant says the procedure took longer than planned and was more challenging because I was slight and there was 'not much breast tissue'.

My throat and lips are so dry, my mouth won't move. I'm asking the nurses questions – Who are you? Where do you come from? What do you love about the job? – and it's coming out as 'mmffffgg' x 3.

My chest feels like someone's jumped on it from a great height. Breathing is laboured, but I want to start recovery so I breathe in and out, in and out. This breathing malarkey will be the thing that gets me better (yeah, I know, not for survival).

I'm trying not to press the morphine button too often. If I can understand the level of pain, then I will know whether to pick things up like cups and pens, or whether it's something that can wait.

Having said that, I had a marvellous, slurred, happy conversation with Joss and Alex and my stepdaughter Emily, so maybe, every time I have a visitor, I'll whack some more in.

Called Liz and regaled her with the story (as much as I know it) and Brett too – this time, with a message on his answer machine: 'Hello, lovely, this is your cancer buddy – I'm out and fine and pressing the drugs button.'

Time is expanding – having contracted in theatre. When do I sleep if they need to check me once an hour? Do a breast exercise: shoulder shrug. Nearly faint. Time for the button.

Tuesday, 6th January

Midnight morphine thoughts.

The kiddies shouldn't come in tomorrow – at this age they should see me strong. Then it strikes me that strong and wired up might be fascinating. I could show them the catheter for wee and the inflating socks and the cannula and drips. Perhaps it'll demystify pain and illness . . . OK, I've changed my mind.

Ask them to give you one of their really special, soft and gentle cuddles so they don't come bounding in and squash the stitches open.

Sort out a cab company so I can take them to and from school, so I don't arrive in a new town as a victim who needs help and that breast cancer at this stage is something you get on with, not succumb to.

Call Paul to talk to the mums on the play date on Wednesday, but make it brief and factual. 'She's got breast cancer. She's had a mastectomy and she's really positive' (morphine may be kicking in here on the 'really positive' bit). Inevitably, I'll have a period when I'm old and tired and look like shit.

When I'm feeling old and tired and look like shit, I shall remember this:

1. *The nurse from the Philippines who had a double mastectomy and showed me her scars (ugly, but she thought they were good. No, not ugly – raw and red. Survival scars). She told me that she'd had no one to look after her through it. Not a partner, or family, or friend. And I have lots, who all sent love on the morning of surgery and who I am astounded by.*
2. *That I had and still have a huge, powerful angel at my side. This may be bollocks. But I'm inclined to believe it.*
3. *That I am filled with light, bright, warm, yellow light. And its warmth floods my body, going into all the parts that need healing. This I believe, also.*
4. *That I will spend my life helping. In small ways, so people who are in psychological pain see a path out, however rocky. I will help them over the rickety bridge – holding their hand, gently and lightly. Not as some kind of role model, but a trusted friend.*
5. *I will be kinder to myself, try (ha!) to be non-judgemental.*
6. *I will be lonely and cranky if need be.*

B/p 131/70, temp 37.2, pulse 73, oxygen 98%.
Drain 1 – 50 ml
Drain 2 – 20 ml
Drain 3 – 20 ml
Drain 4 – 0 ml

Poor old Yolie, my lovely overnight nurse who seems frazzled, was called in tonight when she was off shift. She retired three years ago as an agency nurse. This is her first of two weeks of nights and she has forty-five patients on the ward. That's forty-five people with hourly checks, ringing bells, asking for water. She says nursing has changed. She can't spend time with anyone, she's always running, doing paperwork, chasing beds and meds.

And then she drops my catheter bag and the contents burst all over the floor. A weary sigh. 'At least it's mainly water,' I say, not really making it any better. She's on her hands and knees, wiping it up. We talk after that, for longer than she's probably allowed. I tell her how much I value her care, which I really, really do. I was meant to have a less experienced nurse, but she wanted Yolie to take over. It's a big procedure and there's lots to monitor, what with the heated blanket and my temperature going up and down like a jack rabbit; poor thing was overwhelmed. She told me she knew me from the telly. That was an unnecessary complication for her: 'I was the one that boiled Sian Williams.'

Ow, ow, ow. Chest hurts. Time for morphine and try to sleep. Morning can't come fast enough.

Random unconnected morphine words/phrases that interrupt almost rational thinking.

1. *It's just like B and Q (What is?)*
2. *Domestic violence (Why?)*
3. *Wayne's family is cross (Who's Wayne?)*

My catheter itches and I can't sleep and I keep thinking my hourly check is due. Part of the latter comes from when I had a post-partum haemorrhage and lost four pints of blood, the night after Seth was born (blue and flat). I had been left in a room with Paul, with no checks on my blood pressure. It was only when he woke up and felt wet sheets that he turned on the lights to see a bloodbath.

1 a.m.

B/p 121/66, pulse 89, oxygen 98%.

I had asked Paul what it was like, waving me off to theatre, and wondered whether he'd been reminded of that time.

As he gave me a final hug in the corridor today – me all gowned up, my breasts marked with a Sharpie pen, in my embolism stockings and blue hospital slippers – he whispered, 'I'm with you in there, holding your hand, all the way.' I couldn't talk for fear of weeping, so I mumbled, 'Love you', and turned to walk into the operating theatre reception. Anyway, it wasn't for long – the weepiness, I mean. I was put in a waiting room and watched 'Rip Off Britain' and 'Bargain Hunt'. Contemplated picking up the 'Saga' magazine and decided against it. I'm only just fifty, after all. Which reminds me: as the anaesthetist was checking my age and I said 'Fifty', he said, 'Gosh, I thought you were much, much younger', which thrilled me and is obviously a very effective distraction technique, because I no longer felt all the needles pulling inside me and fell straight to sleep. Nonsense, of course; I looked shocking, like when Paul saw me with tubes up my nose, a bag of wee and greasy hair. 'Am I still sexy?' I said. 'Always,' he said. I meant it as a joke, he didn't. Lovely man.

2 a.m.

B/p 125/70, pulse 58, oxygen 98%.

Send a couple of emails. Well, I'm awake and (almost) compos mentis. One to Paul's sister, Marianne, thanking her for the protective, but rather fierce angel. The other to Paul's brother, Martin, who lives in Canada. He starts another round of gruelling chemo today and sent a wonderful message last week. It followed a chat we'd had about how tiring it is, telling people about your cancer. I slipped in that I had it too, but the conversation was meant to be for him so he could communicate how he was, via me, to the rest of the sprawling family.

He clearly felt he should have asked about me (he shouldn't, that wasn't the intention) so I get an apologetic, beautifully composed, long email full of contrition and goodness.

Speaking of love – I've never had so many people saying 'I love you' in my life. Family (my brothers Dave and Pete, Dad – it's just not something we feel the need to do) and friends (all of them – and I love them back for it).

Words not to use about cancer:

Battling
Struggling with
Tackling

It's not a 'battle' because that assumes it's a war that you can win or lose, depending on your level of skill or your choice of weapon.

You 'struggle' no more than with any other life 'hump' that you encounter. Sometimes you feel as if it's harder than at other times, but I give in to the emotion – bewildering confusion, anger, hilarity – and try not to fight the feelings.

'Tackling' is better because it suggests a project that needs careful thought to manage. So yes, if it's used positively. I suppose you could also see it as a rugby manoeuvre, emerging from the scrum, making a run for the try-line with the ball, getting back up when your opponent grabs your ankles. OK, I've reassessed 'tackling'.

Other words not to use:

Brave/plucky
Victim
Breast cancer survivor

'Brave' because there is no option but to get on with it. I don't feel 'brave' or 'plucky'; I feel, in turns, optimistic, or irritable, or lucky, or grateful, or concerned for how others are coping. But not brave.

'Victim' – urgh! Say no more.

'Breast cancer survivor' – none of us is our disease/symptoms/diagnosis. I am Sian, who happens to have breast cancer, just like I have four kids or brown hair or big feet or small (now non-existent) breasts.

Can't quite believe my small breasts were there this time yesterday and now they're not. I've never felt defined by them – who is? – or flaunted them – why would you? Even when I became a presenter they were, how shall I say this . . . ? Presented to give the illusion of a body in balance and not – as one boyfriend so delightfully put it – the proportions of a teenage boy.

One of the reasons I stayed small when my mother was not, is genetics. Dad is like a whippet, as are my brothers. Another is that my mum's sister, Sue, died of breast cancer at the age of twenty-eight and I thought the bigger you were and they were, the greater the risk. Mummy had mammograms and every time I thought she'd come back and they'd have found something suspicious. So my philosophy was – stay small, stay well.

Yesterday, when the consultant was marking up my breasts, he said, 'We'll take all this away.' I replied, 'What away? There's nothing there! How have I got breast cancer?' and he answered, 'It's luck. Some get it, some don't. It has nothing to do with lifestyle, or size.'

Often, in the run-up to this, I questioned whether I needed reconstruction. I'd said yes without thinking and yet voiced out loud that, as they'd fed four children, they'd done their job and weren't necessary. Then I saw all these pictures of women post-mastectomy and felt they looked completely normal, apart from the scars. In the end I went along with the idea of it, although it seems quite grotesque when I think about the process. I feel I've succumbed to vanity, but that's a bit rich coming from someone who gets her hair dyed and her eyebrows threaded.

Inflate away then, and stop when I reach symmetry.

Is it really only 2.30 a.m.? Speed the night! Please!

4 a.m.

B/p 117/56, pulse 58, oxygen 98%.

It's 4 a.m. and I've written down that I've had 25 mg 16x of morphine but have no idea what this means or whether it's accurate. Is that enough? Too much? The nurse will only say it doesn't matter, it's regulated, I can't overdose on it, just press when I'm in pain. Yolie checked the stitches – 'They look nice': nurse-speak for they aren't bursting open – and reapplied the inflatable embolism stockings.

I am WIDE AWAKE. Not going anywhere, I know, so I can sleep tomorrow.

The last set of imaginings was darker. Up until now it's been 'la la la', great breathing and bright white or yellow light. Then it turned to worry and irritability – not about this, but about work. Why should I be thinking about bloody TV now?

Things are starting to hurt, too. I've been picking up the water jug when I shouldn't; the drugs are masking the pain. As brother Dave says – morphine lies. In all sorts of ways. He should know, he's spent a lifetime working with clinicians in the NHS, seeing it coursing into those who are suffering.

5.30 a.m.

B/p 118/58, pulse 52, oxygen 99%.

Uh-oh. Mood change. Something has worn off. Some nice drug that I'd like again, please. From having the most amazing, positive, full-of-light thoughts, they are back again, these restless ones, full of doubt.

I've drifted off to sleep and the dreams have been of letting people down – the nursing assistant who attached the oxygen clipper to my toe and got a false reading, who I directed to my finger for a more accurate one. Twice. I should apologize to her. I told her boss that the clipper wouldn't attach properly to my foot and the assistant was crestfallen when she saw me last.

My heart races and then slows. I am feeling more pain. My hands are seizing up. I feel nauseous. Help. Not HELP! Just – is this actually what it's going to be like when I'm out of here?

6.30 a.m.

B/p 113/65, pulse 67, oxygen?

I thanked the nursing assistant for her support throughout the night and she told me there were two members of staff for twenty-one patients. Ouch.

Feeling sick and slightly paranoid. This isn't a good mix. Stiff, too, and with a crashing headache.

It's still dark. That was a great night up until about 3 a.m. when things shifted. So, my worry is that I can't be positive and think my way out of this, although I am trying. But no amount of soft, bright, white light seems to shift it. Bone-aching fatigue, too. Wanting to sleep and then my heart racing when I close my eyes. I'll try again. Bit more morphine might do it (no access to that when I'm out of here, though).

7.15 a.m.

B/p 123/67, pulse 51, oxygen 99%.
Drain 1 – 70 ml
Drain 2 – 50 ml
Drain 3 – 60 ml
Drain 4 – 5 ml
Antibiotics, anti-sickness, injection of anti-coagulant in stomach.

7.30 a.m.

Shirley comes to examine me . . . and show me my breasts. Or at least, show me where they were. I have a cursory glance. No dressings, just two dark red scars, starting under my armpits and finishing just past where the nipples used to be. It's extraordinary, really. I feel what's left of my chest and there are two crumpled packets where the breasts were, hard and unyielding. Then two small buttons, each the size of a five-pence piece, protruding from under the skin, just on the bra line. That's where tubes will take in the saline/silicone, injected through a needle.

Nauseous, faint, can't eat breakfast. New nurse comes to move me and I find I can't hoist myself up by the arms – there's no strength there at all. Lots of very painful bum-shuffling to get me off the bed so she can change it (the bed, not the bum). It is excruciatingly slow. Once I'm in the chair, she takes my gown off and begins to give me a bed bath, at which stage, Jo, the surgeon comes bustling in, throwing open the door, with three of her team in tow, to look and prod and poke.

The scars are 'viable', she says. 'You were challenging and extremely difficult' – not the first time someone's said that – and the operation took more than five hours. Lack of fat under the skin is the problem. 'Great pectorals, though!' she smiles. That could make reconstruction easier, apparently. The only fear is the risk of wound infection as there is no tissue or fat to play with.

7.46 a.m.

B/p 96/55, pulse 58, oxygen 99%.
Drain 1 – 100 ml
Drain 2 – 110 ml
Drain 3 – 150 ml
Drain 4 – 0 ml

Last night Joss and Alex came over. I could barely talk with fatigue and pain. Couldn't even shuffle up the bed or hoist myself onto pillows. My arms can't lift my weight – it's extremely frustrating, because I can't move myself.

Some poor junior doctor tried to take my blood three times, tapping the veins, wiggling the needle around, bruising – squirting blood that he was unable to catch.

Joss was getting twitchy, wanting a nurse to do it, as this lad poked about, not getting anywhere.

They didn't see me at my best. Brought me some supper, which I ate, and then left. I drifted in and out of sleep until Liz arrived. Again, I was no company, barely able to talk, kept closing my eyes, slurring speech, feeling uncomfortable.

Nurse has left, bloods taken, tablets given, sleep.

Paracetamol, dihydrocodeine, ibuprofen. Ondansetron, cyclizine, anti-coagulant in stomach.

Wednesday, 7th January

7 a.m.

At last, a sleeping pill and a good night. Wake up feeling as though I can get up (I can't, yet).

I can probably see people today, I was hopeless yesterday. The first test is being able to do things for myself and I've just spilt water all over this diary because the jug is too heavy to lift, so that's not a good start. Small steps.

I get up, first dosing myself with pain medication. Stick one large drain bottle in one pocket, another in the second and pin the third and fourth to a lanyard, together with the catheter, for the ten-foot walk to the bathroom. It's there that I see my chest, properly, for the first time.

It looks like a torso after an autopsy. Two large misshapen scars over skin that's mangled and hard. I can feel the deflated balloons underneath and they cause lumps and crevices across my chest. My breasts feel numb to the touch, as if all sensation has been taken out of them. It looks pretty horrendous, so I take pictures of them on my mobile, for reference.

I've tidied the hospital room and it's taken half an hour to clean myself up. The catheter is out and now all I want to do is sleep again.

Keep going, keep going. Drink water, tea; don't succumb to these overwhelming waves of listlessness.

In one of my earlier morphine moods, I wrote an email to Paul:

Hello lovely you.

It's half past three and I've been drifting through the night. I'm working on my breathing so I can get as much healing oxygen as possible, while opening my chest and lungs.

It's wonderful thinking time although my thoughts are scattered and random. Remind me at some stage to show you my writing – spidery and covered with morphine imaginings, peppered by occasional lucidity.

Thank you for being there today. I realized that although I am 'fine on my own, thanks very much', I do need you and you are tougher than you realize at times like these – allowing yourself emotion and vulnerability is a sign of that, so please remember to acknowledge it – the processing, the talking, will strengthen us both in the coming weeks and months. Please allow yourself that – and allow me to experience it.

This – perversely perhaps – is a gift to us both.

They take my blood pressure on the hour so I've been, naturally, readying myself for it. They're a little late. All the numbers are fine so far and they need a break, working through the night.

I'm hitting the drugs button too, while I'm still allowed access to it and I'm not in any pain, so all is well.

I sent Martin a quick note – his chemo starts today I think, so maybe you could drop him a line to send him love. I sent an email to Marianne too, thanking her for the angel. She was there (the angel) – large and powerful and intimidating and protective. I do believe that (it's not just the morphine).

It might be good to let the kids see me here – I'd perhaps think about how to get them back to Sussex, you may want to stay here longer. On the one hand, it takes the uncertainty away from them, makes illness more fascinating and less frightening (a wee bag – a bed that goes up and down – socks that inflate). On the other, it's cumbersome for you and maybe they'll fret with the tubes. I remember my mum didn't shield me from my grandfather's illness and all I remember were the free sweets and a bed that moved.

I may as well stay awake for the 4 a.m. check-up now. Roll on morning.

Love you masses – ask for help – there's an army of people wanting – needing – to give it.

Here's to our next future, Mr Woowee.

Sxx

I wonder whether the future will be filled with this, or whether it'll be surgery, an uncomfortable few months and then normality. I was struck by something the cancer nurse said yesterday. We were talking about a follow-up appointment, when we discuss the results of the mastectomy and lymph node removal. She said that's when we discuss future treatment: 'We don't think you need chemo, but we don't know.' Before, it was 'You won't need chemo'. I guess the language changes, subtly, as you move from one stage to another, so they can prepare you for the possibility. Before, it was also an 'unlikelihood' that I'd need radiotherapy. I wonder whether that view is changing too. I'll know in ten days. Ten days of waiting to see how bad this cancer is and how much of my life it'll occupy.

Things that you can't do on Day 1 after surgery:

Pick up a pen.
Hold a cup to your lips (lifting anything is impossible).
Move your arms.
Wiggle up the bed (it catches your catheter).

Things you can do by Day 2:

Move your arms.
Get out of bed yourself by swinging your legs over the side (no hitching still, can't lift myself).
Change (slowly and trying to manage threading four drain bottles through arm holes – that's a challenge).
Clean your teeth and brush your hair (although that, and opening door handles, seems a bit taxing).

Shirley, the breast cancer nurse, comes to see me. The catheter is out and they've scanned the bladder – all seems fine. After last night's abortive blood-taking by the doctor who tried (and subsequently bruised) three different areas, a phlebotomist comes and bish, bash, bosh, two vials of blood, done. Sodium is low.

When I ask Shirley what I can and can't do, she said I should manage pretty much most things if I feel up to it. But how do I know if I'm up to it, if the drugs are masking the pain?

Anyway, contrary to the scare stories I read on the Internet, I will be able to wash my hair, lift a jug of water and hitch and nothing will fall out. She promises me that – nothing will fall out.

They'll take two drains out and discharge me when I've got two left.

That could be tomorrow, it could be the day after – 'whenever I'm ready'. How will I know?

Thursday, 8th January

6.30 a.m.

A night full of dreams and awakenings. The dreams are full of fears, pity and cries. The awakenings full of plans, frustrations and trapped wind. Lucidity too, which I forget to write down, annoyingly.

Drain 1 – 140 ml (up 40)
Drain 2 – 150 ml (up 40)
Drain 3 – 220 ml (up 70)

'Draining a lot, but not an obscene amount,' says Vicky, the overnight nurse. I can have another drain out, potentially, tomorrow. They're in for longer than expected because I'm producing and draining too much fluid away.

I could have had sleeping tablets last night but I don't want to rely on them. Having said that, I've just downed paracetamol (1 g, 4x a day), ibuprofen (400 mg, 3x) and codeine (30 mg, 4x).

The kids start at a new school today and I'm not even there to hold their hands, hug them, reassure them and wave them off. It's gutting. I called them last night and Seth said he's 'really, really nervous and very, very shy'. I told him, 'Try not to try too hard. Observe. Know that it's OK to be anxious.' He's going to be at this school for a long time, so he doesn't need to go in with his ta-da! performance face on. He thinks he won't be liked for who he is, which is why he wants to be able to make people laugh. He's worried they won't understand him, or his love of 'Skylanders'. They will love him, he is extraordinary.

Eve is excited, she's fine. I can't wait to see them bound into school, buoyed by the new friendships they've made and experiences they've had.

I have pretty astounding children. Joss and Al were here all day yesterday, chatting, reading, checking their phones, eating the fruit that my friend Sam sent.

It was very reassuring to have them here, chasing the nurses if and when I needed my bladder scanning (I'm retaining water since the catheter was removed).

Every pipe and tube that's taken out of me feels like a victory over something. So the oxygen tubes up the nose went, as did the catheter, as did the cannula for the intravenous drugs.

The worst bit is the bloody drains. I hate these things. Tubes poke out from dressings under your arms and connect to huge bottles, which collect fluid that your body makes in reaction to surgery. It looks like beetroot juice. Once you stop draining as much, you can go home (hence staying until at least tomorrow).

Taking them out should be a relief, yet it's agony. I had one out yesterday, I thought it'd be a tweak under the arms and I lined up my meditation app, so I could breathe through it, started doing the in . . . and out . . . breathing more and more heavily, as I got more anxious and felt the tugging increasing. 'Are you there, yet? Is it out?' I said, not looking. 'No, I'm still taking off the bandage,' said the nurse. 'Oh.'

Then this fearful pulling and a feeling of something ripping across your chest, dragging and snagging on the muscles.

The nurse asked afterwards if I wanted pain relief. Perhaps, next time, I'll have it before you start the tugging.

Lots of visitors. The day before, Sam and Liz came and I made no sense and wanted to sleep. This time I brushed my hair, changed my pyjamas, put some powder on. I still smell. I'm not allowed to wear deodorant so I've got a small spritz of strong perfume that I hope will mask the dank mustiness of sweat.

Everyone says, 'Don't you look well!' Another friend, Sophie Raworth, arrives after she's come off air, having read the 'One O'Clock News'. She's still wearing the studio make-up and buzzing with the adrenalin of the job, reminding me of what it's like, working in a newsroom full of breaking stories at ten to the hour, with its shouting and frenetic typing as the deadline approaches. Journalists are used to quickly gathering facts and pinning down stories. But this is a waiting game, full of questions and different paths. Very little is certain here – it's a difficult headline to write. My cancer may have gone or it may have spread. I may have radiotherapy, I may not. I may go home tomorrow, I may stay.

She mentions our close friend and colleague George Alagiah, who put out a press statement when he was diagnosed with bowel cancer. He did it proactively, she says, but it's different because he was on air every day and you're not. No, I'm not. I used to be, but have chosen a different path for now. I'm almost anonymous, save for being recognized when my name is called in the breast clinic reception. I am now the 'ex-Breakfast presenter' and can become anything. Jump back into the news, become a psychologist. Take the money or open the box. Do both. Do neither.

Brothers Dave and Pete came in with Dad who held me very, very tightly and shook a little. He is relieved and sits in the chair, smiling – no, beaming – with joy, repeating, 'You look so well!' over and over.

I tell him about my morphine imaginings and he recounts a story about the journalist and broadcaster Bernard Levin, who would wake after a night of visions, where he was able to see the answer to worldly problems and wish he'd been able to capture them. One day, he woke himself up so he could write it all down. In the morning, he looked at his notes, expecting to see profound thoughts, and read the word 'Petrol'.

Friday, 9th January

6.40 a.m.

Something has shifted. Yesterday, it was a day of talking with visitors about recovery (Sue, my agent, came in brimming with positivity about future work and press statements), but today I feel really low.

Alex and I spoke yesterday about how this is affecting him. As a third-year medic he has access to so much more information about this disease than he needs at this stage. He's worried about metastasis – that the cancer has spread from one part of the body to another, through the lymph nodes. He cried, he's vulnerable and, in the end, he's still my little boy. He should be back in Oxford next week, working towards his exams on Friday. He should be going out with his friends, laughing, walking over Magdalen Bridge into town for a drink, having fun, and loving life. Instead, every day, he's here, looking at his mum, worrying that the cancer has taken hold.

I can't give him the reassurance he needs. We don't have the path out of here yet, we won't know for a week whether I need more treatment – and he finds that frightening, as do I.

Last night, before I went to bed, the possibility hit me that I might not be here to see Eve get married. Why that should be a milestone marker, I don't know. It's so old-fashioned. But the thought of her being a brave, strong, feisty young woman, without her mum at her side, really scared me. I want to see what the little ones become as adults. They had their first day of the new school today and were bubbling with such excitement when they rang, full of stories about who they sat next to and what they've been doing, what they wore, what stories they read, the maths they did, the points they won for their house.

I can see them as adults. Eve, plunging into new experiences, unafraid to tackle challenges, kind, thoughtful, popular, wise beyond her years, resilient, determined, studious, clever. Seth, bright, energetic, extraordinary. At turns buzzing with imagination, ideas, jokes, performances and then retreating, quietly escaping into a book or anxiously sitting on the sidelines, frightened of failing, worried that people will judge him and turn away. I want to be there to help them grow.

9 a.m.

Feeling better. Up, showered, dressed, checked, eaten.

Mohammed, the registrar, comes to see me. Every time I see a member of the operating team, I feel overwhelmed by what's happened. Maybe because they were there, for five hours, cutting the cancer out, to save me. When the surgeon, Jo, came round last night and checked the drains ('The liquid is changing from claret to Chardonnay'), she did it with such kindness, with her head cocked to one side, yet such honesty, that I cried. I have to be bright, breezy, clean, smelling nice, dressed well, optimistic, for everyone else – Paul, the kids, visitors, family, brothers, Dad – but I can be myself with them: up and down, frightened of the prognosis, flattened by surgery, literally and metaphorically.

The wounds are red and look angry but they're not, they're 'super', 'viable', 'lovely'. Jo even says, 'Look, you have the start of a cleavage. After a while, it'll look gorgeous.' It doesn't now, but that doesn't bother me. The scarring and changes to my body don't worry me at all. I'm not fussed about new breasts, a nice cleavage; I just want to feel safe and that I can live healthily and happily for years to come.

Visitors will start coming soon. A clutch of friends all at once: Liz, Dixi, Zoë. I'll make myself the positive, chatty, optimistic woman they expect.

Lovely seeing them. Funny, made me laugh. Poor Lizzie had her coat on and the zip had stuck near her neck. Trying to get the coat off, over her head, it became wedged and immovable just under her nose. We were hooting with laughter. Then Zoë came with a beautiful scarf with butterflies on it. I mentioned that I'd joined a breast cancer forum group with the name 'Butterfly' – I like its imagery of beauty and fragility.

Paul arrived unexpectedly and it was so wonderful to see him. I read from this diary to illustrate my random ramblings and we both cried. I told him how genuinely grateful and lucky I feel to have people around me who help and love me. That gives me the strength to fight to recover. Others don't necessarily have that and I know how difficult it must be for them to have the motivation to get up, wash themselves, be themselves. I can do it because I want those I love to see me as me, and not as an illness. I'm also able to do it because I can eat well, so have the energy to try. When I walked the ward today, I looked at so many people who were in a worse position than me.

Even here, by this bed, there's a TV. I don't watch much TV so don't choose to see it, but for those who do, do they have to pay? If they have no mobile phone, how do they communicate? It's so isolating, being in hospital, and you feel so powerless. Doing things for yourself, having the tubes taken away one by one, feels as though you are seizing some of the power back. No, I won't have morphine or codeine because it makes me nauseous and constipated. I won't have laxatives because my body needs to learn how to reset itself. I don't need the cannula; I don't want the plasters holding swabs over the areas they've taken blood. Or even the gummy marks left by the adhesive holding down the tubing. Everything has to go. All reminders of medicalization – all examples of a lack of control. Wearing my own clothes rather than pyjamas all day. It's been a struggle, managing the dressings, especially with the drains attached, but how much more reassuring for others, and me, not to look ill. A dab of cheek stain and powder, just to liven up a flat, pale face. A scarf to drape across a bloated stomach. Small things, small steps, regaining control.

Joss said he was proud of me tonight. The boys came over with supper, which has sustained me, along with the fruit and bread and tea, for four days. He was proud of how I have handled this from the start, he said, insisting that he'd found it inspirational, how positive I had been, how I'd approached each step. 'You've just got to get on with it,' I said. 'Well, it's inspiring. I wouldn't be like that, I know I wouldn't.' (He would.) 'You've been amazing.' I remember this conversation well and as he was saying this, I was vigorously shaking my head.

They are fine boys. The way they have handled this has been incredible. Supportive, calm, loving, protective; they are like two sentries, either side of me, marching with me to whatever future we face.

Saturday, 10th January – discharge day

6 a.m.

Drain 3 – up 50 ml to 80 ml
Drain 2 – up 80 ml to 120 ml

They are up a lot, these levels, and I'm draining lots of fluid so I'll have to go home with the bottles attached and monitor myself at 6 a.m. every morning until Tuesday, ringing the specialist nurse with my results.

Discharge drugs:

Paracetamol 1 g (pain) 4x a day
Co-amoxiclav 375 mg (antibiotics) 3x a day
Ibuprofen 400 mg (pain and swelling) 3x a day

I'm all packed up and ready to go. This time on Monday I was in a hospital gown, having circles drawn in a marker pen on my breasts where the incisions and implants would be. I'd had radiation injected into my body to see which parts lit up with activity. I was anxious, really fearful of the knives, constantly trying to witness my own operation from above, willing the angel to be there at my side.

And now I'm dressed in the same clothes that I wore as I walked into the hospital 145 hours ago. I feel stronger, more alive, more resilient, and more ready for a fight. I know how much I value family, friends, and how they provide the foundation for the beginnings of tentative growth. I have a new resolve: to nurture those relationships and give them back the love I have felt. To start looking after myself better, trying not to impose too many rules, strictures, and judgements. Trying to be gentler, more forgiving. To understand my body better and what it's trying to tell me. That means being nice to it, eating well, not punishing myself with over-indulgence, sugar, alcohol, which poisons it, however lovely it is in the short term.

I remember during my Psychology thesis, one of the participants, a BBC foreign affairs producer called Stuart Hughes, started describing his physical and subsequent psychological trauma after he'd lost a leg in a bomb attack in Iraq. 'This didn't happen by accident,' he said. 'This happened not for a reason, like a spiritual reason . . . but something is out of whack in my life. I can correct it, or I can try and carry on like I was before. And if I carry on like I was before, it'll probably happen again. So really, it's up to me to put the changes in place that I need to prevent it from happening again. And there's always a danger, like a New Year's resolution, that six months down the line you say, "Ah, OK, I'm fine now." Even to this day, I've been out of hospital, what, four years? Five years? I have never gone back and I hope I will never go back to the way I was. That has absolutely been the fundamental change – and it has gone from an idea into the real core of who I am now.'

I completely understand that. This didn't happen because my life was too frenetic, self-absorbed, and rigorous. It happened because of a combination of genetics and bad luck. But something was 'out of whack' too. This has given me an opportunity, which I hope I'll remember, to reconsider what's important in life, who is important – and what, or who, is not.

In superficial terms, that'll mean more walking, less running. More juicing, less chocolate. More natural, less painted.

In bigger 'life' terms, it means more family, less work. More saying no, less saying yes. More rural, less urban. More forgiving, less judging.

I will continue to work – I love it and get pleasure from it – but it won't receive the absorption I've given it, thus far. I don't know where I'm going next, either on this cancer path or the work one, whether it'll be psychology or broadcasting or both or neither. And as far as the cancer is concerned, will it be radiotherapy? Chemotherapy? Both? Neither?

It's interesting that I put work and cancer so closely together. I know one didn't cause the other, but a bit of my soul knows that psychological sickness can manifest itself physically – and I thought I was going ill in the head for a while, driven mad by what I thought others were thinking, their opinions and criticisms. That is not a healthy place to live in. So while the cancer is 'genetics and bad luck', perhaps I unwittingly created the ideal conditions for it to take hold. Have I changed enough to prevent it doing so again? I'm not sure. Would I still be as vulnerable to potential vitriol? Not sure. Either way, TV, while occasionally both highly regarded (often I don't know why) and highly paid (ditto), can be destructive to your sense of self and identity.

I could easily become 'that newsreader who has breast cancer'. 'Breakfast' and breast cancer – the two things that precede Sian Williams. If or when it comes out in the press about this, the headlines will be 'BBC's Sian and her battle with breast cancer'. 'Ex-'Breakfast' babe has breast cancer', 'Brave 'Breakfast' star and her breast cancer battle'. So work and cancer are, will be, irrevocably linked.

I know that I can use that for good, to let others know what to expect from this operation.

I've read so many magazine articles recently with well known women talking about their 'breast cancer scares', following a screening. How frightened they were about a positive diagnosis, an early death, the mourning children they would leave behind. How delighted they were to discover they did not have the disease after all. For those living with cancer, it can be hard to read. Maybe it's good to raise awareness and you're glad they're not blighted by illness, but some might be left asking why they chose to make headlines out of their unfounded fears. If you're left vulnerable by cancer, there's a risk you may feel diminished even further, after reading the palpable and public relief of those who've just been told they haven't got it.

What about when they read the stories of public figures that do have the disease? I know I'm lucky to have the resources and support to help me recover from it. Not everyone does, and I am acutely aware of that. Sometimes I feel that people might read my 'cancer story' and feel as far away from me, as I am from Angelina Jolie.

I suppose there are unifying emotions, whoever you are, when you know you have cancer. You are frightened – about the operation, the disease, the future, your ability to cope. You're confused: What led to this? Could I have stopped it? Was it my fault? You are hungry for information about what you should do, eat and drink, beforehand, to improve your chances of getting better, faster. You are anxious about telling friends and family, because you don't know if you have the strength to manage their reactions. And you don't have enough facts to answer the questions, either.

So there must be universal thoughts too: I'm lucky it's not worse / I'm unlucky I have it / I'll live / I won't / I can't endure this / I'm strong enough to cope . . .

I do leave here a changed woman. And not just because whatever breasts I had have gone, to be replaced by wrinkled, deflated pockets, covered by translucent, bruised skin, marked by large red gashes across left and right, with tubes still inside and also outside, trailing from each armpit into a large bottle that fills with liquid the colour of beetroot juice, every day (not Chardonnay yet, Doctor).

Physically different. Psychologically different. Physically weaker. Psychologically stronger.

I hope I get fitter and healthier, and that any resolve I feel now won't weaken or diminish when I shut this hospital door and go back into the cold, harsh realities of life. It's a wibbly-wobbly bridge I'm getting on and I'm about to take the first few tentative steps.

3

Control

'It's a good thing to have all the props pulled out from under us occasionally – it gives us some sense of what is rock under our feet, and what is sand'

Madeleine L'Engle, *Crosswicks Journal 2: The Summer of the Great-Grandmother*

Once, when I was a senior producer at BBC Radio 4, I was working on a story about the Beirut hostage crisis that took days to organize. I had the guests booked, a detailed brief written about them and then, suddenly, on the day of the broadcast they had last-minute nerves and withdrew. It all collapsed and I was left with a huge gap in my programme. A fellow producer, Chris Birkett, trying to sympathize, said, 'God laughs at people who plan.'

We all think we can manage our lives, until something dramatically threatens our perceived sense of control. Initially, like me, you may find you blame yourself for 'inviting' it in. I thought I had cancer because I had lived wrongly, eaten badly or failed to look after myself properly. It was bad karma, a poor diet, and a life of shift work, trying to do too much. 'No,' the breast cancer surgeon insisted, 'it's a mixture of genetics and bad luck.' Not only had my aunty died of breast cancer, but the disease got my mother too, this time in the bowel and liver. Those cells are in there, waiting to mutate. Whether they do, depends on the cards you're dealt.

It's hard to rationalize your feelings when you're caught up in grief or anger or fear, because it seems as though your life has turned into something destructive, dangerous and surreal. Being trapped in a hospital system where you don't understand the language, where procedures are done to you, and you have no choice but to give in, is frightening. When you have lost someone dear to you and the grief knocks you down like a wave on a beach, it feels as though you will never be able to stand up again. Everything outside your world looks distant and alien, as if you're viewing it from behind a thick glass screen. The normality of life shifts so dramatically that it seems as though you can't ever access it. You will never be the same again.

Two emotions heighten that desperation: a sense of blame or guilt, and the feeling you have lost control over everything. They can exacerbate any psychological effects and can be harder to deal with than physical injury or illness.

I'd been studying the impact of stressful situations for a few years, before disease started ebbing away my own sense of control. As a journalist for almost three decades, I mentored junior colleagues and advised them on what to expect if they were sent out to a road traffic accident, or to a disaster zone. I trained as a trauma assessor and began to help those who returned from reporting on the horror of war and disaster. I hosted 'hostile environment' days for those who worked in news, discussing how best to protect ourselves and whether we all needed a 'psychological first-aid kit' before we left the office, a way of understanding how to defend our minds so they can safely process extremely distressing environments. I worked with the national mental health charity, Mind, and produced short films for the BBC on how to speak to the bereaved or those with mental health problems; how to spot the signs of acute stress.

A couple of years ago, when I started my Master's in Psychology, I was also news-reading on the main bulletins, hosting a weekly Radio 4 show, *Saturday Live*, and presenting a prime-time BBC1 show called *Your Money Their Tricks*. It was a relief to escape from the immediacy, intensity and borderline neuroticism of broadcasting to something more reflective, something wider. I studied for the exams in the evenings and at weekends, and it was liberating to be a student again, to try to be better than I was at school: the very average pupil managing to get by without passing a single maths exam. Now I could atone for my paucity of knowledge. I sweated through exams on statistics and agonized over quantitative analysis. I laboured over research, debated with my fellow graduates on theories and argued, ill-advisedly, with my tutor over a disappointing grade. 'You may think of yourself as successful outside this university,' he scolded. 'Here you are a student. You are learning and you must accept your mistakes, which will be many.'

My thesis focused on my journalist colleagues who are working as reporters, producers and technical crew on profoundly upsetting stories. It isn't just those on the front line of battle who can be affected by what they witness. Some never leave the office, yet after screening unfiltered footage, day after day, of images such as atrocities to children in Syria, they can feel numb and become prone to nightmares. I wanted to understand whether there was a way of helping them, by examining the impact of covering these traumatic events. I sent out a survey and more than a hundred and fifty replied. They said how much they loved the job, but many also wrote about the horrific experiences that came with it.

The psychological damage was so great that some had been hospitalized with post-traumatic stress disorder (PTSD). Although the majority of journalists go about their work without incident or injury, for those colleagues, the guilt of reporting on other people's tragedies, yet being able to get on a plane and go home – the fear of working in environments that put them at huge risk – the lack of understanding from others when they returned to base – became debilitating. Often, the sickness in their mind was worse than any physical injury they might have suffered.

Stuart, who lost his leg in a bomb attack in Iraq, told me, 'If I could have lost my other leg and not have gone through the psychological side of things, I would do it willingly . . . The thing that was so devastating for me was that, even when I lost my leg, I was the same person and yet losing it psychologically, I became a different person, and that's much more difficult and scary.'

To see why he lost it psychologically, we need to go back to how he dealt with his trauma, the loss of his limb. Stuart was a member of a busy newsroom – 'not a manager, just a grunt' – but on his return, he suddenly found himself the centre of attention, treated like a hero. He was in the newspapers, received loads of cards and presents, a senior executive visited his family home and gave him tickets to an FA Cup Final, and he was promoted. Stuart tells me with a laugh that being blown up was, perversely, 'the best career move I ever made'.

He returned to his old job, putting himself 'back out there . . . earning a few more career credits'. He had been invisible before, but now he had the 'eye of the bosses'. Still learning to live with an artificial limb, he looked on it as a challenge, something to master. Within a year or two, he was back in the war zones, to prove he could still do it.

Then, two things happened: colleagues thought he was coping and so began to turn their gaze elsewhere and Stuart fell out of the spotlight. He threw his energy into his work, determined to show he could be the same producer that he was before the injury, so he didn't reflect on the fundamental changes to his life and his family. After three years, whatever had kept him going, stopped working and he began to 'run out of road . . . the wheels start to slow down' and he began to 'get into a death spiral'.

Gradually, he became agoraphobic and tried to avoid going out on the difficult and challenging stories he once loved. Then the panic attacks and suicidal thoughts crept in. He'd lie awake at night, every night, barely getting more than an hour's sleep; and the less he slept, the more anxious he became. He saw doctors and psychiatrists, took medication, but nothing seemed to work. He grew more desperate. As the father of a young son, he witnessed the effect of his stress and anxiety on his boy and it frightened him. He began to discuss scenarios with his wife: should he move in with his parents and quit work? Should she take on a new job? Could they cope financially? They knew they were running out of options, running out of road.

Stuart says the first shaky step to his recovery was acknowledging a crisis and 'pressing the nuclear button'. He decided to admit himself to a psychiatric hospital. 'Going into hospital was my way of saying I can't cope any more, this is very serious, you know, like Spike Milligan's gravestone – "I told you I was ill"'. Once there, the professional recognition that he had a mental health problem, the doctor with a certificate on the wall validating his psychological descent, meant he could start to look at what had gone wrong and ask for help. Admitting to himself and others that he was psychologically ill was 'the most therapeutic thing, weirdly. As therapeutic as sitting through a yoga lesson or cognitive behavioural therapy [CBT] class.'

Post-traumatic stress is defined by the National Health Service as 'an anxiety disorder caused by very stressful, frightening or distressing events'.[1] Symptoms include being tearful, angry, numb, guilty, ashamed, feeling helpless or constantly agitated; it may lead you to drink more, eat less, be unable to concentrate, get nauseous and sweaty, become impulsive, argumentative, withdrawn. You may also be plagued by flashbacks, nightmares and insomnia. None of these symptoms is exclusive to PTSD; most of us experience physical and psychological distress in response to a traumatic event like bereavement or divorce or a major loss of some kind. The difference is that with PTSD, the symptoms do not go away.

The NHS suggests the condition may affect 1 in 3 people following a 'traumatic experience', but estimates as to the number of sufferers vary considerably. Indeed, some experts argue it's being over-diagnosed. British soldiers returning from combat in Iraq and Afghanistan have a PTSD rate of 4 per cent; in America, where a diagnosis of PTSD could earn a veteran around $3,000 a month, it's considerably higher, around 20 per cent.[2]

Professor Neil Greenberg, who spent two decades as a naval psychiatrist and is President of the UK Psychological Trauma Society, tells me that the disparity in PTSD diagnosis in the UK and US may reflect the fact that in America, where healthcare is not free, there is more pressure to have a recognized mental health disorder so you can access treatment.

Differences in diagnoses may exist, but those who have the condition say it's serious and debilitating. Stuart had many PTSD symptoms, like his feelings of isolation, irritability and guilt, his problems with sleeping and his difficulty concentrating on simple things. He felt as though he had lost control over all parts of his life. What helped him back to recovery and, subsequently, what led him to growth, was talking to experts in military trauma. And it's war veterans that really helped the psychiatric and psychological communities understand how the mind deals with an extreme event and what works to get us back to stability.

The term 'post-traumatic stress disorder' was first used as a medical diagnosis by the American Psychiatric Association (APA) in 1980 in its *Diagnostic and Statistical Manual of Mental Disorders* (DSM-III), with the concept centring on the reaction of an individual to a traumatic event, like war. But the idea that conflict could trigger serious psychological reactions was recognized years before that. In 1862, during the American Civil War, many soldiers were suffering from an irregular heartbeat, difficulty breathing and trouble sleeping. A surgeon called Jacob Mendez Da Costa saw hundreds of such cases and five years later, by war's end, suggested they all had 'irritable and exhausted soldier's heart'.[3] There was no suggestion that the mental stress of warfare was responsible for the symptoms and the men were deemed either mad or homesick. It was not until the First World War that British doctors began to realize they were dealing with a diagnosable mental illness.

Soldiers there were enduring some of the most horrific forms of warfare ever known; facing death and mutilation daily, witnessing their colleagues being killed or injured, fearing the creep of a silent, deadly, poisoned gas. Just a month after fighting began, many thousands began suffering symptoms like uncontrollable twitching and terrible nightmares and, by the end of the conflict, more than eighty thousand men had been diagnosed with shell shock – defined in the official British military history of the war as 'a severe mental disability, which rendered the individual temporarily, at any rate, incapable of further service'.[4] The legendary British journalist Philip Gibbs put it more vividly after seeing the effect modern warfare had on soldiers on the Western Front; he wrote about the 'strong, sturdy men, shaking ague, mouthing like madmen, figures of dreadful terror, speechless and uncontrollable'.[5] Back then, so little was understood about mental health that some army generals regarded the soldiers' mental disturbances as 'damn nonsense and sheer cowardice'. Medical officers dealt with shell shock with solitary confinement and humiliation, and some British soldiers who could not bear to go back to the front line were shot for desertion.

Others thought bed rest, sedatives and electric shocks would help. But some doctors, like psychiatrist William Rivers, were inspired by Freudian psychoanalysis to focus on the mind as well as the body. He encouraged soldiers, most famously at Craiglockhart hospital in Edinburgh, to talk about what they had been through, fuelling a rise in psychotherapy. As well as reflecting on what had happened, these men began gardening or working with animals; simple tasks that helped tackle their social isolation and diverted their mind.

By the Second World War, shell shock was also known as 'combat fatigue' and psychiatrists were routinely deployed to fighting units, albeit to make sure the men were treated and returned to battle as quickly as possible. A retrospective War Office report estimated that between 5 and 30 per cent of all sick and wounded evacuated from battle areas during the conflict were psychiatric casualties.[6]

The fighting didn't just affect service personnel – it hit civilians too. My own father remembers the trauma of that war but only recently told me about its effect on him. In February 1941, he was a toddler living with his parents in Swansea in South Wales. Over three nights, the city suffered heavy and sustained bombing as the Luftwaffe tried to destroy the port and docks. Incendiary bombs and high explosives fell from the sky, engulfing a huge area in flames. The fires were so extensive they could be seen from seventy-five miles away. More than two hundred people died and more than four hundred were injured in that Blitz, and my dad's family was lucky to escape alive. He was only three years old, but his memory of what it felt like is still vivid, nearly seventy-two years later. They had been bombed out of three homes before the Swansea Blitz happened, so this time they all just hunkered down. My father remembers hiding under a table, holding onto his mum, hearing the noise and seeing her fear. The terror was so great that when the bombing finally stopped and they came out from under the table, he was rendered mute. He didn't say a word for six months.

Imagine – a whole country traumatized by war, not just soldiers but their families too. Most didn't get help because they were busy trying to survive; there was no time to analyse their mental health and it was rarely questioned or explored. No one asked that modern-day journalist's 'go-to' question, 'How do you feel?', and I'd imagine those millions of servicemen, widows and children wouldn't have known what to say in reply. But war saw the growth of some pioneering medical work from doctors who knew that its mental cost was generations of men who were debilitated, psychologically.

The military led the way in psychological understanding because they had to – they needed fighting men, not those who were incapacitated or invalided out. Eventually, though, psychiatrists advising the armed forces began moving towards resilience and in 2008, the US Department of Defense spent $140 million on a preventative programme, devised by the psychologist Dr Martin Seligman. The US Chief of Staff of the Army, General George Casey Jr, had called Dr Seligman (who he described as 'the world's expert on resilience') to join him and his team for lunch. 'I want to create an army that is just as psychologically fit as it is physically fit,' he said. 'You are all here to advise me how to go about this cultural transformation.'[7] The US Army recognized that the way forward for modern-day soldiers was proactiveness – not waiting until they are destroyed and then attempting to piece them back together, but sending them out with an idea of how they can manage in difficult circumstances.

Service personnel were asked to complete confidential tests, called the Global Assessment Tool, where they answered a raft of questions as honestly as they could about their strengths and weaknesses. As well as asking how satisfied they were with life, their work, their friends, their unit and their families, the survey posed questions about actual situations where they may, or may not have used 'open-mindedness', 'good judgement', 'creativity' or 'persistence'. They were asked how much enthusiasm they showed for their everyday lives, how much love they showed their families. At work, how often were they fair? How often did they display leadership, teamwork or loyalty? How emotionally fit were they? Did they feel they had any control over bad events happening to them?

A training plan was rolled out – the Penn Resiliency Program – which teaches resiliency techniques to soldiers as part of the Army's Comprehensive Soldier and Family Fitness scheme. These skills include trying to think differently and not falling into the habit of 'catastrophizing', or expecting the worst to happen. The training encourages a sense of optimism, asking soldiers to 'hunt the good stuff' by acknowledging three things that have happened to them during the day, however small, that made them feel better.

It builds on research that suggests that those who express gratitude by counting their blessings daily, and thanking those who have helped them, see benefits that extend to their sleep, their satisfaction with life and their general well-being.[8] [9] In a meta-analysis into the impact of the program on civilians – in other words, a study of all studies – it was found to reduce depression, although the effect was small and it didn't lessen, delay or prevent future psychological disorders.[10] The overall effectiveness of the course is questioned by some; others embrace it and in the UK it's being used as part of a one-hour-a-week pilot programme in thirty schools, along with mindfulness, to see what difference teaching resilience skills can make.[11]

It's important to note here that trauma is about how we *perceive* and react to an event. Psychologists say a 'seismic event' can challenge or invalidate how we lived before.[12] When suddenly everything changes, the ground shifts and the insecurity can be frightening and bewildering, but not everyone will see it like this. Responses to difficult life events can be dramatically different. My brother-in-law, Martin, has Stage 4 invasive cancer but does not see it as 'traumatic'. Yes, the diagnosis was surprising and sometimes having the illness makes him angry. He hates the chemotherapy and the way it limits life, but he doesn't view his cancer as 'traumatizing'. When I ask him whether he feels he has changed because of it, he looks quizzically at me. 'I don't think so,' he says, while at the same time his partner Inge shoots back, definitively, 'Yes!' 'Well,' he says, 'I've changed certain things like my diet and the way I spend my time, because the chemotherapy regimes mean I've had to. I've changed how I view spirituality, too. But the fundamentals of who I am haven't really shifted.' Inge disagrees, saying he is different, altered by his experience, that he's 'grown'. Why the disparity? It's all down to the way 'trauma', 'change' and 'growth' are perceived by the individual.

Martin thinks the impact on his life is restricted to certain amendments that he's had to make to it, but he doesn't view these as 'traumatic' either – just something that he's had to get on with. However, he does reflect on his experience – and that very act of examining it is important. He's not locking it away in a tightly shut box and burying the key, because it's ever-present. He discusses it with his partner, he explores new ways of living and different medications, and he embraces alternative therapies alongside the more traditional ones. He is active and taking control of the things he *can* manage. He's stopped eating sugar because he thinks it's toxic. He stopped chemotherapy for a while because it severely reduced his quality of life. What helps Martin through what any of us would *think* would be a challenging time, are two things. Firstly, he thinks about his illness, adapting his life accordingly and trying out different ways of managing it; and secondly, he tries to exert control over some of it while remaining flexible. He's choosing not to ask about his prognosis, for example. He's asking to join medical research trials that may provide a clearer path through his disease, but if he doesn't get on one, he'll find another approach. He cannot ignore this cancer, so he is actively thinking about how to incorporate it into a fulfilling life.

We may or may not believe we've experienced 'trauma' because of the loss of our health, of our mind, or of someone we love, but unless we begin to think about *how* that event affects us and understand the emotions that are caused by it, any recovery will stall. How we do that safely, without causing further injury or distress, is crucial. It's not about ruminating on the event, getting stuck in those repetitive, negative, self-flagellating thoughts about why it happened – it's more of an honest self-reflection, examination, and exploration. Martin is doing that, even if he disagrees with his partner that it equates to him 'striving' and 'thriving'. He is not stuck in an endless loop of 'Why me?' or 'Why can't I make it stop?' He's thinking, 'OK, there's no cure for this, so what can I do, during a tricky time, to make life more bearable, even enjoyable?' If we can all do that, we can build up resilience and be better prepared if and when adversity strikes.

We *are* resilient creatures, we just need to know how to tap into it. Resilience can be expressed as those who overcome adversity while experiencing 'transient and mild disruptions in functioning'.[13] This description comes from Professor George Bonanno of Columbia University, whose research suggests we are naturally resilient in the face of horrific life events and, controversially, that the absence of obvious grief may be normal. Bonanno came up with the phrase 'coping ugly', to describe how we can use strategies to deal with a life stressor that may seem counter-intuitive, like laughing, for example. He interviewed New Yorkers, seven months after the September 11th Twin Towers attack and then eighteen months later. Previous statistics on how populations react to a traumatic event suggested that at least 7.5 per cent of them would be showing signs of post-traumatic stress disorder. The overwhelming majority did not experience any symptoms of PTSD, even those who had been at close proximity to the attack site. Bonanno says his study provides 'important evidence both for the prevalence and robustness of resilience in the face of high exposure to a potentially devastating terrorist attack'. He goes on to suggest that while most of us have this resilient streak, it can be strengthened and positive emotion developed after a loss in our lives. There is no one route to health, he says, but many pathways, with benefits and costs to each.

Here in the UK, Professor Sir Simon Wessely, President of the

Royal College of Psychiatrists, agrees with Bonanno that resilience has not been properly acknowledged:

> Stretching right back to the Second World War, there has been a tendency for people in authority to underestimate the people's essential resilience. Doctors, politicians, the media, you name it, underestimate the strength of the public. They believe they will panic in situations when they don't, and forget that most people have good coping mechanisms in the form of social networks.[14]

If we all have this well of resilience inside us, how can we reach into it and use it to promote development and growth in a time of uncertainty, even catastrophic change? Coping strategies differ from person to person, just like the perceptions of adversity, but some techniques are universal and quantified by science and experience.

It's not straightforward and easy, as those who've been through it will tell you. Stuart's path to health after he lost his leg and then his mind, sometimes stuttered. He tells me you could almost predict the peaks and troughs of it: two weeks good, two bad. But then two weeks of feeling better became two weeks and a day, two weeks and two days, and he could see things were shifting. His social network helped with that. Others who had also been through trauma popped in to see him in hospital and he says that is still 'the most important thing' to him, 'the support of a number of senior and trusted colleagues who've been there and came and chivvied me along and understood and kept me going'. He was 'very, very vulnerable' and even five years later, still feels that fragility. But the first day that he got through a day's work and ate and slept normally was 'brilliant'. It was an achievement. He believes he's been given a second chance and that means he looks anew at his life and those within it, he's 'more selective' about how he chooses to spend his time. He goes to football matches with his seven-year-old son – something he never used to see as 'valuable'. He manages his work–life situation differently, and his view now is, 'I'm not going to waste my time doing crap.'

What's fascinating about Stuart's story, and many others I'll introduce you to, who've been through traumatic, life-changing events, is how many of them feel they've grown because of it. They haven't gone back to who and where they were; they are different, they've gone beyond resilience, to growth. Stuart says although his experience remains the 'most horrible, terrifying, most awful thing that has ever happened to me', it made him a stronger man because it forced him to reassess everything about himself: his family, his work, his life. He's seizing back some control of his life and he's doing it because he wants to, not because he's been told to. 'When you get to that sort of mindset, then the growth kind of kicks in. You think, right, OK, if I'm in a state of mind where I can make changes, then where can I make changes? Maybe I'll do more of something I wasn't doing much of before and less of something else. And then you feel kind of, OK, well, anything's possible.' He laughs about sounding 'too self-help book' but acknowledges his desire for change affected everything. 'If we're going to renovate this house,' he says, 'we may as well do the lot, rather than just stick a slap of paint on the walls.'

This does not negate the awful, paralysing, damaging effects of trauma, and to suggest that every life crisis has an upside would be naïve, patronizing and simplistic. However, while horrific experiences may have a deep emotional cost, there is increasing research and recognition that growth may emerge from the *processing* of that trauma. If we have to endure it – and we do, whether it's injury, loss, bereavement or illness – then how we make sense of it, and what meaning we attach to it, will determine whether we feel we have grown as a result. We do not just 'bounce back' to where we were – we change, we adapt, we can become stronger.

This concept of perceived benefit is not a new one – it's an ancient idea, found in Hebrew, Greek and Christian theory, as well as the teachings of Buddhism, Hinduism and Islam. It's been variously described over the past decade as 'benefit-finding', 'stress-related growth' and 'thriving'. Growth after trauma and adversity means going beyond the absence of distress, recovery or benefit to a transformative change, beyond mere resilience to new levels of functioning. But what helps some individuals stay effective and grow after loss, illness, or trauma? Do they possess something inherent, or can we all learn from them? Do we all have it within us and how do we tap into it?

I ask those questions of Professor Stephen Joseph, who has worked with survivors of adversity and sufferers of post-traumatic stress for more than twenty years. He suggests between 30 and 70 per cent of trauma survivors report at least some kind of benefit.[15] He's based at the University of Nottingham, where he specializes in the science behind well-being and personal growth. Professor Joseph tells me about a very influential American psychologist from the 1950s and 60s, called Carl Rogers. As a boy living on a ranch outside Chicago, Illinois, Carl would go down to the cellar, where they stored potatoes. There was a small shaft of light coming through the bricks, which splintered the darkness, and the tubers from the potatoes would always reach towards it. Those sprouts would be long, weak and spindly, but they would find a way to seek the light, to achieve growth in the best way that they could. Rogers likened this to what he called the 'actualizing tendency' in humans. We may be in the darkness but we are trying to reach out towards the light, to grow. Is that the same for all of us? I ask. In the depths of gloom are we all trying to find the light? Professor Joseph says there is often adversity in our lives and we react to it 'as biological organisms': 'We're trying to fulfil our own potentials as individuals, of what it's like being a human being and that is ultimately to be socially connected, to be autonomous and to have a sense of mastery.' In other words, we grow because we want to regain the sense of who we are. That means shifting our perspective to accommodate the new experience, reassessing, developing and strengthening our relationships, examining our identity and our place in the world, trying to exert some control over a life where that control seems to have spiralled away.

Does everyone grow, however awful and traumatic their experience? 'People are always trying their best in trauma to grow in these purposeful directions. They may not always be very successful and it may not be that obvious to people, but that's going to be their motivation. Growth is a process, not an outcome, so it doesn't make much sense to ask "has a person grown?" because in a sense everybody will grow, everybody is trying to grow.'

When I suggest that there are many of us who have been through difficult life events who don't feel they're developing or progressing, or indeed, thriving, he refers back to the potatoes in Carl Rogers' cellar. 'Like the shoots reaching out in the darkness, the potato looks very unhealthy. You wouldn't say that's a nice-looking, healthy potato; you'd say that looks very distorted, and if you looked at a person who was similarly trying to grow, you may not see lots of lovely, positive things – it may look quite nasty, but it would still be that person, striving to grow.'

It can look quite nasty, Professor Joseph is right. It means letting go of belief systems that we've spent years building and defending. Changing, transforming, accepting and accommodating this new experience takes a long time and I'm still learning. I really wrestled with the whole concept of thriving after trauma when I felt ugly and bitter and bruised. 'Struggle doesn't feel like growth,' I say. Professor Joseph replies that even if levels of distress are high and we are feeling destructive, we can still be thriving. 'How is that possible?' I ask. He pauses. 'Look around at the trees outside your window,' he replies. 'They may be skewed or bent over to one side, because they've been damaged through storms. Or they may be very sparse in some places because they've been struck by lightning. They are not all beautifully healthy, flourishing as a perfect tree. Most will look distorted, twisted, thwarted and distressed, but you'll always see a tree striving to grow. People are the same.'

That's what surviving and thriving means. That's what rising after trauma is. You may feel distorted, twisted, thwarted, skewed and fragile. I did – and often still do. And certainly for me, those first weeks after surgery were among the hardest of my life. It was a time when I found it hard to reach towards the sun, but there were glimpses of light and hope and I clung to them, like a twisted tree, battered and damaged but still striving. Still trying to grow.

4

Going Home

'You're braver than you believe and stronger than you seem and smarter than you think'

Christopher Robin, to Pooh

Saturday, 10th January

Home. Wherever that is now. Paul and the kids are back in the empty London house which we can't seem to find tenants for. Good job too – he and the kids have been kicked out of the Sussex holiday let for the weekend. He was going to collect me from hospital but Neale, my ex-husband, had dropped by the ward, so he drives me back instead. When I walk through the front door, Paul shakes his hand, says, 'Thanks, old chap,' and when the door closes, bursts into tears. He's been doing a lot of that. Sometimes I'll look at him and he's weeping, silently.

Seth comes running downstairs with a new haircut and a big grin. 'Mama! Mama!' I automatically hunch to protect my wounds as he throws his arms around me. 'Careful! Careful!' Paul says. It's OK, it's inevitable and I don't want them to think I'm ill, or breakable.

Eve is out on a play date, Seth is about to go. I have a couple of boiled eggs, some painkillers and sit on the sofa, totally whacked. Seth, knowing something's wrong, keeps wanting to squeeze up, right next to me, maybe to test how ill I am. He's curious about the bottles. I explain how the drain system works – liquid collects like it does under a blister and it needs draining. He's fascinated. He watches the tubes intently before crying, excitedly, 'The juice is coming out! The juice is coming out!'

I snooze when he leaves and then Paul and I make a gentle move to the top of our road. Suddenly, you're conscious of how busy London is, how many people jostle and bustle. I'm fiercely aware of my fragility and whether I'll get unintentionally hit, or bumped.

We go to an organic food shop – me to the takeaway section, Paul to get tea. I agonize over the choices. It all looks dried-out and unappetizing, but I need to eat in order to heal. I order a hotpot – beans, chickpeas, spinach, tofu. Start as I mean to go on? A green juice, too. 'What's best?' I say. 'This – if you're under the weather,' she says, pointing to something with apple, cucumber, spirulina, kale.

Obviously, it's clear that I look sick, but then Paul says everyone in that shop looks peaky.

Walking back feels like the last few miles of a marathon. I ache, I want to lie down, I can't even cross a road at a decent walking pace, I've slowed. So much for my idea of brisk walks to recover and rejuvenate. This is going to take weeks – months, even.

Get home, read a book cover-to-cover, ignore family life, stay on the sofa. I'm full from the meal, those warm beans coagulated under a hot plate didn't seem particularly fulfilling but the bulk of it did the job. I look six months pregnant; my belly sticks out of my new shirt, my drains like gun holsters, either side of my waist. Then a hollow chest and a white face with lank, yet flyaway hair. This will be a long, slow road if even the stuff that normally holds together is falling apart. Seems a tad unfair that when your upper half looks ravaged and torn, like some scene from 'CSI', your body revolts all over, so there's no solace to be found in any of it.

Watch a film and then bed at eleven. It's been wonderful to be surrounded by the children (Eve was equally fascinated by the drains and worries, constantly, about them overfilling). I hid them when my stepdaughter Emily arrived. She's eighteen now and entering womanhood, I don't want to scare her into thinking that it can be something disgusting, debilitating.

Monday, 12th January (seven days after surgery)

We stayed at my brother Pete's last night, as our nomadic existence means we can move back into the holiday let in Sussex, but can't check in until later. The kids' school day starts early and, luckily, it's not far from Pete's so he suggested we come for supper and a sleepover the night before, so the children could play and laugh with their cousins, without being preoccupied by the fact that they don't have much of a home – or, to be honest, much of a mum. Seth wanted to show off my bottle of 'juice' to my sister-in-law, Katy, and her three boys, but I hid the drains away in my jacket. Sleeping was complicated and hot. I cried last night and the night before. On Saturday night I was overwhelmed by being out of hospital – frightened of the results and the future. The tears didn't last long and Paul was there. I can have a 'moment' with him, without the fear that he will think I am constantly wobbling. I'm not. I'm strong during the day and waver at night. It happened again last night. I got undressed in Pete and Katy's bathroom and, with the harsh lights and strange surroundings, together with the swollen stomach, the puckered gashes that make up my chest and the tubes leaking blood, coming out from under my armpits, it made me feel . . . grotesque.

So I came into the bedroom and rather self-pityingly cried, 'I'm hideous! This is hideous.' I was angry too – if I hadn't had all those biopsies, all that invasive needling, would the cancer cells have taken hold? Is it better, sometimes, to let things lie undisturbed? Would my body have sorted it all out without the poking and tissue removal?

I do not recognize myself. I hope growth comes of this. At the moment, I feel bruised beyond repair. Brittle, contorted, punched, ugly, old, damaged, diseased, thin, bloated, alien.

I drained between 30 and 40 ml each side – my fear is these buggers will be accompanying me for some time.

Morning comes – up and out with the kids to get them to school on time. Bit of make-up (but very bad Suzi Quatro-type mullet hair) and a coat that doesn't quite mask the two huge drain bottles. I poke the alarming, see-through tubes into the back of my trousers, so no small child hooks them out and says, 'What's this?' Those tubes carrying beetroot-coloured juice – it looks like I've just left the ward as soon as you see them. Something a geriatric patient would have, attached to a drip.

Various mums know about 'an operation' (both Seth and Eve appear to have mentioned to some of their teachers that 'Mum has breast cancer, she was in hospital and having it cut out'). Everyone was charming. I was nervous and halting. Usually, I'll bowl in, all smiles, diary open, contacts made, play dates arranged. I couldn't wait to drop and go.

We head back to our holiday let, the cottage in the grounds of a castle near the village of Wadhurst. It's small, sweet and isolated, just where I want to hide while I recover, somewhere new, away from inquisitive eyes. I need to be right away from London, people and curiosity at the moment. Until we find somewhere more permanent, it feels perfect, like a little burrow in the middle of nowhere. After unloading our suitcases, Paul and I head to a nearby coffee shop to check emails and shelter from the rain in companionable silence, digesting, quietening, normalizing. We visit estate agents, go to see a house, start dreaming of a life here in the country, surrounded by wet fields, here in Sussex perhaps, or the blustery Weald.

I'm still 'oozing', so I pop into the local doctor's to get my dressings changed. Sitting in the waiting room, I look at the table full of women's magazines. A newsreader is on the front of one of them, smiling, confident. 'How does she juggle her busy life,' the headline asks, yet 'still stay so glamorous?' I continue to ooze. My name is called and is recognized by some. Heads turn, patients look with surprise – what's she doing here? Is it her? It reminds me of when I went to the theatre with my mum on a day off and while in the queue for tickets, two women behind us muttered: 'That's Sian Williams, she's not much in real life, is she?' I hide my drains in my coat and tuck the tubes, vacuuming the blood away, down the back of my jeans. No, not that much in real life at all.

I see a nurse. She knows who I am, that TV presenter, but doesn't know why I'm here. 'I've just had a double mastectomy and need my dressings changed,' I say. She fails to rearrange her face in time, so I see the shock and wish I'd softened it a bit. She whips off the bandages with typical, reassuring efficiency and calls a doctor to have a look at the wounds. As he's examining my scars, he asks how I'm feeling. 'It doesn't matter,' I say, 'just get me a route map out of here.' The doctor starts telling me an anecdote. Oh no, I think, please don't, I'm picking up the kids from school soon. He begins describing a walk across a field. The field is deep with snow, without hedges or edges and he can't find the path, so he tentatively sets out, just putting one foot in front of the other, hoping he'll get to the other side. Eventually, he does. He looks back and – as the snow melts – he sees he's taken the right path anyway. His path. Winding and uncertain, but he still got to the end of the snowy field.

I'm at the start of my walk, I can't see the end, I worry I'll double-back on myself, that I'll give up, sit down, have a cry, wait to be rescued. Lace up your boots, he's telling me, it's going to be hard yards from here and there is no map. But you will get to the other side and you'll have taken the right path: your path.

I phone the hospital. My appointment is tomorrow at 12.45. Have the results from the pathology of the breast tissue and lymph node come in? Yes. Will you tell me over the phone? An astonished laugh. No! Later, an email from the breast cancer nurse, Shirley, saying they'll take out another drain (does she know there are two?) and a chatty last few sentences. 'Glad you feel OK! Hope it goes well!' What does that mean? Do those exclamation marks bode well?

To sleep, perchance to dream. Tomorrow, I'll know which path I'm taking – or at least in which direction I'm headed. It's either: cancer is out, tumours have gone, see you for your reconstruction, mind how you go. Or: it was more complicated, we've seen some changes in the lymph node, we have to have more surgery/radiotherapy/chemotherapy. I feel like a leaf in the wind.

Tuesday, 13th January

12.45 p.m.

Results. I'm with Jo the surgeon and I'm scribbling down everything that I'm being told. Get the facts, hold off on the emotion. Right side – 60 mm, ductal carcinoma in situ (DCIS). No invasive disease, no micro invasion, normal lymph node. Disease in another area, where they took the biopsy, right under the skin, can't make skin any thinner, so scraped as much as they could. Will be recommending radiotherapy every day for three to five weeks. Have to wait six weeks to heal first. Worry about how thin the skin is. Bring skin in from somewhere else. Concern about skin flaps. There is no clear cancer-free margin of tissue and skin.

Left side. Also DCIS; 50 mm. All out. No evidence of micro-invasion. No sign of invasive disease. Didn't take left lymph node as didn't know there was cancer in left breast, didn't see it on imagery. Chances are, still some cancer there, maybe 1 per cent in armpit.

Paul sends a text to the boys and everyone is mightily relieved – except me, for some strange, unfathomable reason. I don't feel like shouting, 'Rejoice! Rejoice!' I feel a bit numb, contemplating the next hurdle. Alex is outside the consulting room and we go to a café for lunch. I take some painkillers to prepare for the drain removal and I pop my pills with my super-food salad. Alex senses me being quiet and spends a long time reassuring me about what good news it is. And it is. The cancer is gone. I worry about the lack of a clear, cancer-free margin, the fact that the disease goes right up to the skin, the healing process, radiotherapy, potential skin grafting in the likelihood of the breast skin being damaged with further treatment. It's overwhelming; I don't feel I can shout, delightedly, from the rooftops, yet. That seems to make Paul sulk, angrily, for hours. I know it's because he wants completion and a sense of safety, but I'm not there yet.

Once Joss arrives, I explain it all to him and talk it through, trying to manage his excitement too, not tamp it down, but cautioning that the journey is a long one. This breast cancer will take months of my life, maybe even longer, even though it's out (is it?) and that feels strange. I don't know how to plan, what I can achieve, whether I can work.

I ask Jo the surgeon about going back to work and she says it'll be fine. No one need know. Once the drains are out, no one will be aware of the radiotherapy, it won't be obvious or noticeable. When I'm healed, in about six weeks, once we see what's happened with the fluid, the scars, the reconstruction, have a timetable for radiotherapy, then we'll know. She says she wants to 'inflate' my chest larger than is necessary, with silicone and saline, so it can then settle naturally. That'll be interesting.

She whips the drains out with a couple of brisk tugs. Thank God, thank God. Those bloody things – I hated them. They tie you up, physically and mentally, tether you to infirmity, a reminder to all that something is wrong.

I was more relieved when the drains came out than being told the cancer is out. That's weird. I think it's because I haven't processed it properly yet. It just seems like a series of future paths, next steps, hurdles. I want to be thrilled, I really do. Why can't I feel it?

Joss and Al leave for home. I have a minor domestic in the station with Paul, who is still sulking three hours later because he thinks he's been told off for being relieved. Wrong. I said I'm glad he's relieved and I'm sure I will be, but I'm not feeling it yet. He's surprised by my reaction. Fine. I'm fed up with having to explain why things may feel different to me than to others. Best thing really is not to talk about it too much, which is a shame, but if he can't handle what I'm feeling then let him just handle his own emotion. I can't be dealing with trying to pick him up like a spoilt, cross child. It's needy, selfish behaviour so I'm best off dealing with this myself from now on.

Friday, 16th January

I've calmed down. Considerably. I was harsh and unfair. I should have known Paul would grasp any piece of good news. I did feel relief of sorts, but looking at my chest – which still resembles a war zone, with its livid scars, blisters and lopsidedness, its partially fluid-filled, deflated and wrinkly implants – I know there is so much more of this to come.

I'll mend in six weeks and then every day I'll have radiotherapy which, according to the websites, hardens the implants and discolours the skin. Which is why my surgeon discussed further operations, a possible tissue and skin transfer from my back or thigh. Highly complex, needing further hospitalization, anaesthetic, pain, as they stitch together the arteries and nerve endings of different parts of my body, which will be welded onto my chest. Ugly.

Most of the charity websites say radiotherapy isn't needed after a double mastectomy and that reconstruction takes place after your body has tried to burn away the vestiges of cancer. This is happening because the margin of disease-free tissue is almost non-existent, which increases the risk of recurrence.

What if we had done nothing? Would this cancer have sat there, innocent and inconspicuous? Did I need to go through this?

The mastectomy happened last week. Is it really only last week? I was diagnosed on 18th December – no, 12th December. The following week I got the MRI results and then it was wait, wait, wait. Then the double mastectomy last week and now wait, wait, wait again until radiotherapy. Everything is on hold: work, holidays, move, life.

My appointment today is with Jo, the surgeon. She takes off a few dressings, marvels at my breasts – 'You've got a cleavage!' – and tells me they've been discussing me in great depth. The Woman With The Abnormally Thin Skin. I need to talk to the other specialists, but her view is we may not need radiotherapy after all. Monitoring might be the most effective form of treatment. Empirical evidence is mixed about the effectiveness of radiotherapy for those who don't have invasive cancer after a mastectomy. If I'd had a lumpectomy then she'd say it was the most obvious next step. Having had all my breast tissue taken out, there's nothing for the cancer to re-emerge in, although it may still be under the skin. The chances of it being in the left lymph nodes are slight, she says, as there was nothing in the right lymph nodes to suggest a spread there.

What are the chances of reccurrence with such small margins of error? I ask. She says there's not enough evidence to really know for sure. In the left, the margins are 0 mm, in the right, less than 1 mm.

So there we are. It may stop here. A bit of inflation, minding the scars, tending the wounds, but in a few weeks, some breasts back. Then, eventually a nipple or two. Hopefully two.

I'll talk to the oncologist – the cancer surgeons say the choice is mine, but it isn't, really. With a lack of evidence, I'm relying on their expertise and guidance. It's not a decision I can take.

Monday, 19th January

It's 4.30 a.m. I can't sleep. Neither can Eve – she got into our bed at 3 a.m., fully dressed. Poor thing. We are all a bit anxious about our new life, new school, new friends, new house. Knowing to bring the right kit, live in the right place, be the right people.

These are the thoughts buzzing around my head: Where should we live? Why haven't I done my meditation recently? What can I make with my new juicer? What job should I do? Should I start the Radio 4 series now, or later? Should I spend more time recovering? Have I remembered my niece's birthday? When is Seth going to start his Roman artefact? Where will I get the materials? Why is it so hot in here?

Got to start a list, start prioritizing, otherwise it all becomes a bit overwhelming.

It's two weeks today since I woke up and got dressed, ready to go to hospital. Wheeling that suitcase up the road, worried we'd be late for the 7 a.m. admission, irritation masking the deeper concern, that soon I'd be laid out and 'etherized upon a table', as T. S. Eliot would say. Then, carved up. Later, marker-pen slashes on my breasts to denote the target areas for the knife, radioactive dye coursing through veins to the lymph nodes, gown on, anaesthetic in, blacking out.

Waking in recovery, tubes everywhere. An intravenous drip feeding me morphine, another delivering saline, a catheter draining urine, four drain bottles collecting blood. Tied to a hospital bed by lines and tubes and drugs.

Seeing the scars for the first time and being shocked by the livid distortion. As if I'd been attacked, my breasts severed, and then I'd been captured and tied up.

Being unable to raise a glass of water to my lips, my voice husky with lack of use after five hours in unconsciousness.

Feeling nauseous, woozy, unbalanced. Unable to move my body because my arms wouldn't shift, let alone support me to swing my legs around or sit up.

Bloodied, sick, immobile, in pain.

Two weeks on and I can raise my arms above my head, wash my hair, walk for forty-five minutes on my own, drive, carry a handbag. I can't pick the children up yet – I miss that. I rather optimistically bought a pair of running shoes and an outfit to jog in, thinking I'll be able to start soon and get back to full health. Running before I can walk, probably. Yesterday, I tried to go a whole day without painkillers. I got to the evening and my breasts were so swollen and hot that I gulped down the paracetamol.

The kids are up, I can hear them padding around upstairs. Unsettled in our rented house, wanting the things around them, their friends, their toys. When Seth had a meltdown a couple of days ago and said, 'You didn't consult me about this move! I hate the new school! I miss my friends and my house and my old school! Why have you done this without asking me?' I felt he had a very good point. Why have we done this? Will it work? We are all trying, making new friends, organizing lunches, trying to craft a new life, but I feel for them – little people trying to be brave, putting on their uniform to face another day of new experiences.

They have to be unsettled by all this, too. Even though they cheerfully tell their friends, 'Mummy's been ill, but she's getting better', they know they can't hug me yet without me wincing. I can't sweep them up in an embrace when they're upset. The physical evidence of disease has gone for them, although Eve has seen – and touched – my scars. Dressed, mobile, make-up on, you wouldn't know anything had happened two weeks ago. But they would have felt it.

Tuesday, 20th January

Rereading this diary for the first time, I'm aware of how quickly I've lapsed into old ways of thinking.

That intense feeling of gratefulness, of a life that has shifted, of priorities recast – it can't be so easily forgotten, can it? Why did I wake at 3 a.m. with thoughts of what I 'should' do? Why am I thinking about work already? Angry that I cancelled jobs this week when I now feel up to doing them? This time should (argh! That word again!) could/might be used more profitably to think, reflect, absorb, accommodate.

Remember those hospital thoughts. Don't go rushing towards your old version of normality, with its concerns about judgement, both yours and other people's. Rest a while. Ease off. Old Sian, TV Sian, was full of 'shoulds' and 'should nots'. I should run. I should eat more healthily, I should try to look less like a fifty-year-old woman, I should, I should, I should.

Perhaps New Sian can be slower, if possible. Gentler, more forgiving. I vowed that my new 'no more cancer' diet would be full of green juices. Dairy-free, wheat-free, sugar-free. In the past few days, I've had a lot of cake, walked a bit, watched some films. It's OK. Chocolate cake, every now and again, will not encourage the cancer to come back. Eating two enormous, very posh cupcakes from my lovely sister-in-law Katy, one after the other, was immensely pleasurable.

I've always equated a diet that excludes 'bad' foods with a guarantee of good health. Look at me! All green tea and salmon! And still, I got cancer.

Maybe easing off will be beneficial in all areas of life. No more 'shoulds' and 'should nots'. Maybe, as my doctor says, 'mights' or 'might nots'. Or even – 'fuck it, why not?'

It'll all be fine. That was the subject heading of the email I sent out when I discovered what was going to happen. And it will. If you can handle this, when you have been at your most vulnerable and damaged, physically and mentally, and you can get up, rise up, straighten your shoulders and look squarely at the world, you'll be OK. It'll all be fine.

Except when it won't. Because sometimes, it won't be fine. There will be other things like this – injuries, sickness, loss, bereavement – and once again, I'll be felled by the sudden, painful hell of it. Just like everyone else. Do I feel stronger now, than before? Yes. Do I feel able to get back up? Probably. But that doesn't mean everything is sunshine and roses. I know recovery is hard work. That there are emotional relapses where you shout and feel sorry for yourself (and in my case it was two days ago and the target was Paul, who I unfairly blamed for lacking engagement in the intricacies of my illness).

I remember in the months – and years – after Mummy died of cancer, I would feel OK and then suddenly, out of nowhere, I would crumble, as if my knees had given way. I grew up by the sea and find much solace there, but it felt like when you're standing in the shallows with your back to the ocean and a wave hits, unexpectedly, knocking you onto the pebbles, gashing your knees. That's what 'recovery' feels like. Fragile. Capable of unravelling at any time.

The family is up. Less introspection. Time to get on with life.

5

Reflection

'Be patient toward all that is unsolved in your heart and try to love the questions themselves; like locked rooms and like books that are now written in a very foreign tongue. Do not now seek the answers, which cannot be given you, because you would not be able to live them. And the point is, to live everything. Live the questions now. Perhaps you will then gradually, without noticing it, live along some distant day into the answer'

Rainer Maria Rilke, *Letters to a Young Poet*

Thursday, 29th January

My friend Dixi sends me that quote as reassurance that feeling wobbly is OK. We're in the Wellcome Trust café on the Euston Road, just next to University College Hospital where the clinicians whipped my breasts off. The café is full of mumbling erudition – lots of clever people sipping kale and ginger juice, wondering whether to buy another book on the brain. Dixi has brought a present in a small, shiny red bag, stuffed with pink tissue. 'Don't get this out here,' she warns, looking around. 'Wait until you get home.'

'Don't be daft,' I say. 'I've had a crap morning having my miserable

chest manipulated and you've brought me a gift. I want to open it now.'

I take out the tissue and, looking quizzically at her, delve inside, taking out two soft, round, pink balls – with very perky nipples. 'It's from my nan,' she says, suppressing a giggle. 'She's knitted you some new breasts.' We start to howl with laughter as I hold the ridiculous woollen boobs, one in each hand, up to my chest, catching the eye of a café dweller, who's clearly wondering whether two middle-aged ladies-who-lunch have become hysterical on early white wine.

This whole thing is absurd. I've decided to be wheat, dairy and sugar-free after the operation to try to stop the cancer returning. This, despite knowing there's no solid clinical research to suggest diet makes much difference to it coming back. The deprivation, if that's what you'd call it, results in an almighty eating session of bread, cereal, pudding and giant spoonfuls of chocolate spread.

The thing is, even though my studies tell me how hard it is to stand up when you're being battered by tumultuous waves, I want to stay steady, I want some control over this. But illness and disease aren't ordered neatly. They don't respond to me getting angry and trying to marshal them in one direction. Medical decisions are sometimes tortuously slow and lacking certainty.

Of course I'm going to try to impose some ridiculous dietary restrictions upon myself, I'm desperate to reassert some authority over my revolting body, even while knowing it won't make much difference. It's a bit of genetics, a bit of bad luck and there's not much you can do to stop it happening to you. That's what the surgeon said. How frustrating – a life rushing to deadlines, managing work, children and study, keeping fit, eating the right things, being good. And it still gets you. Cancer, waiting behind the door, sniggering at your pathetic attempts at planning, guffawing at your desperate desire to retain control of your life. It waits, it laughs, it gets you anyway.

But feeling as though I have some control over my recovery, even if it's illusory, negligible, is helpful. It's about managing the things I can handle now. I can't manage the big stuff, but at least I can decide what I eat.

Wednesday, 4th February

Tomorrow, it'll be exactly a month since surgery, and today I had my feet massaged and my breasts inflated. I cried in front of a psychologist and talked tough in the middle of a business meeting. I tell myself I am strong, yet am vulnerable and weak. The trouble with appearing capable is that people assume you don't need help, so don't offer. 'I'm quite able to drive/lift/walk/work/do this myself,' you say. And then, when they let you, you get upset because you're not being 'nurtured'.

I read too much into others' intentions, getting irritable when an email pings into my inbox, asking how I am, quickly followed by 'Can I ask a favour?' This from a family friend, who knows I've just had a double mastectomy and who didn't contact me afterwards, yet now wants 'celebrity endorsement' for a business plan.

Another irritation – a friend comes over and spends most of the time whining about their cold. I know I'm expected to be sympathetic, and I am, but am also bubbling with indignation. I want to say, I may be having radiotherapy in a few weeks, which could, as one doctor so beautifully put it, 'fry your skin, damage your implants and mean a skin and tissue graft when you have more spare, followed by all this reconstruction again'. Sod your bloody cold, I think. Your poor thing, I say, how ghastly.

At the moment, it all seems to be, Can you work on this? Sympathize with that? Speak at this? Send me that? Redraft your thesis for publication? Come up with a lecture we want you to give on trauma? Think of a business plan for resilience courses? Some days I think: yes.

Yes, I can because I know all about resilience and how to bounce back, I did two years of research, I know the pattern. And other days I think, I can't bounce and, even if I did, it won't be 'back'. I can't go back, now. I don't know how to do this. Will you all please go away and leave me in peace.

I'm healed, aren't I? I'm lucky and I certainly look the same – clothed, at least. So why do I feel so lost and angry? Certainly more emotional and experiencing this intense sadness, which comes in unexplained, unbidden. Weaker, easier to knock off balance, confused.

Paul comes with me to see the oncologist, Dr Blackman. I feel he looks at me like a cancer lightweight. 'We used to call this pre-cancer,' he says. 'There's some evidence to suggest surgery is not the right option for it.' 'Was it for me?' 'Yes.' He tells me there was cancer in both breasts. It hadn't been detected in the left, by the hospital's world-class, gold-standard technology. Some of the cancer, quite a fair bit of it, is high grade.

Lots of questions: as my aunty died of breast cancer in her twenties and had her ovaries out because of fear of the disease, and as my mother also died of cancer, should I be gene tested? Would hormone therapy make a difference? I also ask him about radiotherapy. Three weeks, five days a week to start with, says the breast surgeon. Maybe five weeks. But the oncologist and the operating team have met and discussed the case of the woman with perhaps the thinnest skin they've seen and they suggest radiotherapy may have more risks than benefits. The whole skin-frying, tissue-damaging, implant-buggering thing, I suppose.

I ask my last series of questions. 'Is there any cancer still there?' 'No,' he answers definitively, 'it's out and it was non-invasive'. I query how he can be sure it won't come back, how he knows the surgeons have got it all if there is no clear margin between the disease and the healthy part of me. 'The cancer won't come back,' he says, with incredible certainty. He gives me the options: blast the chest with radiation, make sure none of those unpredictable cells is lurking, ready to divide, make a mistake, create cancer again. Or leave things be and monitor, in the hope that division, the mistakes, the cancer, are picked up by the technology that missed them, at least in one breast, the first time.

I ask if I can have a second opinion and immediately feel dreadful, as if I've insulted his expertise. He says it'll be interesting if I did, from an oncology perspective. And if they disagree with him, it'll also be 'interesting' to see what decision I take. Is he trying to mask indignation with curiosity? The scientist in him is interested, I know. The experienced leader in his field may be a little affronted. I spend a long time apologizing and explaining, trying to alleviate any wounded pride.

Will mine be a path that takes me into hospital more, or less? I don't believe it's all gone. Every time I speak to a medical professional, I learn something new. Today it's that some cancer cells have inevitably remained, that they couldn't 'scrape them all out'. Scrape. Along with 'ooze' and 'moist', the words that rank as some of the more grotesque in the almost-medical lexicon.

Meanwhile, my breasts. At the moment, I look like a woman who's preparing for her next fight. Who's hacked off the parts of her that get in the way of victory. I look like a Mad Max, futuristic, scarred, fighting drone. Or a defiant, self-mutilated, Amazonian warrior. On the good days, that's what I feel I look like. The 'otherness' looks alien, but not wrong.

Other days, I can see the puckering and the uneven, indented, red slashes across each breast and the missing nipples, and I feel differently. I feel ridiculous, as if I have two deflating balls on my chest, with the skin covering them so thin that I can feel the wrinkles of the implants beneath my fingers. I hide myself from Paul when he says, 'Give us a look!' Not yet. Not on demand, not on your terms, I think. Then I stop myself for being so precious and show him. Not as bad as he thought, apparently, although he says that my breasts have always been 'irrelevant' to him. Swell, thanks.

Last night, I went onto the Internet and typed in 'mastectomy scars, one month on'. I saw such beautiful women, standing proudly, looking into the middle distance, black-and-white shots, their scars looking a little like mine, their faces radiant, at peace, comfortable, accepting. I wondered how long it had actually been since their operations, their scars were not as livid as mine – a year perhaps? It looked as if they were really comfortable in their bodies, accepting the changes.

Friday, 6th February

Two days later. Remember this, you are bloody remarkable, Sian Williams. And don't EVER let ANYONE persuade you otherwise. You have come through one of the most terrifying experiences anyone can imagine – and you might have more to come – but if you can face this and ride the pummelling waves, you can face most things. A month ago, I could barely lift a cup to my lips, hold a pen, embrace my children. Today I am walking tall and I feel strong and resilient. That doesn't mean that I'll feel the same way tomorrow. But at the moment, this is where I am and it feels OK. More than OK. It feels like the foundations are getting a little more solid.

Tuesday, 10th February

Today they've shifted again. Logically, everything's healing and I'm nearing the 'six weeks and you're all healed, then' marker. Paul doesn't understand why I am so confused about all this. They cut the cancer out, job done, no? I look like I did before the operation (at least, clothed). Once I wash my hair and put lipstick on, I look, almost, like before. Tired and pale, but almost there. Why am I so emotional? If anyone is nice to me, a friend, a breast cancer nurse, a woman at the gym I've laughably joined, then I'm liable to well up and start crying. There is no reason for this, I am healthy. I am lucky. Yet hearing about work from colleagues unsettles me. I should get back in the game, I think. Where did I go? Whatever happened to . . . ?

This is myopic, because everything has changed since last month, but sometimes it feels as if nothing has. Kids get grumpy, Paul sees me as 'normal', house needs sorting, my agent asks if I want to work. Bypassing all this is a feeling of being fundamentally altered. Diminished in many ways, more emotional, experiencing visceral sadness, unexplained, unbidden. Weaker, easier to knock off balance. Confused.

Wednesday, 11th February

I'm seeing a psychologist at UCH who specializes in breast cancer care. When we talk, I cry – about past traumas, my mother's fast, undiagnosed cancer, which killed her within four months. Giving birth to a blue, flat baby and then losing more than half my blood – being told that we almost lost our son, before almost losing my life, too. Even earlier traumas of being trapped, feeling threatened, aggression. She has a lot of untangling to do.

Talking to her, I realize that in our family we suppress emotion and get on with things. Pull your socks up, snap out of it, pick yourself up, dust yourself off. The morning after my mother's death, my dad, my brothers and I had organized the funeral and taken all her clothes to the charity shop in black bin bags by midday, just a few hours after she died. So I'm not really used to indulging in emotion, and no one expects it of me. I'm known as being capable, strong in a crisis, psychologically literate. Not this.

The psychologist recommends I address priorities. The first is the treatment decision. When I know about radiotherapy, I can decide what next about life, home, work. I draw up a list of pros and cons. It's complex. The 'pros – no radiotherapy' column includes: continued physical recovery, don't have to go into hospital every day for five weeks, it keeps others like Paul and my oncologist Dr Blackman happy. The 'cons' column has: constant cancer worry, back on the bike sooner. The 'pros – have radiotherapy' column has: kills remaining cancer cells. The 'cons'? Frying the skin, hardens implants, possibility of further procedures, daily trips to hospital. I do the same with going back to work, a whole page, divided into pros – going back (might be fun, keep occupied) vs cons (sucked back into a world with judgement, egotism, competition, narcissism. Less time with Paul and kids. Need childcare). The work decision is different to the radiotherapy decision and they are entangled in my head. The psychologist tells me to find my voice and listen to it. Separate things out. What am I ready for? What am I not? Life is not the same. Life will never be the same. The tectonic plates have shifted.

Monday, 16th February

It's half-term and six weeks today since the operation. So this is meant to be a milestone. The literature says recovery should take at least six weeks. Yet it still pulls across my chest to close a car door, or take off a pair of boots. I lie down and the construction where they cut and sewed and inflated feels strange. The implants are rippled, I can feel them just below the skin, filled with saline: two little, almost full balloons of water. How odd it feels. And looks too, with the slashes across each, the puckering of the skin, the strange androgyny of it. I look like a creation, patched up after battle, sexless.

Paul and I stand on a beach, looking out to sea, and I can't quite believe that this has happened to us. Not in a self-pitying way, just slightly bewildered. 'Does it seem odd to you?' I say. 'Lacking the substance of reality? "Sian Williams has had a double mastectomy." That statement seems too incongruous to belong to me. Does it sound weird to you?' He looks at me and seems tired, worn, resigned. It's not weird to him because he lived it. While I was surviving, he was watching and feeling – what? Impotence? Anger? Fear? And my emotions focused on getting through, small steps towards recovery, raising a cup to my lips, lifting my arms above my head, hiding the bottles that drained the blood from my wounds. It's like being in a bubble where all your energy is directed back upon yourself, you're clutching onto tiny victories as proof you can build back up, grow stronger. The shock of it, mentally, is outside that bubble, suffered by others, looking in at you struggling to do the things that a small child could do, yet unable to help.

Tuesday, 17th February

The presenter Carol McGiffin has breast cancer. It was in the Sunday papers and it's still going today. She had a mastectomy ten months ago, then fifteen rounds of radiotherapy, then chemo. She kept it private because she didn't want sympathy. I'm amazed – and heartened – that no one tipped off the press in that time. It meant she could present her story from a position that might have felt more manageable for her. Or maybe not. Other newspapers pick up the news but bury it in a story about her colleague going shopping. So, this life-affecting personal trauma becomes an adjunct to an article inviting us to look at a celebrity not wearing make-up, buying food. Her cancer is described as a 'secret heartache' and I become irrationally angry. 'Secret heartache'? What does that mean? Somehow the phrase does exactly what Carol wanted to avoid: it victimizes her, she becomes someone who we feel sorry for, struggling with her 'secret heartache' when she's probably just getting on with things as normal, but with this odd, constant subtext, a soundtrack, a background story, running underneath the everyday. Cancer becomes something you try to live with, along with everything else, like work, home and all the flotsam and jetsam that accompany both. Appointments to discuss radiotherapy are slotted in around the rest of life. It becomes normal, something you roll with, not something that flattens existence. It is not a 'secret heartache'. It's a bugger and perhaps it'll even be a blessing. The Janus face of cancer. Losing breasts and gaining – what – insight? A vivid appreciation of life? I don't know. Maybe I'm looking for something, anything, positive to come out of this. Don't let anyone call me 'brave'. I'm not. Don't call it 'heartache'. Losing someone you love is heartache. Losing your breasts is not.

Wednesday, 18th February

To mark six weeks of being wheat-free, dairy-free, sugar-free, I had two large bowls of muesli and four Mini Magnums, after a restaurant meal of pasta and chocolate mousse. I finished the evening eating Nutella with a dessert spoon.

Thursday, 19th February

Work dreams, the ones I had when I was actually working, are back. I can't blame the Nutella. This is anxiety about returning to some broadcast work on Friday. They all collided, these dreams, so I was sweating about being in the wrong place, half an hour before the 'BBC One O'Clock News'. Not being able to contact the output editor, or find a jacket, or an earpiece. Looking ghastly and irrevocably tired/old/shabby, the hair thin and flyaway brittle, the eyes yellow instead of white, the wrinkles deeper. Ouch. Judgement. Rusty 'skills', missing deadlines and pissing off bosses. Then, a Radio 4 dream where my show had a new presenter, who was all perky, with loads of confident competence. How easy will it be to put the mask back on? Can I slip back into it naturally? The bravura that I had has been cut away and I wonder whether it will be spotted, this change in my nature. Everything to do with the BBC seems overwhelming, as if the tasks that were once simple and innate have been lost. That's the searching element of the dream, that and being erased, not being able to find the tools to get me on air. I'm scrabbling around for the uniform, I've missed my slot, I've been usurped. I don't know if I can still do this. Although no one will know I've had my breasts cut off and that I'm waiting for news on radiotherapy, will they? No. Stay bright, bright, bright.

Monday, 23rd February

Seven weeks since the operation and I'm kneeling on the landing at our cottage, pounding my fists on the floor again and again, and wailing. I haven't wept like this for months, my face is contorted, eyes streaming, angry – no furious – with the bloody NHS. The NHS that has nursed me so carefully, which spotted the cancer and cut it out. The NHS, with its nurses full of empathy and its surgeons full of expertise. The NHS, where my grandfather, grandmother, mother and brother spent their working careers. Where my son will work as a doctor. Letting me down because I'm no longer a priority. Whip 'em off, send her out, watch for lumps, cancer's back.

I'm waiting for a second opinion about radiotherapy and I call the hospital daily. The secretary, tapping away at her computer, tells me again that someone will call back. No one does. Then comes the news that my case will be discussed at the fortnightly meeting. I wait for two weeks, delay decisions about life and work, ring up after their meeting and hear that my case has been postponed. It's 'dropped off the list, for some reason'. What reason? What could be the reason? It's like being in a Kafka novel, or an Orwellian nightmare: no one telling you anything useful, authoritarian figures in white coats, saying nothing. Secretaries and nurses with mouths taped up. No one knows, no one explains. Bouncing around a hospital telephone system, trying to find someone with information and running up against the bland defences of the innocent. 'I don't know, I can't say, it's not my position, I don't know your case.' 'Then find someone who does know, or can say or may understand,' I howl with self-pity.

Oh, the teeth-grinding frustration of it all. I start to cry on the phone and regret it. The nurse says sorry and I realize that she could be a member of my family, run off their feet, dealing with the pain and anguish of other cancer patients, perhaps those with terminal prognoses, and yet now she has an angry, demanding patient who has unanswerable questions. I get back into my box. It's OK to howl, just don't blame others.

Tuesday, 24th February

I'm on a train to London to get my hair cut and go to a big event. Last night, I told Paul I wasn't going, but I've agreed to turn up, to sit and talk to important people, to look like a TV person, to work the room. My eyes are still swollen from the howling and my dresses won't fit. My breasts are, rather comically, rather irregular. One is more than an inch lower than the other. The vast, flat expanse of chest between the two not-quite-inflated, lopsided balls has a huge blister across it, the result of wearing an old underwired bra that rubbed and dug and scraped the skin. How to transform myself back to who I was? I'm nothing like that now. Jobs I would have jumped at, I push away. Commentate for the BBC on a big national event? I should, I know I should. Putting on make-up and dress won't take me back though, it'll be so obvious I'm different.

Dipping my head back into the basin at a celebrity-stuffed, blonde-highlighting Kensington hair salon, with the news on televisions thoughtfully placed near the ceiling so you can catch up while the conditioner is doing its stuff, I almost feel like the old me, eyebrows threaded, grey hair hidden, ready to go. The artifice that we create, believing it's necessary. What would happen if we stopped all that threading, plucking, waxing, colouring? Always painting our hair, nails, skin with chemicals to try to look better. What if we didn't do it? The sky won't fall in. I may be a snapshot in a crappy magazine, 'embracing' my 'natural self', tapping into our neuroses. Other than that, who cares?

Mask on, new bouncy hair, high heels, sticky false eyelashes, blistered chest, red lipstick, a dress with maximum torso coverage and I'm back on the underground, heading for the Guildhall in London for my first event since surgery: the University of Cardiff's Annual St David's Day Dinner. As I totter out of the station, I glance at the invitation. Wrong day. It's the wrong bloody day. I'm out by a full week. How ludicrous. Standing in my short dress, fully made-up, at seven o'clock, ready to go to a posh 'do' that's not even on tonight. I get back on the train, home to a cold empty house in London, peel off the eyelashes, jump into pyjamas and a dressing gown, laughing at myself with my scarred, lopsided breasts and my 'Alexa choppy bob', looking and feeling absurd. Sian – you are not ready for this. It's not you. You can't be who you were with a slick of paint and an expensive hairstyle.

Is cancer everywhere? Or do I think that, purely because I have it? Like being pregnant and seeing babies everywhere. Nick Robinson, the BBC's Political Editor, has it. A cancerous tumour in his lung. He'll be back by the General Election, he says. Everyone seems to say: good for you, deal with it and get back to work. I feel for those who have a different cancer, a different mentality, who feel so altered that they can't get back on the bike. Perhaps they can't slot back into who they were and what they were as easily as others. Will that make them feel lesser, weaker, worried that they're not coming up to the mark?

It's that Angelina Jolie effect again. Look at her, all glamorous, caring, a global ambassador, fighting for women's rights, lauded by politicians and the most admired woman on earth, according to one poll. And all this after having her breasts removed. Brave, beautiful Angelina.

What if you can't be 'better' after surgery? If you slide and go under? How do some become pioneers of stoicism and others slink into solitude? How helpful is it for public figures to talk about getting back to 'normal' so fast? I wonder – and I count myself in this – if it's actually quite alienating. I have privileges that others don't – good support, a decent salary and the research background to understand what may work and the space and resilience to try it.

I hope that Nick's journey is one that's easy to navigate and that his path leads to where he wants it. I imagine his work is a huge part of his identity; without it, his life and sense of self might alter. I can see why he wants to return, fast. Back to who he was as quickly as possible. Excise disease.

I lost it with the kids tonight, so badly that my voice went hoarse with the shouting. I told my eight-year-old son to 'shut up'. I've never done that before. Never screamed in anger at them, my face contorting with fury. Poor little Evie started crying, suddenly frightened and confused. Seth kept repeating, 'I'm sorry, I'm sorry, I'm sorry.' I'd had enough of their bickering. Seth had sung a song about Evie's bum being big, Eve hit him, Seth said he hated her, I told them to stop squabbling, they continued to yell, I warned them I was about to lose my temper and BANG. It went, quickly and spectacularly. Leaving them both open-mouthed, before dissolving into tears.

My nerves are frayed and I don't know why. My brother-in-law Martin, the one with a cancer that's a lot worse than mine, has written to me to ask how I am. How completely selfless and loving of him. What am I to say? I have my life, thanks, but I'm still a moody, ungrateful cow. Seems a bit myopic to be moaning about your circumstances to someone who may have a clock ticking, marking the minutes.

Tuesday, 3rd March

I'm on my way to a work interview and I'm sick with nerves. We're recording a Radio 4 series in an anechoic chamber, a small room devoid of sound and light. It's like an isolation chamber, a flotation chamber for the mind. We've recorded one interview already and it went well. Today, I'm anxious, feeling incredibly low. Here we go . . .

It went well. How can I quieten and reassure my mind about these things so I don't spiral into anger, irritability, ineptitude? The brain is plastic, the 'father of psychology' William James said so in 1890, I remember it from my lectures. Surely the mind can alter the brain? I know mental activity can lead to changes in the brain structure because I learnt about it during my neuroscience studies. Am I not concentrating properly, then? Am I not firing enough new neurons to facilitate change? There are a hundred billion of them, are they working together positively or negatively?

How to think differently? To see these aberrant and abhorrent versions of myself – shouting, depressed, frightened – and rewire them into something else, something more nurturing, forgiving? Nicer? I have to alter my brain's neurochemistry.

I stay overnight at our empty house in London and meet Paul in the morning at the Royal Marsden Hospital. We are in the radiotherapy department, with lots of others who have cancer of one sort or another. Many greet the receptionist like an old friend. One has spent three hours getting here, to be told her case hasn't yet been reviewed and she has to turn around and go home again.

I'm anxious. I went for a run after I woke up today, my old route around the woods, and it was tough going. I was tired, my legs didn't want to do it but I thought I needed to get fitter, stronger, for whatever comes next. On my jog back, I bumped into my ex-husband, Neale, who lives around the corner. His smile and hug made me cry. 'I'm OK!' I kept saying. 'Really, I'm fine . . .' while tears were coursing down my cheeks. I don't know why I suddenly felt so sad. His face, bright but full of concern, maybe. Not needing to be in control and on top of it all for him, like I am with my family, to protect them from worry. Not needing to pretend.

I'm called in to see the oncologist, a consultant in her fifties, Gill Ross, who has leopard-skin trousers, high boots and mad hair. I like her immediately. She tells me she's looked at the 'pathology' of my breast tissue; in other words, she's examined the cancer that was taken out. She says some of the analysis shows I have low, intermediate and high grade ductal carcinoma in situ, or DCIS, the cancer that lurks in the milk ducts, and that it's unusual to see malignancy in all three grades.

The doctor with the funky trousers gives me three options. One: do nothing. 'You can leave everything be and hope the cancer doesn't come back.' She gives me a fascinating statistic which I hurriedly scribble down. If DCIS is still there and is left untreated over ten to fifteen years, about 0.5 per cent of patients will see it develop into invasive cancer. A half of one per cent. They are ballpark figures, she says, and most evidence is around lumpectomy, not mastectomy. My risk is an area around the muscle and skin; mammography won't work now, so in future doctors will work with their hands on me, searching for lumps.

Two: five weeks of daily radiotherapy. This only inactivates cancer cells in some cases and is not 100 per cent. In my case, she says, it is a 'completely theoretical treatment'. We don't know whether cancer cells still lurk under the skin and, if they do, whether blasting them will kill them. It's a 'shot in the dark'. The consultant is not worried about the 'flaps' of skin, they look healthy and she doesn't think radiotherapy will damage them unduly. She talks about reconstruction. At the moment, I still have these odd, round, temporary implants with two buttons, or ports, under my skin, just on the bra line. She says they feel rigid and may become more so with the radiotherapy, that I'll need cosmetic surgery to replace the implants, that the operation is 'not as severe' as the mastectomy and that some women will need their implants replacing after five years.

Three: we sacrifice the reconstruction, get rid of the 'skin envelope' around both my breasts and reconstruct new ones by using tissue from elsewhere. There will be a bigger set of scars, as they'd take the dorsal muscle from the back.

I don't have the information to make the right choice between the three options. She asks why I haven't been gene-tested, as my family history means I'd qualify for it. If I do have the test and am genetically predisposed to cancer, then the third, most dramatic option is the best, followed by operations to remove my ovaries and fallopian tubes. She tells me about the test for the BRCA gene mutations. In the mid-1990s, the Royal Marsden helped develop state-of-the-art gene-sequencing equipment to identify them in breast and ovarian cancer patients, and that groundbreaking work now informs treatment for prostate and pancreatic cancers, too.

The BRCA test costs the NHS around a thousand pounds, with lab fees and a couple of counselling sessions to prepare you for the implications – and it's about an eight-week wait for the results. You can get them much faster by going privately, but it's more expensive. In England alone, fifty-six thousand women get breast cancer every year (and more than 350 men will be diagnosed, too). There are also seven thousand cases of ovarian cancer annually. That's a lot of people wanting to know if they have a hereditary pull towards the disease. Some say it's cheaper to test those who may have the mutated gene rather than treat them later for an invasive cancer, because all that surgery, chemo and radiotherapy costs the health service around thirteen thousand pounds per person. It doubles for what the NHS calls 'more serious metastatic cancers', where the disease spreads to another part of the body. Yet a positive genetic result, which leads to a 'risk-reducing' mastectomy and reconstruction, is a quarter of that price.[1]

If I have a BRCA mutation, I'd need to tell everyone in my family that they are at risk too, so they can think about testing. There are implications for our children, too. Hopefully, by the time the little ones reach puberty, doctors will have found a way to deal with cancer that doesn't involve sawing bits of your body off. Already, researchers are looking at which other gene markers may predict cancer, and scientists are continuing to improve screening technology as well as looking to see how to target chemotherapy drugs to specific cancers. Breast cancer is leading the way towards more sophisticated treatments. Until then, for some, the scalpel seems to be the best option.

Wednesday, 4th March

I'm inspired by a woman in the darkness. I'm recording my Radio 4 series, 'The Thought Chamber', in a room devoid of light and sound. In there, alone, is space scientist Dr Maggie Aderin-Pocock. She had an incredibly disruptive childhood, bouncing around thirteen different schools as a youngster, dealing with dyslexia, wanting to become a scientist, exploring the universe beyond Earth and being told she could become a nurse 'because that's a scientific job'. (Worthwhile, yes, and with much science in it; my mother and grandmother were both nurses. But scientific? Surely if a child says she wants to be an astronaut, you encourage her to reach for the stars?)

Maggie spent forty-five minutes in the room, looking up. Even though there was nothing to look at. Her default is to look beyond, to lose herself in clashing galaxies and exploding colours. To go beyond the universe and the beginnings of time to explore and delve into who we are and where we fit. She is the epitome of not just resilience after challenges, but joy, excitement, seizing life with both hands, pushing beyond the boundaries and strictures of earthly life. To find answers in the stars and inspiration in constellations. She could have looked back at her past, been downcast, or set her eyes on a clear, defined, forward path. She chose up. To infinity, to endless possibility. She teaches me to try not to be shackled by earthly concerns and minor trauma. Life can spin on a sixpence, can change in an instant and be rendered terrifying and destructive within a day. But while the sun shines and my only real worry is getting balloons for Evie's sixth birthday party, I shall count my lucky stars. Along with Maggie. Keep looking up, Sian. Look beyond.

Thursday, 5th March (two months after surgery)

I'm on a treadmill for the first time in months. I used to run. I say 'used to', as if there's a 'before' and 'after' to cancer. The irony being that I ran a marathon for Macmillan Cancer Support, the very people who are offering me help now. Then the training runs involved up to eighteen-mile distances. Now, I'm struggling to do two. My chest pulls, my lungs drag, my legs ache. I fix my gaze on a spot beyond the window, trying not to look at the speed, slow, or the distance, which is negligible.

Anyway, Joss and Alex had put together a music track-list when I was slogging towards the marathon and I always thought their choices were so fabulous and the intent behind them so pure and kind, that it spurred me on through grinding runs in the rain. Prodigy and T-Rex, the Red Hot Chilli Peppers, Jamiroquai, Rizzle Kicks, Josh Osho, it's a great list. That last artist, with his song 'Redemption Day', always leaves me sobbing through the grisly, grimacing last mile. 'You're a soldier, you're a fighter, don't go and waste another day, just take what comes your way . . .' Plod, gasp, sob.

Here's the odd thing about life in or after trauma. You can have these positive, 'seize the day'-type thoughts one minute – Look up, Sian! Look up! And the next? You're back to feeling weary and battle-fatigued. Wrong word, maybe, as I always rail against using 'battle' anywhere near 'cancer'. You'd think my mum, with all her decades of nursing, could somehow arm herself against the disease, with all that knowledge, tools and technology. But it got her anyway; no amount of dodging or fighting changed that. There wasn't a 'battle'. It wasn't a fair contest.

The real battle is with the mind; the real 'fight' is the one with your sanity. The war only gets under way after you've survived and crawled from the wreckage, still breathing. You look back at the damage and think, What the hell was that? Why am I still here? Why do I continue to hurt? The bleeding stops but the tears continue to flow, churning up old memories, reminding you of your own fragility. This doesn't feel like growth. This feels raw and painful.

When I started writing a book on resilience, I knew recovery wasn't smooth and that it wasn't a linear process, but backwards and forwards with many stumbles, because that's what my research subjects told me. So I know it and yet, resilience seems so far away. I can't seem to do it; I can't seem to heal myself fast enough. When will I start to get better? Which path shall I take? Too many unanswered questions. Do not now try to seek the answers. Live the questions.

6

Finding Our Voice

'The best way out, is always through'

Robert Frost, '*A Servant to Servants*'

What happens if the trauma is so vast and all-encompassing that it doesn't feel as if you can bear to live the questions? I lost my breasts, my colleague Stuart lost his leg and even though the subsequent effects on our minds were quite different, we both had to adjust our view of ourselves, our relationships and our place in the world. You try to live the questions, even though it hurts. Can everyone, though?

There is no pecking order of trauma. Someone else's experience may seem more, or less, severe than ours, but what is important is not the event itself, not the suffering per se, but how we make sense of it, afterwards. Many people survive extremely challenging life events that, at the time, they did not think they could get through. Those, for example, who experience profound grief after death robs them of their loved ones, leaving them with a gnawing emptiness that makes everything seem vacuous, a pain that overwhelms and threatens to destroy. How do they get better? How do they learn to embrace life again, to the extent where they emerge with a renewed sense of purpose and growth?

In the weeks and months after my surgery, I meet some extraordinary people who have gone through very distressing periods in their lives and their stories really help me. These were times that felled them, experiences that knocked them flat, and many thought they would never be able to pull themselves up again. But they did, and now they use their knowledge and insight to influence and help others. I write all their advice down hungrily, for me and for anyone else who needs it. It'll be invaluable – I just wish I'd sought it out many years ago.

~

> The pattern of all losses mirrors the pattern of the gravest losses. Disbelief is followed by numbness, numbness by distraction, despair, exhaustion. Your former life still seems to exist, but you can't get back to it; there is a glimpse in dreams of those peacock lawns and fountains, but you're fenced out, and each morning you wake up to the loss over again.
>
> Hilary Mantel

It's early on a Saturday morning in October 2006, when I get the phone call from my boss. It's not a working day for me and my heart falls to my stomach when I hear his voice. Something's happened. 'Sian, there's been an earthquake in Pakistan. I can't send Dermot [Murnaghan, my then co-presenter on *BBC Breakfast*] because he's recording a new series of *Eggheads*. Get your passport and head to the Pakistan Embassy.' I'm struck by the absurdity of someone not being able to go to a news story because of contractual obligations to a game show, and that I am second choice to present the coverage. It contrasts sharply with the horror of the tragedy. My boss tells me all he knows: a few dozen killed, many injured (it would become eighty-seven thousand dead and more than seventy-five thousand wounded). The infrastructure's damaged, but we have to get as close to the epicentre as fast as possible, finding shelter where we can. I'll present *BBC Breakfast*, the *One*, *Six* and *Ten O'Clock News*, with the rolling news channels in between, for however long is needed.

I spend all day sorting out visas and talk to a producer, Farah Durani, who knows the area and is coming with me. Grab a few shirts; buy some packets of dried fruit and nuts for sustenance and run to the airport. It's a long flight and it's packed with British charity workers heading to the scene. My colleagues from ITN are on the same flight and we nod acknowledgement. We'll all be hitting the ground running as soon as we touch down, yet know very little of what to expect. When we arrive in Islamabad, there's chaos. My camera crew has arrived with a satellite dish and before we've even left the city, we pass an apartment block, the Margella Towers, which has collapsed and is covered in a seething mass of locals and rescue workers, delving through large stone slabs to try to find survivors.

We start our journey to the epicentre but the roads to the mountainous region of Kashmir are broken – blocked by mudslides, trees and rocks, they're very difficult to navigate. It takes all day to get to the regional capital of Muzaffarabad and when we arrive at dusk, we're greeted by a vision from hell. Everything is destroyed, with hospitals, hotels, shops, schools and houses now huge mounds of bricks. People wander from pile to pile, picking, scrabbling and searching for loved ones. Some wander aimlessly or stand before collapsed homes, paralysed with shock. Hundreds of bodies lie, twisted and trapped in the rubble. Saturday's a school day in Pakistan and many of those who died are very young. The sight of parents using picks, shovels and their bare hands in a desperate attempt to find their children is haunting.

At 9 p.m. GMT, I file a quick update for the BBC. 'This is a city almost completely destroyed. Over two-thirds of the houses are rubble. Thousands are still without shelter and it is getting colder. There is no food, power or water. Up until now there has been very little help too. But aid is starting to arrive. Everything is silent here; people just sit and stare, wondering what to do. Tonight we saw some dead bodies, which had been left outside tents along the roadside that are being used by the survivors. It is clear people are still dying here, the help is not getting to them.'

I keep broadcasting until after *Newsnight* finishes and sleep in a car together with Farah; she takes the front seat and I'm at the back with the camera kit. My shirts are hanging by the car window for tomorrow's broadcast. A few hours later, we're up and presenting on *BBC Breakfast*. There's a large area of scrubland where families are congregating under trees. They have nothing. Aid is coming in so slowly that there's little water and food, few tents, no medicine. Farah speaks Urdu and we move from family to family, asking whether they mind being filmed 'live' for the BBC. Some seem vacant and bewildered, unable to talk. Others are full of energy, their eyes flashing with anger as helicopters clatter overhead, taking aid to remote villages elsewhere. 'Show the world what's happened to us,' they say. 'Bring help. Fast.'

It's impossible to show the audience at home what it's really like. It is the very depths of human misery; survivors struggling to find shelter and some food to give their children, while the bodies of those who died wait to be buried. The smell of rotting corpses, together with the stench of faeces and decay, is everywhere. We live in this community of the dispossessed for days, reporting on efforts to get the aid through. When grain and rice start to trickle in, families ask us to sit with them and share their meagre rations. Even those who have almost nothing offer what they can – we decline, overcome with gratitude and guilt. Our discomfort is temporary; after this job, we'll be returning home to safety, warmth and our families. But the contrast between our life and those we report on comes in the most shocking way, during one 'live' broadcast for the BBC's lunchtime news.

Standing in the rubble, updating viewers on casualty figures while rescuers pick through the wreckage behind, I hear shouts over my shoulder, followed by gut-clenching moans of sorrow.

I don't look round until I hand back to the studio, but when the cameras stop rolling, I turn to see a group of young men standing, wailing, heads in their hands, having pulled their mother's body from the wreckage of their home. Being there suddenly feels intrusive and insensitive.

After a week of broadcasting, I return home, unable to articulate what it's been like, remembering that fear and desperation of the brothers in Pakistan, the grasping for the broken life of someone they love. A similar grief is to overwhelm me, less than a year later.

~

No one ever told me that grief felt so like fear.

C. S. Lewis, *A Grief Observed*

My mum, Kathy, is almost seventy. She's organizing a family party and as she opens her wardrobe and looks inside, she sighs. 'There's nothing here!' she laughs. 'I buy all this stuff from M&S and when I get it home, it looks awful!' I tell her we're off up to London, to Selfridges, to buy her a new dress. It's booked as a birthday treat – there's a room in the personal shopping department with a couple of glasses of champagne waiting for us and a very camp assistant who'll bring in lots of inappropriate and wildly expensive outfits, for her to try on. When the day comes, it's fabulous fun. Mummy, for the first time in decades, is a size 12 and she's thrilled. 'The weight's dropping off and I haven't had to do anything!' she says, delightedly. After all those years of different diets – Hay, grapefruit and egg, F-Plan (renamed F . . k-all Plan, by us) – she's now lost her appetite and is slinking into dresses she's never worn before. I buy her a beautiful green, sleeveless Missoni dress, a brand she's never heard of, and she loves it. We head off for lunch, where as usual, she orders something with prawns and a large glass of white wine. She touches neither but constantly reaches into her handbag for another indigestion tablet.

At her party, she's lost more weight, is eating next to nothing and tells me she thinks she has a gallstone. She's been a nurse for almost four decades, so she should know. It sounds easy to manage, nothing much to worry about. A month later, scans show shadows in her bowel and on her liver. We visit the hospital together and the surgeon tells us the shadows are cancerous growths and they're inoperable. My mum is stoic. She knows she doesn't have long. I'm in shock and me and my brothers make calls to hospitals, specialists, anyone who can cut this thing out of her. No one will.

She's admitted to the very same hospital where she spent most of her nursing career. She starts out looking fine, although tired. After two months of radiotherapy and chemotherapy, plus endless courses of steroids, she asks for the treatment to stop. Less than four months after that silly, giggly shopping trip, she's dead.

The day after she dies, I write this:

I called her Mummy. I'm forty-four years old and I still called her Mummy.

Mummy died yesterday at 7.22 on Tuesday morning, 17 November. I had been holding her hand since 4 a.m. It felt so fragile, like the wing of a small bird. I was stroking her arm and I could feel the bone through her skin. Her skin was so mottled and bloodied. And I looked at her arm and thought – that was her tennis arm – where's the muscle gone? Where's the tan that she spent so much of her life encouraging? What are all these little blood spots? Then – can she feel me stroking her arm? Hear me talking to her?

'You're my best friend and I'm going to miss you so much,' I said. 'You do know how much you're loved, don't you? Everyone loves you.' Then she smiles, with her eyes closed – and I know she's heard me, so I

go on: 'I see your smile in every single one of my children every day I look at them.'

I'd been with her just a few days before, but was late, tied up practising for the BBC's annual 'Children in Need' night. I'd always said no to it, it seemed too showy-offy, but she wanted me to do it. 'Go on, just one time! It'll give us something to smile about.' And it did. I practised for weeks with my newsreader colleagues, all of us bumping into one another, pouting, strutting, and feeling ridiculous. I'd go into rehearsals after presenting 'BBC Breakfast' and, afterwards, get on the train down to Sussex to see her. Practising my moves, telling her what it was like having five women presenters of a certain age falling over one another in an attempt to 'do sexy'. We'd be crying with laughter.

I'd just done a photoshoot for the 'Mail on Sunday' to promote the show – wearing a tight smile, military jacket, tight black jeans, and high heels. I left the shoot and caught the train back home to Eastbourne to see her. Arrived – and she was in bed. A bad sign because, up until then, she'd made an effort to get up and go downstairs, even though that exhausted her and left her breathless. She didn't want to be bedridden. Now she was. Her legs were heavy, swollen with fluid and it frustrated her. I noticed her toenails needed repainting. That was the only thing I could do for her in those last months. Talk to her and paint her nails. Now she was in bed and couldn't move. I tried moving her when she got uncomfortable but she was so heavy. 'You're too small,' she said. 'Get Daddy.' 'He's sleeping – shall I wake him?' She looked disconsolate. She knew he needed sleep, that he'd been looking after her, moving her, washing her, cooking for her, cleaning for her, for months and now he was sleeping and I had to wake him to move her. She hated it.

She said that she wanted to go into the hospice, so all day we waited for the consultant to tell us if they had a place. That night, I found some poems that her mother had written in the back of a book and I read one to her. It had been written to my grandfather as he left his family to go abroad, to serve as a doctor during the Second World War. I read the first two lines and she inhaled sharply and started welling up. 'Shall I go on?' 'Yes, yes. You know me, I cry at soaps, I cry at anything.'

Then she told me about meeting my dad and how good he'd been and that she was tired. I left her to sleep. The following morning, the Macmillan Cancer Support nurses who'd been popping in every now and again, told her she was going to be admitted to St Wilfred's Hospice. It sounded so final. Don't worry, she said, it was temporary. It would give my dad a break. We collected a few of her things – I'd just bought her two pretty nighties and a dressing gown – a couple of soft sponges, and put a selection of bits in a bag. Her make-up, which she rarely used, although I noticed she'd put on some eyeliner – rather haphazardly – to go into the hospice. I put in the hand cream she loved that smelt of vanilla and almonds. The lavender heart pouch she had on her pillow, her comb. It all looked like nothing much. Her last things amounted to nothing much.

She couldn't walk, so she was stretchered down the steps of the house to a waiting ambulance. She shut her eyes. The journey was difficult, she was strapped to a chair and she felt every bump in the road, she was wincing and muttering, 'Oh dear, oh dear.' Repeatedly. The hospice seemed like a relief – she'd been a nurse for so long, now she had the security of having her indignity managed by fellow professionals – but once she was in her room, in her bed, she knew she wasn't coming out. The first thing she said when she went into the room was 'Oh, there's a telly. Does it have Sky Sports?' But she was saying less and less.

A couple of days later the picture from the 'Children in Need' photoshoot appeared in the papers. One of the hospice nurses held it in front of her. 'We're in the news, Kathy!' she said. 'Me?' she asked, confused. 'No! Sian!' 'Oh,' she said quietly. 'My celebrity daughter.' Her speech was slurred by the drugs. Was she angry? Sarcastic? Proud?

I couldn't understand her. I left the room, shed a few tears, chastised myself and went back in.

That night I slept, restlessly, at home and went back in at 7.50 a.m. on Sunday morning. I told her I couldn't sleep and wanted to be with her. She said that she had watched 'Strictly Come Dancing' that night and saw that my 'BBC Breakfast' colleague, Chris Hollins, had gone through to the next round. That made me feel unutterably sad. I couldn't believe we'd been at home eating while she'd watched TV on her own. Then she fell into a sleep.

I took Eve down to the seafront and the rain began to lash down. The storm was so fierce, the rain was horizontal. We sheltered in the bandstand and I looked out at the huge waves and the dark grey skies and cried. Then, strange thing, there was a break in the clouds and the most intense sunlight, which came all the way over the sea and lit us up. And standing there, bathed in this light, I felt stronger, like it was willing me on. Be strong for her and strong for the children. I waited there for a few minutes, talking to myself, and then made the call to work to cancel all next week. Cancel the awards ceremony I was meant to be giving on the Wednesday, the dinner I was going to on the Thursday, the 'Children in Need' performance I was doing on the Friday.

I went back to the children and Paul. Got them up, took the big boys to see her. 'When's your interview?' she said when she saw Joss. So excited about the possibility of him going to Oxford University. She hugged them both, they both told her they loved her and she told them she loved them too. It's taken years for any of us to say we loved one another and here it all is in the last weeks and days, flooding out. I stayed for ages – then got a text asking me to go back – Daddy had cooked a meal. 'It feels odd to leave,' I said. 'Dad's made supper, go home,' she replied. So I did. Ate and returned. When I got there, Mum looked pained. 'I'd lost the bell,' she said. 'So silly, but I couldn't call and I needed more pain relief.' I felt guilty that I hadn't been there. Again. The doctor took me to one side. 'I think you may want to stay overnight,' she said. I rang Daddy and told him. Put up a camp bed in the room opposite. He came over – 'I need to be there too,' he said. He put a bed up next to hers.

We went to sleep at 10 p.m. I kept popping in, asking Mummy if she needed more pain relief. She said no, asking her doctor, Jo, whether the end was near. 'I don't think it's too far away, Kathy,' she answered, holding her hand. 'Good.' Jo was so caring. She told Mummy she was dignified. That she'd done really well – here Mummy shook her head – that she was so strong – she nodded – and that her family were all around her and that must be a huge comfort. Here I wanted her to nod. But she didn't. I put a cold flannel on her forehead and she smiled. I told her she had the most beautiful smile. And she smiled. I kept putting my hands in hers. 'Cold hands,' I said. 'Cold hands make good pastry – isn't that what you told me?'

I combed her hair. She wanted a back massage but I couldn't get to the place where it hurt. The doctor said the tumour was so big, it was pushing up into her diaphragm and that was causing her neck, back and shoulder pain. They gave her more morphine. She was becoming less able to communicate.

By the Monday morning, she was almost unconscious. Her breathing was so laboured, it took such an effort just to breathe in and then breathe out. Sometimes she slept. Other times you knew she was awake but her eyes had rolled back. She saw her best friend Wendy – made a huge effort to reach up and pulled her towards her to thank her for being such a good friend. For a while, she'd squeeze my hand when she needed something. More pain relief, usually. After a while, she couldn't acknowledge me, not even to squeeze my hand when she needed the fan on, or have her neck rubbed. I wanted to hold her hand all day. So I did. Kissed her forehead, whispered in her ear. No nods, no smiles, no squeezes. The last two words I heard her say were 'Pain' and 'Tired'.

I went to bed when she dropped off, although her breathing was long and laboured. Came in at 2 a.m. and then again at 4 a.m. I moved the chair next to her bed and stroked her arm and held her hand. We both slept like that and I found it enormously peaceful, her hand just resting in mine. Her breathing softened for an hour – her hour of need? I hoped I'd been there to administer some love and it had helped a little. Though maybe that's just me wanting to feel like I helped in a small way. Then her breathing became rapid, rattling. From 6 a.m. till 7 a.m. it got worse. I sent a text to the rest of the family. They arrived at 7.22 – walked through the door, just as she took her last breath. It was almost as if she'd waited for them to be there. I was on one side, holding her hand, Daddy on the other and my brothers at the door. She exhaled and then – nothing. I could see a pulse in her neck. 'It's OK – I can see a pulse,' I said, desperately, but she'd stopped breathing. I hugged her, kissed her forehead and watched as the blood seemed to leave her face. She was still warm. She looked tiny. We left her room and didn't go back.

~

> It's so curious: one can resist tears and 'behave' very well in the hardest hours of grief. But then someone makes you a friendly sign behind a window, or one notices that a flower that was in bud only yesterday has suddenly blossomed, or a letter slips from a drawer . . . and everything collapses.
>
> Colette

I behave very well in those 'hardest hours'. Two hours after her death, we are organizing the service (no fuss, flower donations to charity, simple urn, scatter the ashes in the memorial garden). When the undertaker asks about readings, Dad says, 'Sian will do it, she's used to that sort of thing.' Not this sort of thing, I think.

During the reading I thank everyone for the joy and friendship they shared with Mummy over the years and the love and support they showed her in the last few months. I tell them that I don't think she realized how much she was loved – although we all knew it, of course. That towards the end she told me she had no regrets – she'd had a fantastic life with so many good friends – and there was no fear about approaching the end. That typically, she was worried about how we would cope – rather than about herself. Then I read that poem, the one that my grandma had written to my grandfather the year he went to war, the one that I read to her the night before she went into the hospice. It's called 'To All Who Serve':

> I know as your life speeds onwards
> Towards the Eternal Quest
> The road will be long and you have to be strong
> If you're going to stand the test
> And midst all the tears and laughter
> That are with you on your way
> You must not pine for what is after
> But live only for today
> And in those few but precious hours
> Snatched from a care-worn day
> You will live to love again, my dear
> In the grand and glorious way.

After the funeral, after I've cleared the house of all Mummy's clothes and handbags, I go back to work on the *BBC Breakfast* sofa, with no one but my editor, Alison Ford, and my co-presenter, Bill Turnbull, aware of the loss. Weeks and weeks of being on autopilot, interviewing soap stars and singers about their latest projects, hoping no one will make a 'friendly sign' that might lead to an embarrassing, highly public, on-air collapse.

One day I interview a man about living through bowel cancer. I tell him I'm glad to hear he's now well and when the interview finishes and we cut to a filmed report, I run to the toilets, telling Bill to hold the fort. None of the viewers notices anything over the following months, apart from a loss of weight. I feel, if I start talking about it, I'll never recover.

My psychologist friend, Dr Chloe Paidoussis-Mitchell, works with many people who have been through traumatic loss and told me recently how grief can affect them. She says they experience such a powerful reaction to the news of the death that their view of the world is profoundly shaken. Their sense of who they are alters. They can feel disorientated and isolated, experiencing a deep, but temporary, loss of meaning about life where they can't seem to get back to 'normal'. And yet, eventually, they get through it and, more than that – at least with the many people she's heard from – there's growth, too. They all talk about a need to create meaning in life, so they re-evaluate and find ways to focus on what's important to them. For most, that means nurturing and prioritizing relationships with friends and other members of the family. It also means living their lives more 'authentically', so they revise work, or other projects. They re-engage, but in a different way.

They continue to live with their memories of those they lost, perhaps remembering them with others, keeping hold of some of the relationships that were important to their loved ones, treasuring some of the items that belonged to them and finding ways to include their presence in important life and family events. Everyone that Chloe has counselled over the years has found these things to be helpful in coping with loss and maintaining a life that feels meaningful.

In other words, although it is catastrophic at the time, death and grief can lead to a deeper understanding of how to live a fulfilling life. Growth can come from reflection, from examining how it affects us. When our 'old' life is rocked or destroyed, the act of rebuilding means it has to become something new. The best way out of grief – or as Robert Frost said, the *only* way out – is *through*, but it can take a very long time. Six years after Mummy's death, I can still be knocked over by loss. It's not as desperate, it doesn't batter me every day, but it's there, waiting to unsteady me again. The children remember her in their prayers every night, I bring her into conversations and she is still present. This morning, running along a familiar coastal path, with the sun breaking through the clouds and streaming across the sea, I thought about that moment with my baby daughter, when the same light shone, when I summoned strength to get through Mummy's death. I stopped, shed a tear and then ran on. I know that when I'm knocked over again, I will stumble back onto my feet. I can steady myself, I will run on.

The death of a parent is inevitable. The grieving is hard but you find your way through. The death of a child, though, goes against the 'proper' cycle of life. How would you cope?

It's April 2015 and I'm preparing to deliver a lecture on trauma to King's College, London. I'd agreed to it ages ago and when asked for a title for it, less than four weeks after breast cancer surgery, I rashly and rather tersely suggested: 'Reporting on trauma: when will there be good news?'

I'm using a broadcast clip of an interviewee that I'd spoken to for BBC Radio 4: David Rathband, a policeman who had gone through a violent gun attack and who had lost his sight. It's there to illustrate the roles and responsibilities of journalists when they talk to people who are going through a profound trauma. News is always looking for the personal story to illustrate a global catastrophe, the more emotive the better. Even as a child, I knew journalism could put you in difficult environments, asking uncomfortable questions of people who are still in shock. My father, John, was a Fleet Street hack for years before going into broadcasting. I was raised in a house full of newspapers and a radio permanently tuned to the news. After university, I applied for the BBC traineeship scheme, was accepted and dispatched to earn my stripes in Liverpool. There, I first saw tragedy on a huge scale, interviewing survivors of the 1989 Hillsborough football stadium disaster as they flooded back from the scene in Sheffield. They were hollow-eyed with bewilderment, their thoughts going straight into my tape recorder. The horror they'd seen was overwhelming. The guilt I felt, asking intrusive questions of those who had lost someone they loved, was masked by reassurances that it was crucial to get their story across and their voices heard. Yet it sat uncomfortably, sometimes it even felt exploitative. That feeling would come back often, over three decades in news.

Tomorrow's talk title – 'When Will There Be Good News?' – feels like a rhetorical question. It was designed to reflect my research on growth after trauma. Sometimes it sounds like it'll never happen, as I run through the checklist of disaster coverage over the past thirty years.

I'm speaking on the same platform as Julie Nicholson, the mother of Jenny, who died in the 7/7 London bombings. Julie rings me this morning to chat through how we'll structure the lecture. I've spent the weekend designing my first ever PowerPoint presentation, because the conference organizers want clips and it's the only way we can play them. Julie says she's just speaking to the delegates, naturally. Suddenly, my talk seems wrong, forced, artificial. What do I know about trauma, sitting next to a mother who lost her daughter? A mother who was called to the Church yet whose faith was shaken to the core, forcing her to renounce her ministry as a vicar. How dare I mention the word 'growth' after the word 'trauma'? We talk and talk.

Julie explains what helped her when Jenny died, how she believes therapy is often given to those who see grief as a disorder or condition, and that listening, just listening, is better. I hesitate to mention my part of the lecture, but she asks and so I start talking about how the media engages with people who are traumatized. Are we fair? 'Sometimes,' she says. Then she mentions a programme she appeared on, where the presenter was asking questions about the bombing and Jenny's death. Yet the eyes of the TV anchor were constantly darting around the studio, she was not engaged and her questions were facile. To a mother in trauma, that was hurtful and disrespectful. I remember Julie coming in for an interview for *BBC Breakfast* – please let me have dealt with her fairly, I think. Even if I didn't, would she say so?

I talk, hesitantly, about reconfiguring your life after a trauma. Julie says the media has helped her ask questions of herself, enabling her to piece together the event and its impact upon her life. The more sensitive journalists encouraged her to challenge herself and her thinking in a way that the Church, with all its tea and sympathy, didn't feel able to. She thought very carefully about who she spoke to after that incident in the television studio where she was treated like the next thing on the running order. 'You choose with whom to share your story,' she says. So, I choose to share mine. I'm careful to minimize it, I don't want to suggest that my cancer is, in any way, similar to what she has experienced. Julie is warm and wonderful, gently questioning. I tell her I'm writing. 'Good,' she says, 'control your own story. I did, even though I was criticized at the time.' She talks about how writing her book, *A Song for Jenny*, helped articulate what she was thinking and strengthened the bond with her daughter. Julie says Jenny would have understood why she wanted to share her experience of grief and loss, that she would have encouraged her, realizing that it would help others. It's a mother's tribute to her daughter, a way through grief, a semblance of control exerted over an event in which Julie had none. It felt like a choice.

Then, something extraordinary happens. 'Hang on,' Julie says, 'I have someone here who wants to talk to you. She's an old friend of your mum – they trained together as nurses at St Mary's in Paddington. She helped me after 7/7 because she lost her daughter too, Laura. We have so many shared experiences.' My breath catches, I know who it is. It's Hazel. Despite the two of them going separate ways after training, Hazel and my mum met every year with other St Mary's nurses. Sometimes I'd gone too. Hazel comes on the line and her voice sounds familiar and strong. I try not to sob but tears stream down my face. She talks about when I came with my mum to their last meeting. She had cancer then, but none of us knew. She was still 'chatty' Kathy, the life and soul of the party. 'Your mum was so proud of you,' says Hazel. 'So, so proud.' I think about tomorrow's presentation at King's, my mum, grief, loss, trauma. I cry a lot and need to wash my face before I pick up the kids from their Easter sports camps.

I'm hopeless during the presentation the next day. Standing in front of academics and peers, next to Julie Nicholson, who'd just delivered the most passionate, heartfelt speech on bereavement and loss, I crumble. Suddenly, what I'd come to talk about – the role of a reporter on difficult and challenging stories – growth after trauma – seems insignificant in the light of her testimony, as she speaks about her struggle to see the body of her dead daughter, against the wishes of the authorities. How, when she did get to see Jenny, they had 'tidied her up', wrapped her body in white muslin, when Julie really needed to see her daughter's death in all its rawness. How she questioned her faith and wondered whether she could preach about forgiveness, when now she understood how hard that was to do in practice.

I interview Julie at the end of her presentation and she describes being so organized in the first few weeks, feeling as if she had control of it all. She 'behaves well in the hardest hours of grief'. The focus on seeing her dead daughter and then sorting out the funeral when her body was delivered back to the family prevented her from falling apart. She did that later, after Jenny had been buried.

When it's my turn to talk about trauma and growth, I hesitate. I plough through the presentation but feel sick with the inappropriateness of it all.

I'm curtailing the lecture as I go along, conscious – and relieved – that our time's running out. I turn to Julie; her story feels more appropriate than my research. 'How has this process changed you?' I ask her. 'It's changed me, fundamentally,' she replies. 'I have more focus, I don't do anything I don't want to do, I know what matters and what doesn't. I'm stronger, nothing can ever be worse than what I've gone through and I have a strength from that. I appreciate life, I'm bolder, I've found my voice.' Of course, she can't bring Jenny back. She's had to go through her grief. And she is a completely reconfigured, different, bigger person on the other side.

C. S. Lewis was right – grief does feel like fear. It gnaws; it's untidy, snotty, racking. It creeps up on you just when you think you're 'dealing with it'. As the novelist Hilary Mantel puts it: 'You fear to focus on your grief but cannot concentrate on anything else. You look with incredulity at those going about their ordinary lives. There is a gulf between you and them, as if you have been stranded on an island for lepers.'

Yes, embracing loss is tough. It makes you look at yourself – your weaknesses and failings, your insecurities and shortcomings, and it also reminds you of your strengths. It is the way into the self and the way out of it, and while we work our way through the impact of death we must also remember to live, among those we love.

INDIAN PRAYER (TRADITIONAL)

When I am dead, cry for me a little.
Think of me sometimes, but not too much.
Think of me now and again, as I was in life.

At some moments, it's pleasant to recall.
But not for long.
Leave me in peace and I shall leave you in peace.
And while you live, let your thoughts be with the living.

7

Finding Our Identity

'Every radical adjustment is a crisis in self-esteem: we undergo a test, we have to prove ourselves. It needs inordinate self-confidence to face drastic change without inner trembling'

Eric Hoffer, *The Ordeal of Change*

Tuesday, 7th April

I'm sitting in the busy reception area of the Macmillan support centre at University College Hospital and my stomach is jumping with nerves. It's crowded with people with cancer, in their various stages of health and hair loss. Their supporters, friends and spouses bring coffees and small talk. I'm here alone, as usual. It's my choice and it's better like this – it means I'm not trying to manage someone else's concern. I don't have to engage, reassure, be upbeat.

I look up at the screen announcing the clinics that patients should head to. My name flashes up. Here we go. What am I expecting? A review of my war-torn chest. Some pointers towards whether radiotherapy is likely. Or whether – as the oncologist with the leopard-skin trousers from the Royal Marsden suggests – to take the more radical option – embark on major surgery again, take everything off, 'harvest' some tissue from elsewhere on my body and patch it all up in the hope that it'll eradicate any remaining cancer – if it still exists there at all.

I'm sent to another waiting room and it's a little quieter here. The day after bank holiday and cancer is on hold for some. The nurses are talking among themselves, about a running regime and a new diet; brown rice and organic wine. There's life here, among the shuffling patients and mortality, but it's a vivid contrast between the vitality of those who are well and those who are not.

I can kid myself that I am healthy. I ran yesterday and a half-hour jog still pulls at my chest and leaves me breathless. I am like everyone else here, shuffling, shuffling, eyes full of weariness and wariness. When I'm called in, I'm told I've been a 'model patient'. The 'skin flaps' (add to 'ooze' and 'harvest') are 'very healthy'. The surgeon, Jo Franks, believes she got all the cancer, she can't be 100 per cent but 'I've taken every precaution. There's nothing in your pathology which looks aggressive.' She understands there isn't enough hard evidence to make a decision about what to do next; she knows it's frustrating but I'll have to go with what feels right. How comfortable am I with risk? In the end, I'll have to make a decision about radiotherapy or surgery. You make it, I say, you're the expert. She sighs – medicine has changed, the patient is now given a choice. I don't want choice! I say. I don't even have the scientific evidence to make a decision. You choose!

I want to please her, show her that I've been trying, so I say that I've put on weight, around my stomach and my back, in case they need to do a 'fat transfer'. They agree that I have, that there's enough there to do it. Horrible. I start to well up and get cross with myself. 'I know I'm lucky,' I say, dismissing the upset. The doctor says it's a tricky case. With a small tumour, they take it out, give radiotherapy and then reconstruct. The path can be obvious and straightforward. There are still many debates about what to do after a case of DCIS, when you have no breast tissue left but when you know there still may be cancer cells lurking under the skin. The thinness of my skin makes it complicated but at least if it comes back we will be able to feel it, she reassures.

When she examines me she asks which of my breasts I prefer. I laugh. 'Look at them!' I say, glancing down at the little, uneven balls with a wide expanse in the middle. Hmmm, she agrees, not much there, no. She squints at them – yes, that one is too far around to the left. The reason they look unnatural is because they are round, not tear-shaped implants, so not really breast-shaped. Also, because she had to move the chest muscle on one side to get to the worst affected area, one is now higher than the other. She was working with a colleague too, not alone, and her side of the operation was more challenging due to the biopsy scarring. I like her a lot, she's straight and honest, even though she knows it's a long road ahead – first let's deal with the cancer management, she says – then we'll tackle the aesthetics. We can talk to plastic surgeons.

I have lunch with Joss, who has half an hour free, and we eat a fast takeaway while he asks questions about the hospital visit. He's starting to scale the lower rungs of the career ladder so has a small income. He offers to pay the £1,500 it costs to get a BRCA test done quickly, rather than wait for months. 'It's your health, Mum,' he says. 'What's more important than that?' I thank him and decline. I don't want him spending what he doesn't quite earn on me, just to speed things up, and I don't want to jump the queue anyway. In the NHS you get world-class expertise and endless waiting. It's part of the deal.

I run for a train that's about to leave. The barrier guard stops me as I go through, waving my ticket – It's OK, he says, you'll get on. By the way, is this your mother behind you? No, I say, glancing at the stranger behind me. He asks again – Is this your mother? Does she have a ticket? I don't know! She's NOT my mother! I'm running towards the train now and jab the button to open the door, but the whistle goes for it to pull away. I burst into tears. Uncontrollable, hot, angry sobbing. I'm self-conscious enough to hope that the commuters at this busy London station won't know or care who I am. But am not controlled enough to stop crying. I'm furious with the guard and go back to the gate, looking at him, bemused. Why did he tell me I'd get it? Why did it pull away early? He blusters, obfuscates. It makes me more frustrated. Shamefully, I say I've been for an appointment at the hospital, that I'm unwell. Am I looking for an excuse for him or for me? Am I expecting pity? Is that what I've become? The strong survivor seems to have left the station, the victim has run up against the buffers.

Cancer doesn't discriminate; it targets anyone, regardless of age, gender, race, religion, wealth or colour, it is an equal opportunities disease. And just like any other life crisis, we all have a private and public face when we're dealing with it. No one wants to be a 'victim', or a 'sufferer', and no one wants pity, either. Reconfiguring ourselves takes a good deal of time because we have to accommodate this new perspective, this rather fragile, impermanent state where we are constantly reminded of our initial trauma. It can mean emotions burst to the surface at inappropriate moments, when the public mask slips and the raw, wounded hurt on the private face is exposed.

Assumptions about who we are, or who we think we're supposed to be, can shatter after trauma. Everything about our life, our relationships and our sense of self, tilts. It's like being in a house of mirrors, where we see distorted sides of ourselves or find ourselves on an uneven floor where we can't seem to regain our footing. Yet some of the fundamentals can still hold fast – just like they do with my brother-in-law, Martin. He says he still feels the same, Stage 4 cancer or not, although he is reworking a lot of his life and rethinking some of his previous beliefs.

We discover new parts of ourselves during adversity. They are not always pleasant (making a ticket collector feel crappy just because I'm upset? Really?). But often they are powerful (I didn't know I could be this strong/flexible). There's little doubt that for many people, there is a radical reassessment after a crisis, because we can't go back. We are re-versioned and updated, both the public and private versions of ourselves, because we have to be.

No one can take my experience of breast cancer away and I'll probably always fear it returning. Even after regular three-monthly checks, even if I get a five or ten-year all-clear, it'll remain part of me and I can't escape that. Nor would I choose to. No one can. Not even the most glamorous, privileged people in the world. Not even they can undo what's happened to them. Does that mean we're defined by it, then?

Last Saturday night, Kylie Minogue was on *The Jonathan Ross Show*. When she was introduced, she floated down the stairs in a beautiful, flimsy dress to rapturous applause. I've interviewed her twice – the first time after she'd just brought out the single 'I Should Be So Lucky' when she was all dungareed and wide-eyed. We were in a hotel in Liverpool, one of those press junkets where the celebrity sits, royally and rather reluctantly, on a gilded chair while we grubby hacks shuffle in, one after the other. We're allotted fifteen minutes each and ask our inane questions, knowing the star would rather be anywhere but here. I remember thinking she was tiny, with fine wavy hair. I was bigger, with a similar, rather rough perm. I was at the start of my career and she was at the start of hers.

The second time I interviewed her was more than twenty years later, when the 'princess of pop' had turned into a global superstar. She was buffed and smoothed and delicate. The interview was inane, again. It may have been my fault. Or maybe it was because she had spent decades avoiding questions, smiling around them, wincing inside as journalists ask whether INXS front-man Michael Hutchence 'turned her to the bad', or if she still sees Jason Donovan.

Tonight, on the TV chat show, Kylie sweeps in with a big grin, a wave and her almost see-through gown, split to the thigh. She's got a great body. Think of those videos. Kylie in gold hot-pants, spinning around, showing her luscious bottom. Kylie in a hooded top, cut down to the stomach, slashed up to the hip, showing her amazing legs, her fabulous breasts. There are a few innuendoes from Jonathan to kick off with – the adventurer Bear Grylls is on the show, sitting next to her, and Jonathan asks him whether he's 'familiar with the Australian bush', to general hilarity. It's having Kylie there, it just encourages men to be louche, she's so sexy. Then he asks her a question about having been in showbiz most of her life and whether it feels as if it's always around her. 'Weirdly,' she says, 'when I was ill and in hospital quite a lot, one of the surgeons said to me "Oh, we play your music when we're stitching up on other surgeries." Apparently, they whack my music on.' Ooh, illness, slamming into the interview. Where will this go now? Jonathan follows it up: 'It's been ten years since you were diagnosed with cancer, are you all clear now?' 'I'm good,' she says, shifting a little, getting nervous, unsure of where this is going, perhaps regretting the fact she's alluded to it. 'I'm yet to reach my ten-year mark . . . I imagine when I do, I'll be having a glass of champagne and crying a lot, and being very happy and joyful and thanking all my friends and family.' Everyone claps. I turn to Paul – why are they clapping? Why the applause? I don't understand. He says it's because she's seen as a survivor. But why clap illness, I think, or moving on from illness? It's something you have to do, it doesn't make you remarkable. I feel cross. Don't clap please, audience, you're making Kylie uncomfortable. Jonathan moves on to talk about courage, how enormous it is to face the diagnosis, mentions Angelina Jolie – does she feel a kinship with her? Understand what she was going through? Kylie hesitates, stumbles a little over her words. 'To a point,' she says, maybe thinking about the 'right' response. 'Cancer has many forms, she doesn't know my story, I don't know hers, all the stories are different. Certainly, in that she felt it was her duty to talk about it. Never did I think about not saying what I had, it was about making it real to say what I had.' Jonathan congratulates her on speaking out openly about it. She gives a half-smile. 'It's quite difficult to talk about it in interview situations, because it's deep and it's long and it's involved and it's hard to talk about it in an interview package. Yeah, it's . . . pretty strange.' The audience claps her again.

All of a sudden, Kylie's in a different place, in her see-through gown. She was exuding sexuality and now she isn't. She's vulnerable, exposed. The Kylie-tiny-seductress suddenly disappears, replaced with Kylie-fragile-cancer-survivor. It's an uneasy juxtaposition. When illness ravages a part of a woman's body that has been adored and slathered over, what happens to her? What happens to the identity she's spent a career building? For the audience, holding the two views of one woman feels incongruous, dichotomous. In psychology, it's called 'cognitive dissonance' – the 'discomfort experienced by an individual who holds two or more contradictory beliefs, ideas, or values'. What is she now? Cancer survivor or sexpot? Can you be both?

When I was strapped to a hospital bed with tubes up my nose, a catheter and greasy hair and had asked Paul whether he thought I was still sexy, he looked at me with serious intent and replied, 'Always.' It wasn't a joke to him. Throughout this process, he's viewed my chest with nothing more than quizzical concern. He's told me it's an 'irrelevance' to how he feels about me or whether he still finds me attractive. I've lost trust in my body, it's betrayed me and let me down when I thought I was healthy, but he still sees it as desirable. I have issues with how I look, not him. For a woman, nothing seems to knock your sense of confidence and self-esteem quite like breast cancer, nothing makes you feel as vulnerable and exposed as this obvious wound, when your breasts are threshed from the body, when your femininity seems wrested from your identity. Paul doesn't see this. He has never wavered in his affection. Not once. My issues about how I look and whether my breasts are still part of my sexuality remain my issues, not his.

My exuberant friend Alice is now a teetotal adventurer living in Morocco but we were often drunkenly misbehaved during her previous life in London. Then, she used to call her breasts her 'fun bags'. Today I flash her mine, over Skype. Not much fun, but she says they look 'really, really good'. Remember, she says, 'you are not defined by them, or by not having them, or by having a different pair'. Alice jokily describes herself as a 'fat, middle-aged woman from the Peak District', yet that's not her – she's run the toughest running race in the world, the Marathon Des Sables – that's six marathons in six days. She is indefinable but, I'd say, über-tough. Anyway, we've shared a lot of stuff, including giving each other a very inebriated snog one night after we had drunk the entire contents of her flat. Including all the rough, bought-on-holiday spirits that had sat, dusty and ignored, at the back of her kitchen cupboards. We were delightfully, riotously blotto and so we thought we'd test out what we kissed like, on each other. A bit sloppy, it turns out.

Alice had recently been coaching some Lebanese women in confidence. She asked them for their female role models and was told: Amal Clooney and Angelina Jolie. Again. Then she asked them for words, any words, to describe Angelina. 'Inspirational', 'leader', 'compassionate', they said. 'Cancer' came in at number eight. 'Be known for something more than your diagnosis,' Alice said.

The problem is that if we are continuously questioned about our illness, we can become identified with it, categorized by it, known for it and nothing else. The social scientists Peter Conrad and Joseph Schneider wrote extensively about this so-called 'medicalization' of an individual, when they are so narrowly defined by what's happened to them that the richness of their experience becomes limited by the language used around their diagnosis.[1] I wrote about it in an essay about mental health issues when I started my Psychology Master's and it applies to any illness, including mine. The cognitive scientist Douglas Hofstadter says we define people by their diagnoses because 'default assumptions permeate our mental representations and channel our thoughts'[2]. It's automatic thinking and once stereotypes are activated – 'victim', 'survivor', 'fighter' – impressions are formed quickly, without conscious thought.[3] It's reductive, a subjugation. You are 'judged, condemned and classified' by the language used about you, and thus excluded from whatever is considered 'normal'.[4] That's what the French philosopher Michel Foucault said, fifty years ago. Who knew that half a century after he wrote that, and three years after I quoted him in an essay, I'd think he was referring to people like me?

I will not be defined by an illness. How to stop that, though, when you talk about it? I suppose by being known for more than this. Angelina is a goodwill ambassador for the UNHCR, Kylie produces great pop tunes and is fun and sexy. Me? Hmmm. I'll have to find something else that's bigger than all this. It may take a lifetime of looking.

Alice wraps up her conversation with, 'Look at you! You're gorgeous!' Yes, I am gorgeous, I think, heading out on a bike ride with Paul and the kids with a spring in my step and the wind at my heels. However, as I pant my way up a cycle track and stop to let the others catch up, I'm overtaken by another mum who shouts cheerily, 'Are you waiting for your granddaughter?'

I hesitate, winded by the insult. 'Er, no,' I say. She pauses before elaborating, 'It's just there's a small girl in a pink tutu, being wheeled by her granddad.' That'll be Evie and Paul, then. Ouch. I'm wearing a helmet and sunglasses, so she must have aged me by the bottom half of my face and what I am wearing. Ouch, ouch. I spend the rest of the bike ride doing calculations. So, if I'd had a baby at twenty-five and that child had a baby at nineteen, yes, I suppose I would be Eve's grandmother. It hurts. And that has nothing to do with the cancer. That's just getting old.

We make such swift judgements about people based on what they look like, their age, their illness, their life crises. But we are always changing and we are all a work in progress. What we are not is our illness, or our past, or our experiences. They are all embedded within our identity, but no one part represents the whole. I'm not a 'cancer survivor', any more than I'm a 'broadcast journalist' or a 'psychologist' or, for that matter, a mother, or wife, or friend. Sometimes, one part seems more prevalent and prescient than others and that can depend on what's preoccupying us. For me, when I'm in hospital at another appointment, I feel a bit more like a cancer patient and a bit less like a journalist. That's when I have to remind myself they are both parts of me, I haven't lost the ability to do the job, just because I'm dealing with this, however it may seem at times.

Thursday, 16th April

The General Election 2015 is three weeks away and the BBC's presenters are out in force, stamping their experience and authority all over it. The televised trails show them walking through newsrooms with scripts, holding politicians to account – 'Look how on top of this we are,' they're thinking as they gaze down the camera lens at the viewers, looking confident. 'Why go anywhere else for this?'

The BBC's TV opposition leaders' debate goes on for an hour and a half. As it finishes, the 'Ten O'Clock News' devotes almost its entire bulletin to it and no less than five correspondents analyse it. The broadcast is followed by trails to 'Newsnight' and more of those TV ads with presenters striding around, purposefully, urging you to watch the coverage on the BBC. This morning, Radio 4's 'Today' programme is scrutinizing each sound bite; 'BBC Breakfast' is on the road with the sofa, getting the reaction of 'ordinary voters'.

Five years ago, I was caught up in all this and knew every policy manifesto and politician's manoeuvre as I prepared for one of the biggest nights of my TV career, the General Election of 2010. My experience was solid – I'd spent decades covering elections, the first as a cub reporter in Barnsley, watching Labour sweep up in northern cities. Followed by seven years producing at BBC Radio 4's 'World at One', 'PM' and 'The World This Weekend', steeped in political minutiae. For the 1992 election, we pulled apart each party's manifesto, to the chagrin of the spin-doctors who phoned me up to tell me that I was foolish to focus on a certain policy flaw and would be made to look stupid when the following day's newspapers took up a different angle. In 1997, I studio-produced the General Election for Radios 4 and 5, the one where Blair won and Major lost.

When I became a presenter, I hosted many dead-of-night political discussions on BBC2 and endless party conference coverage. I was once asked to be the BBC's Deputy Political Editor but was told by an experienced correspondent at Westminster not to accept the job. 'Don't come here, it's a piranha pit, you'll have a ghastly time and rarely get on air,' he warned. I took his advice and continued to cover each election for the BBC and do the political interviews I loved, on 'BBC Breakfast'.

It's addictive, that roller coaster of election night. Both brilliant and frustrating. Even on the 2005 BBC General Election night programme, when I was part of the frippery, hosting a TV stunt in Gateshead in the northeast of England, along with a group of students, who were spray-painting in the constituencies one by one on a large map on the pavement as they were gained and lost. When the camera cut to us, there were indistinguishable splodgy abstracts of colour on concrete, telling you not very much. It was nonsense but fun. Frankly, I was lucky to get the air time. In 2001, I was in Tony Blair's constituency of Sedgefield as he was voted in again as Prime Minister, waiting for his triumphant arrival from London to talk to his party supporters. I'd been there since the day before, prepping, talking to constituency members, and getting the essential background detail that's vital to good commentary. We waited and waited for our on-air slots, the 'scene sets', which kept getting postponed because of a flurry of results. Then there was a shriek from the London TV studio producer – 'He's on his way! Coming to you soon!' When Tony Blair walked into the working men's club, to waves of hysterical applause, I started my commentary but my microphone wasn't opened. The presenter in London, David Dimbleby, continued to talk over the pictures, the producer took Mr Blair's speech live, and that, ladies and gents, was my 2001 General Election. Still, if I'd been that producer in the gallery, I'd have done the same.

There were many moments when frustration gave way to exhilaration, like when I had a main role in the 2010 election. Me and my co-presenter Jon Sopel (now the BBC's North America Editor) anchored the BBC coverage as the final results came in, just after David Dimbleby wrapped up his marathon Election stint. We were on air for hours and hours, trying to analyse a new and spectacularly confusing political landscape – a hung parliament. The day afterwards, I host 'BBC Breakfast' from a studio that's been built in front of the Houses of Parliament, dissecting the results. In the weeks that follow, I'm always outside in the freezing cold, on a makeshift stage on College Green, with the backdrop of the House of Commons, spending hours every morning interviewing politician after politician. I loved it all.

So, this feels strange, this General Election. It's the first since my early twenties where I'm not required. No one has asked and I haven't offered. It feels gauche to go knocking on doors to ask for a job. Over the years, women often seem to have played the part of the magician's assistant – standing aside as a grey-haired male does the Important Announcements, being the one to do the 'reaction' pieces – or 'this is what viewers are telling us'. Not being entirely trusted to hold the show, direct the flow. It reminds me of when I started as a presenter on

'BBC News 24' in 1997. At Radio 4, I'd studio-produced the General Election, various Budgets, most of the party conferences. A few months later, as a presenter on TV, it was Budget day and we were devoting hours to it on 'News 24'. My male counterpart Gavin Esler was fresh from a stint as North America correspondent. 'This is your area,' he said, 'I'm just catching up with British politics.' Yet the programme's running order, drawn up by one of the team, had Gavin doing all the political heavy-lifting, all the announcements and interviews. My role was confined to the 'other news now' section. I fought and fought that one, just to get parity, for me and for all the other women producers and presenters alongside and behind me. I've been told that the public 'preferred their serious news delivered to them by a man'. I've been taken off a news bulletin at the last minute when a big story happened, so the male anchor could be parachuted in instead. I've been asked, when chipping in with story ideas on a slow news day on the 'One O'Clock', 'Why do you need to be here at this meeting? You're just the lips.' Once the words were out, the room chilled and the other producers looked at me, horrified. Later, that junior manager said he was joking and clumsily tried to give me a hug, which I dodged.

Despite all the ups and downs, I'd love to be there for this election. The BBC doesn't know I have/had cancer, so I could have asked. I did drop into a conversation with a boss the other week, the fact that this is the first election in thirty years at the BBC that I'm not part of, and he looked a little panicked, probably thinking, 'Oh no, a woman over fifty with political experience and we forgot to include her.' He suggested, vaguely, 'doing something', which seemed worse, to be crowbarred into a role. I declined.

What frustrates me is that I'm at home, waiting for a BRCA test result next week, wondering whether I need further surgery, while the merry-go-round is in full swing. I want to be on one of the painted horses, whipping around on the carousel, with the ups and downs of it all.

Nick Robinson, the BBC's Political Editor, is on one of the horses. He's having chemotherapy for lung cancer. In an interview with the 'Mail on Sunday', he says he's prepared to live 'with uncertainty – everybody does' – but the chemotherapy 'feels worse than having the disease, the surgery and even losing my voice. I hate it, hate it, hate it.'

He echoes my thoughts on cancer – and those of my psychologist colleagues – when he says, 'You cannot control what happens with cancer. All you can control is how you respond to it. You delude yourself you're in control because you're used to it in your everyday life, but cancer makes it clear you aren't.'

He speaks of the philosophy that cancer reminds you there's more to life than work: 'I can hear the hollow laughter of family and friends in the distance but I hope that I will learn that it is probably quite sensible not to give your entire life to your work . . . having lain in the garden and read a novel, I realize I need more time to lie in the garden and enjoy books.'

It's this next paragraph that I find most moving, when he writes of trying to speak, post-operation. 'That's my old voice, the one I had before all this happened. Hot tears start to flow. Cancer didn't make me cry. Nor has surgery or chemo. Losing my voice and struggling to get it back has proved to be much more traumatic. It's not about illness. It's not about pain. It's about who I am.'[5]

Who he is has changed, but the relief of getting something of his old identity back is intense. Cancer erodes us and it takes time to find ourselves again.

Tuesday, 12th May

I'm asked to do a corporate event discussing why almost half of young women say they don't have strong female role models to look up to.

Research suggests nearly 50 per cent also say they are ashamed of the way they look and around 75 per cent know girls who self-harm.[6] *It's at the British Academy of Film and Television Arts (BAFTA) in Piccadilly in central London and we have five fantastic women on the panel, all chosen to represent extraordinary strength and talent. Women who've run dozens of marathons to raise money for cancer charities, or won Paralympic gold medals despite being told as a child that their cerebral palsy meant there was little chance of surviving to adulthood. Mothers who've volunteered to go to Sierra Leone to look after ebola patients, a teenager who set up a blood-donating drive among her friends. They are inspiring and their messages are clear:*

'I was so close to giving up, but I didn't, I grew to hate the words "no" and "can't" and I kept going.'

'Life is too short to care about what other people say – do what you love.'

'Focus on other people, make a difference every day.'

'Leave something fabulous for the world to enjoy, even if you're not here to see it.'

These women have made a difference. As the American poet Maya Angelou once said, 'I've learned that people will forget what you said, people will forget what you did, but people will never forget how you made them feel.' The audience feels well and truly motivated.

After the discussion, BAFTA shows the latest version of Thomas Hardy's 'Far From the Madding Crowd'. Carey Mulligan plays Bathsheba Everdene, the formidable heroine, who's at its centre and she's complex, witty and independent for the time. 'I shouldn't mind being a bride at a wedding, if I could be one without having a husband,' she says, 'but since a woman can't show off in that way by herself, I shan't marry – at least yet.' One of her best lines is delivered to a suitor and it's one you can apply to all the women on my panel – and, in fact, to anyone who gets back up onto their feet after adversity, refusing to be defeated. 'I shall be up before you're awake, I shall be afield before you're up, and I shall have breakfasted before you're afield. In short, I shall astonish you all.'

I agreed to do this event long ago, it looked interesting and I thought I could bring my best mate and chat to some great women. I didn't know the sponsor, Panache, and when I research them I discover they're a lingerie firm. Not just any bra and pants company either, but one that specializes in the larger-breasted woman. All these fine, feisty females on my panel have been photographed, with their kit off (and the Panache products on), for a video that plays before we launch into the topic of role models. You couldn't make it up. A woman with cancer, who's just had her breasts removed, fronting a campaign for a firm that makes double-D+ bras.

The following day and I'm back in the hospital, having my very much smaller ones sized up. I don't really need a bra now and when I've got my top off, they just sit there, smirking, the scars turning into pink half smiles. Unlike the women in the video, I won't be posing proudly, just yet. Give it time.

Shirley, the breast cancer nurse, talks about further tests, more surgery, and laughs when I tell her where I was the night before. She reaches into her cupboard of tricks. 'Try these,' she says, holding out a small plastic bag. 'What are they?' I ask. 'Stick-on latex nipples,' she says. 'Give them a go, all the breast cancer ladies love them.' Gosh, we're a long way from lacy lingerie. But you know what? I may astonish you all.

8

Finding Compassion

'When we are no longer able to change a situation, we are challenged to change ourselves.'

Viktor Frankl, *Man's Search for Meaning*

I'm at the Sandford St Martin Annual Awards ceremony in the beautiful surroundings of Lambeth Palace – the home of the Archbishop of Canterbury. It's an event that recognizes excellence in religious broadcasting and I'm there as chair of the radio judging panel. We've heard some programmes of exceptional quality, which tackled issues as diverse as a loss of faith, the search for enlightenment, sustaining love across a spiritual divide and how to find peace among warring nations.

But the story that affects me most comes from an elderly woman, a lady who took part in one of the programmes, who's here from Leeds with her sister and who asks for a picture because she remembers me from the TV. This woman is Trude. Trude has lived through unimaginable distress – yet seems to brim with life and positivity. She stands tall, smiles and laughs often. To hear about her past and see her approach to life is a lesson in surviving and thriving after trauma.

Trude is eighty-six and is still trying to find her mother. She's been searching all her life, ever since her parents bundled her into a taxi with her aunt and cousin when she was just nine years old. Her mother and father were Czechoslovakian Jews and desperate to get their children to safety before they fell into the clutches of the Nazis. Trude can't really recall that day – she tells me she can't even remember kissing them goodbye. 'The trauma was too great; I just couldn't cope with it. I can't remember any feelings whatsoever.'

All the children made it to England to live in different parts of the country. Trude was horribly homesick and cried for six weeks. She couldn't cope with the language, the weather or the food and she missed her family terribly.

Every week, they played the national anthems of the Allies on the radio before the *Nine O'Clock News* and hearing the Czechoslovakian anthem helped her a little. 'It was a bond,' she says. 'None of us knew what was happening back in Bratislava. A child of nine doesn't understand and didn't know the horrors until after the war. For many years, I said little prayers hoping we would all get together again.' They didn't get together again. The day she got into the cab, when she was driven away from her parents, was the last she saw of them.

What got her through six years of war, without knowing whether she'd see them again? 'You just get on with your life,' she says. 'I always had hope and I just kept on hoping.' Of course, neither she nor her siblings, nor millions of others who said goodbye to their families at the start of the conflict, knew about the Nazi persecution that was already under way, or could have predicted the genocide that would unfold. There were letters, at first. They arrived several times a year, not saying much but so prized by the children, they'd be passed around from one to another. After three years of the outbreak of war, the letters stopped. Trude kept herself useful, studying hard, doing domestic cleaning in her boarding school, helping on a farm as part of the war effort.

At the end of the conflict, the children heard a rumour that their father was alive. Then came the cruel news from one of her cousins who'd survived Auschwitz. Their father had been taken to the concentration camp in 1942 and had died within three weeks of arriving. There was no information on her mother, so they continued to wait for her to contact them. Eventually, the hope that she would return to take them home began to fade. 'If she had been alive, she would have made some sort of sign, she knew where we were. Nothing happened, though. So we had to make the assumption that she was dead. But I couldn't let that stand and I started looking for her. I have found a lot of information but unfortunately I still haven't quite reached the end. And I think the end is that she probably died either by being shot on a death march or she died of ill health; at the moment, I've got to accept that.'

She says 'at the moment' because she is still hoping for answers. I ask her how long she'll keep looking for her mother. 'I'm quite driven,' she says. She knows that the last reported sighting was in the Sered labour camp, just outside their hometown of Bratislava where she was registered on 16 December 1944. Many of the Czech women were taken from there to the Ravensbrück concentration camp in Germany, and a fragment of an index card was found there, which could be her mother's. It has no name on it, but it does have her birth date.Whoever held it was listed as a 'Slovak Jewess'. Occupation: Nurse. 'All those things fit,' Trude says.

Trude was invited to that camp at Sered, which is now being turned into a museum. 'Horrible thing about it,' she says, 'they asked if I wanted to visit the cellar, where they shot the Partisans [the Slovaks and Jews]. I wouldn't go down there. There's a mass grave at the camp too, it's grassed-over now.' She's also been to Auschwitz, where her father was held before he died. She says she visited on a wonderful day, when it was sunny and bright. She was taken down to the lake where they'd thrown the ashes of the victims and then, 'I found myself walking entirely on my own along that railway track that took them there and I felt much more at peace. I had closure. Mother will never have closure.'

Her siblings have processed the loss differently. Her older sister Charlotte 'won't watch anything to do with the Holocaust on TV, because she can't cope with it', and at one stage, found it difficult to eat, because with every morsel of food that she put in her mouth, 'she would think of our father starving'. Trude's elder brother Paul, who had promised their father he'd look after her and sent her pocket money as she grew up, found it so difficult to accept what happened during the Holocaust that he eventually destroyed the letters they'd been sent.

Trude thinks she has managed the trauma because she never hid it or locked it away. 'I don't think I ever really closed the box; every single night I said a prayer and after the war there wasn't a day when I didn't think of my parents in one way or another.'

The battles she's fought to stand on her own two feet have made her stronger, she says. She's learnt that 'life is unfair and you've got to cope with it, you've got to see how you get around it, if you sit down and do nothing, it gets worse'. It has not been easy and there have been setbacks. After her 'ping pong' childhood, Trude went on to have a happy marriage and two children, but when her husband died eleven years ago, she asked herself, 'What's the point of living?' She found the point, by plunging herself into voluntary work and it 'means I never have a minute, it's doing something useful and it's keeping me alive, it works both ways'.

She spends her life helping and teaching others about the lessons of the Holocaust, keeping memories alive. 'I know we say "never again", and "never again" is a useless phrase,' she says. 'We've got to change the culture of human beings and we can only do that through education. Children are too segregated in schools, they don't learn about other societies and if we keep them separate there's no way we'll ever learn.'

I ask how her experiences have shaped her. 'I'm pretty determined, I'm pretty stubborn and I'm pretty bolshie,' she laughs. 'On the other hand, I like to be fair. I try to be tolerant and helpful, particularly for those who are unable to help themselves.'

Trude is not downcast, she is not a victim, she does not wallow: she frames her experiences with stoicism and positivity. She was desperately sad when she lost her parents – and again when her husband died, but she diverted her energies into helping others because 'I wouldn't be where I am, without all the outstretched hands.'

There is a power in adversity that Trude recognizes. It's made her thankful for all those 'outstretched hands', it's encouraged her to help others, it's driven her to spend her life teaching children about the horror that took her parents. Viktor Frankl, the psychiatrist who offered succour to others while being held in Auschwitz, the same concentration camp where her father died, put it like this: 'What is to give light, must endure burning.'

Trude has endured – and she gives light, gives back, gives hope.

Another day, another platform and today I'm sharing it with a woman that millions of British children in the Seventies called 'the lady with the blue beads.' I watched her too, on programmes like *Playschool* and *Playaway*. Floella Benjamin was one of the first black women on TV. She had blue-beaded hair, the biggest smile and the most welcoming manner I'd ever seen. 'Hello, children!' she'd grin, widely. 'What shall we do we today? Let's go through the round window . . .'

Floella was born in Trinidad and her parents left her and three of her siblings on that Caribbean island to come to Britain in the 1960s, where they'd been told, as part of the British Empire, their labour was required and the Queen and her subjects would welcome them in with open arms. Floella was left in the care, if that's what you'd call it, of a couple who would make her brothers fight for one plate of food and would physically abuse them, making them clean their toenails while they taunted them. Nine-year-old Floella wanted her mummy and daddy back and fifteen months later she and her three siblings were finally summoned to join their parents in the UK.

The sisters and brothers arrived in Southampton after a two-week sea journey, walking down the gangplank shivering in their thin summer dresses and shorts, collapsing into the arms of their mother and father. They were finally together. But Britain was not warm and not welcoming. It was harsh and cold and brutal. Every day was a challenge. Sometimes, men would lift up little Floella's skirts and sneer 'Where's your tail, monkey?' She cried every night. At school, her accent was mocked, not just by the other children, but by a teacher, who called her a 'guttersnipe'. When she won an athletics trophy on sports day, she wasn't allowed to take it home, because she was black. The family had lived in a one-bedroom flat in Chiswick, but her father, an accounts clerk and jazz musician, and her mother, who did many jobs, including cleaning and ironing, raised enough money to buy a three-bedroom house in Beckenham, Kent.

On the day they went to have a look at it and as the children ran excitedly from room to room, working out who was going to sleep where, they heard sirens outside. Three police cars, several motorbikes and a Black Maria were screeching up to the house. The neighbours had called them because they thought the 'black people' were breaking in to steal from the property. 'Right,' Floella's mother said, 'this is where we are living. We will change the minds of these people. We shall live among them and they shall respect us.'

It was still a daily battle for Floella. So she learned to fight. She'd raise her fists if anyone called her names. They backed off or fought her and she got stronger. One day, a boy was swaggering towards her, spitting out insults. He had a lollipop so Floella grabbed it and shoved it down his throat as far as she could. The boy fell to the floor, gagging and choking. Floella said at that moment, a voice came to her: 'What are you doing? Because of this boy's stupidity, ignorance and prejudice, you are going to get into trouble. You can't change the colour of your skin – if he has a problem with it, it's his problem, not yours. Start loving and respecting yourself.' She helped him up, pulled the lollipop from his throat, and sent him on his way.

It was the day she began fighting back with her smile. That, together with a quick mind and a lot of self-belief, helped her grow stronger, more resilient and more able to tackle prejudice without fear.

Floella became an actress and singer, then one of the most recognized and best-loved children's presenters of all time. She speaks out against discrimination and bullying, stands up for the weak. For decades, she fought for equality, for more rights for women and children. She ran ten consecutive London marathons to raise money for the charity, Barnardo's. In 2010 she got a phone call from the Deputy Prime Minister to ask her if she would like to become a peer, to be 'elevated to the House of Lords', to wear the ermine robes of a baroness. In her maiden speech, she said, 'Children need to be valued, shown unconditional love and taught how to have the confidence to love themselves.' That was, and remains, her mission. 'Hear, hear,' they muttered. She chose the title Baroness Benjamin of Beckenham in honour of 'my beloved, wise mother, who was the symbol of the celebration of perseverance'. The mother who had 'decided that Beckenham was the place for us to live because we would find the best healthcare, the best education and the best jumble sales to clothe us' and who is now buried in the local cemetery. She chose Beckenham, 'not just as a legacy for my mother who told me education was my passport to life and for my father, who was a great philosopher, but in recognition of just how much Britain has moved on'.

Floella and I sit and talk about her life in front of an audience of more than a hundred people at the prestigious Royal Geographical Society. We've known each other for a long time, as we both support the same children's charity, Sparks, and she'd asked for me to host the evening as a 'dear pal'. Before we start, she embraces me, holding me tightly, then looking into my eyes, to tell me I'm beautiful inside and need to believe it myself, to stop listening to the voices of others, to value who I am. She senses fragility.

The lecture begins and Floella charms the crowd. At the end, she finishes by talking about a meeting she had with the Queen, where they sat and chatted about the time Floella arrived on a boat, with the sure and certain knowledge that Her Majesty would love her.

'Who'd have thought?' she said. Indeed, who would have thought that little girl in the thin summer dress, who believed the streets of Britain were paved with gold, who believed that she'd be embraced with love and gratitude, who fought for herself, against ugly racism and brutality and then spent a lifetime fighting for others – who'd have thought that one day, that little girl would be having lunch with the Queen? She stops and looks up to the ceiling. 'I wish my mum could have seen me.'

Eyes now brimming with tears, Floella stands up. It's unexpected, I'm not quite sure what she's going to do and neither is the audience. We hold our breath as Floella stands, then opens her arms wide and starts to sing an old Nat King Cole song. 'Smile,' she begins, 'though your heart is aching . . .' She's shaking her head, placing a profound and heavy emphasis on every word, letting the audience know that she understands their fear and sorrow, reassuring them that even when there are clouds in the sky, they'll get by – they'll see the sun shining through. When she reaches the end, she's beaming, eyes lifted heavenwards, a break in her voice. 'Smile, what's the use of crying? You'll find that life is still worthwhile. If you just smile.'[1] I look at the audience. They're smiling and crying, as is Floella. They burst into applause as she continues to stand, arms wide, as if she's scooping up all the love and warmth in the room in a big hug. Middle-aged men are wiping tears from their eyes, the clapping doesn't seem to end and Floella doesn't seem to want it to. She looks at me. 'Wow,' I say, 'I wasn't expecting that.' 'Neither was I!' she grins. 'I've never done anything like that before, but it just felt . . . right.'

The guests start to file out of the room, still buoyant, and as they pass Floella, they all want to shake her hand, or thank her. Every time someone comes up to her, she grasps their hands in hers. It encourages intimacy, so I hear people exchanging confidences, as if she's a friend. With each one, she gives her time and a piece of herself, homing in on whatever it is they need from her, making them feel special, confident, loved. It's as if she's back in a room full of children, who all want a mothering embrace from the lady with the blue beads.

The organizer tells me it's the most extraordinary event they've had for a long while, the atmosphere was 'something truly special'. Usually, the talks are engaging and sometimes passionate; rarely though, are people so enraptured. More than half a century ago, that little girl arrived in the UK hoping that the arms of Britannia would wrap her up, but they were tightly folded. She will not do the same to others. 'Adversity could break my spirit or make me strong,' she says. Floella chose the latter path and now she shares that life philosophy with all she meets. Live life to its fullest, give out as much joy as you can, don't hold onto bitterness or resentment, tell yourself you are worthy even if others try to make you feel less so. Use your experiences to make you stronger, to move forward and to blossom. And smile, though your heart is aching.

9

Finding the Words

'Sell your cleverness and buy bewilderment'

Rumi

Floella and Trude had a choice: to let adversity break them, or use it to make them strong. Now, they give light, give back and give hope but it took a long time. Any life crisis can threaten what we believe makes us who we are. When we lose our health, or our mind, or our sense of self or our loved ones, it feels as if we've completely lost control. I know a colleague who was once dealing with the loss of *all* of those. A series of horrific assignments in war zones left him with uncontrollable anger, panic attacks, a feeling of isolation and a terrible memory. He couldn't eat and he was getting just two hours' sleep a night. Although functioning at work, at home he wasn't coping. He couldn't talk to his family and eventually his wife threw him out, leaving him alone, frightened, homeless, guilty and ashamed. That was in 2010. Now, he tells me, his life is better than it has been for years. What brought him so low and how did he get from there to here? With enormous effort, he says, as he reveals with great honesty what works and what doesn't.

When we first met, neither of us knew the other was dealing with adversity. It's been a terrible, cultural unspoken rule in journalism, that you just get on with the day job, no matter how messed up your head is. For me, the death of my mum and the fact I hadn't processed it properly, meant I was seeking out ways to claw back to health, months and months later. I'd boxed away not only the grief but also the earlier experiences of different deaths; the smells, the sights and the cries, from a lifetime of reporting on other people's tragedy. The lid of the box flew open later, as it inevitably would. I knew something was wrong when I lost the ability to drive a car, midway through a journey. I've been driving since the age of seventeen yet suddenly, en route to do some shopping, a wave of panic hit me. What do I do with the pedals? Why can't I touch the steering wheel? How have I suddenly forgotten how to do this? It didn't last long and, luckily, it was a straight road so I pressed a few pedals until something stopped the car. The brain does the strangest things in grief. I was still presenting *BBC Breakfast* during this time and some autopilot functions remained. The hurt, anger and incomprehension bubbled away behind a rictus smile but I was obviously not well. I asked to go on a trauma course for journalists, primarily to help others who'd been through similar experiences on assignments, but also, selfishly, so I could learn techniques to do something about my own mental state.

Physician, heal thyself, right? I'd already made futile efforts to talk to a professional, but when I rang up an employee helpline, the tone of the woman that answered was so soft, so annoyingly cloying and sympathetic, that our conversation lasted less than a minute. I banged the receiver down, angrily. Right, give me the tools, what do I do? I know – go on a course, get a handbook, train for a certificate to say I can deal with trauma.

I asked my editor, Alison Ford, if she could spare me from hosting the daily TV show to spend a few days on a Trauma Risk Management (TRiM) course and that's where I met Patrick Howse, the man broken by thirteen tours of duty in Iraq; years of working long hours, protecting his colleagues from attack as they filmed the grotesque and barbaric effects of relentless bombing. During his time as the BBC's bureau chief, he'd developed post-traumatic stress disorder. On this course he was still working towards recovery. His memory of the training is of mixing with people telling horrific stories and finding the whole thing quite harrowing. Patrick remembers a colleague talking about the body of a baby, washed up on a Sri Lankan beach after the Asian tsunami. It may have been me. I was one of many journalists there after the waves hit, walking through bloated corpses, wondering what lives they had, wondering whether anyone would care enough to bury them. I probably talked about it, dispassionately.

The course is a good one, lots of colleagues dealing with facts, not emotion, and listening to the experience of military personnel who're engaged in humanitarian operations as well as war. I know the man behind that TRiM course, Professor Neil Greenberg. As President of the UK Psychological Trauma Society, he understands how people react in shock or grief, and the reason Professor Greenberg thinks TRiM is so effective is because he found that in the first month after a distressing incident, most people didn't need trauma counselling. In fact, they were more likely to be damaged than helped by it, because of the risk of re-traumatizing them. Many of those going through trauma are well equipped to deal with the emotional consequences themselves, as long as they have friends, colleagues and a good support network of people who understand what they've been through. He feels that's much more beneficial than a routine psychological debriefing, where some might feel a counsellor is 'forced' upon them, making them relive all their nightmares and distressing experiences. The trainers on this course stress that peer-to-peer support and mentoring within the first few months can mean distress is managed better. The normal reactions in the first few weeks after a traumatic incident are those that could be associated with post-traumatic stress disorder (PTSD), such as nightmares, flashbacks and avoiding some situations, but most of the time, they're normal and thought to be useful in processing the experience. Again, a 'traumatic event' is one that is perceived as being so and there's a huge difference in the way people may react to it, but many people will have similar responses – so the event will seem threatening and provoke anxiety, and if there's exposure to death or injury, they can have difficult and intrusive thoughts, memories and dreams. Although most may have those reactions, they will not go on to develop mental health problems. However, a small number will, and unless they're helped, their symptoms can lead to PTSD. That's what we are being told to look out for. If our colleagues are still suffering six to eight weeks later, there's something amiss and they need help.

My TRiM handbook says one of the characteristics of trauma is a sense of loss. It goes on to define it, suggesting it's 'when a key aspect of self is lost. This may be a material loss such as personal belongings, or emotional loss such as self-esteem, self-worth or a shattered belief in personal safety. It may also be the loss of a significant person, friend, or partner and individuals are likely to experience complex bereavement reactions such as grief.'[1]

Complex? I should say. The training instructor reminds us we are not being turned into experts. We can make assessments of others, decide when to intervene, help understand what might lead to recovery. We take our handbooks and our scribbled notes home with us. Some of us probably have a good cry. My recollection of the course is being a bit stand-offish, observing, quietly dipping into what trauma means, protecting myself. Two years later, when I was writing about trauma and growth in journalists, I sought Patrick out and sat with him for a couple of hours, to talk about what had happened to him in Iraq and how he came through it.

*

Patrick's post-traumatic stress disorder was a culmination of experiences over a number of years in Baghdad. He speaks vividly about being the head of a team, terrified of sending them into areas where he knew they'd be at risk. To Patrick, the office back at the London base seemed to have little idea about just how frightening and perilous it was out in the field. He once told them that if his crew went into a particular hotspot, 'everyone involved would end up dead'. A query came back, he remembers, asking if that meant he wouldn't do it. 'Not can't, won't,' he says, angrily. Another time he refused to take his team into a volatile area after talking to some colleagues on rival networks who had decided it was too much of a risk, and also on the advice of his own security advisers. He says he got an 'angry call' from base which he felt questioned his commitment; he even believed he was being accused of cowardice. Now the BBC has very good systems in place to train its staff to recognize when someone is under too much pressure, or if they're suffering from acute stress because of the nature of the job. Then it was different. Patrick felt a keen sense of anger, guilt and failure, even though he knew he'd taken the right decision to protect his crew. That, and the 'background radiation of fear', created a toxic mix that bubbled up and over the top. Spectacularly.

He describes it to me like this. It's the day before his current tour of duty in Iraq is ending and Patrick's in the middle of a dust storm at the front door of the office, when an air-raid siren sounds. He punches the code into the combination lock, but one of the numbers sticks and as he's pressing and pressing, he can hear the whistle of a rocket get nearer and nearer. 'It's like one of those car crash things, you know: time stretches. And I'm thinking, "Actually that's gonna hit us."' The rocket goes overhead, through the office ceiling. Patrick realizes if that button hadn't stuck, he'd have been inside. He opens the door and all he can see is billowing dust and black smoke. 'In a flash, I thought, "Everyone's dead, I'm the only one alive. Everyone's dead."' Miraculously, no one was. The incident of the BBC Bureau in Iraq being struck by a rocket attack became a news story around the world and Patrick began organizing his team to film what had happened. 'I felt really good at that point because nobody had been killed. I was in charge. I felt really in control of things – you know, "You go and do this, you go and do that." And everything worked, and we were broadcasting two hours later.'

The following day, Patrick headed back to London and handed in his flak jacket. He says not a single person asked him about what had happened. Not one. I'm staggered. 'Not even "How are you?"' I say, incredulously. 'How are you?' he replies, gazing off into the distance. 'That would have been an excellent question.' It was, he says, one of the most psychologically damaging days of his life. 'I was in bits at the end of that.' He says no one had acknowledged what he'd been through, no one persuaded him to talk about it, no one bothered.

That weekend Patrick and his family headed to Scotland, where he was running the Edinburgh marathon, with him 'feeling that no one cared whether I lived or died'. They had a couple of days off in the Trossachs, a small woodland glen in Stirling, and Patrick was bathing in a lake. 'I was standing up to my waist in a very cold loch. It was May time in Scotland and I'm up to my waist in water and suddenly, I saw a wave coming down the loch and I thought, "Oh, a gust of wind's going to hit me." And then I made the connection between that approaching and the rocket and then suddenly I was back – I was opening the door, seeing the black smoke. Maybe you'd dismiss that as a memory. But the thing that I found remarkable was that I got hot. I got really hot. I was standing up to my waist in a lake, in Scotland, in May, and I was hot. I was sweating.'

Flashbacks of previous events in Iraq started to crowd into other areas of his life after that. Back in London, intrusive thoughts would barge into a seemingly ordinary day, thrusting him back into the terror, the heat and the horror of watching bombs hit civilians. 'I'd be on a train and something would spark off hearing the screams. So I'd be on my way to work, and for me it would be forty-five degrees and I would have wafts of revolting smells coming to me and I would be hearing the screams.' It was much more than re-experiencing something, this was Patrick feeling as though he was there again – and these moments of panic were becoming more frequent. During all this time, he didn't take a day off work. He didn't allow himself to reflect, he didn't really know what was going on, he bottled it all up, boxed it all in. 'You know, I was coping,' he says.

Finally, he exploded. He was in the BBC office at Westminster, listening to the inquiry hearings into the Iraq war. Just as William Hague, the future Foreign Secretary, walked past his desk, Patrick heard a statement from a witness to the inquiry that enraged him so much that he got up and 'smashed my headphones on the desk, bits flying everywhere. I started swearing, uncontrollably. I completely lost it. And from that day, for three months, I didn't sleep more than two hours. I would go to bed exhausted, pass out, and wake up two hours later in huge sweats, usually having had a nightmare, often crying . . . completely broken, basically.'

His lack of sleep made him irrational and angry. His son was sixteen at the time and his daughter eighteen, but he didn't confide in them, or his wife. He spoke to no one about how he felt because, as he puts it, if he couldn't understand what was happening to him, how could anyone else? 'Understandably,' he says, 'my wife threw me out.' Patrick says it was 'courageous' of her to admit their marriage was over, and it gave him the impetus to seek help. He told a work colleague that he was suffering and she pointed him in the direction of a psychiatrist, starting a long and difficult process back to recovery, finding ways to process and understand the trauma that would work for him.

He discovered that writing poetry, describing his mental turmoil and the events that led to it, helped him process what had happened;

and that very act of reflection, having the courage to allow his mind to be curious, open, accepting and forgiving, was enormously beneficial. Rather than avoiding thinking about it, he says he 'opened a dialogue with myself', accepting that some of the feelings were uncomfortable. It's hard, accessing memories that hurt, without causing further distress, but Patrick says he now recognizes the importance of exploring 'the labyrinthine sewers in my mind. I'm shining some light into them. It's not always easy, but it's much better than the alternative.' This is a man who thought he was destroyed, who was isolated, angry and desolate. He knew he hadn't dealt with his experiences and he finally sought professional help, so he could talk to someone, without judgement.

It's fragile, though, this sense of growth. Just a couple of years ago, on holiday in Italy, an ambulance drew up alongside Patrick as he was walking over a bridge and the sirens suddenly started blaring. In a flash, he was back in Baghdad. A few years earlier, it would have affected his week, his month, thrown him backwards. This time he was able to put himself outside the experience and look in on his feelings, observe his thoughts. 'I thought, "Oh that's triggered *that* sort of reaction. This isn't about Florence, this is about Baghdad." It was a fifteen-minute process to entirely put it behind me. And I'm probably going to have sensitivities to these things for ever. But at the moment . . . I've got a way of managing them, and it's OK, it's all right.'

Another way of managing is shifting his perspective on life. He's now much more discriminating about how he spends his time and who he spends it with. He says he makes 'calculated, hard decisions' about everything, from where he lives, to where he goes on holiday, to his friends. He has cut out anything he considers 'toxic'. He also tells me he's stronger now and much more open to new experiences. He has a partner, Inge, an artist with a background in psychology, who helps him understand his experiences and allows him to talk about them. When Inge describes the colour red, she tells him it never fully dries. Patrick replies – that's like blood. He knows he's still living with his bloodied experiences and they'll always be part of him. When he writes about it, he talks of his post-traumatic stress disorder as being something that'll never go away, completely. It's like a sleeping lion, he says, occasionally flicking its tail to remind him it's there, sometimes howling in the night. He wishes he could get rid of the lion, but 'he's mine for life'. Nevertheless, when I ask Patrick whether he would still go through that experience to be where he is, he is emphatic. 'Yes, I would, I would, I would.' I ask him why. 'Because I am in a much better place than I was then. I'm open to life's experiences. I can't think of a single way in which I'm not better now than I was then. Everything's better. So that's got to be worth it, hasn't it?'

After that moment in the loch, in the icy cold waters, when the wind took him back to a rocket attack in Baghdad, Patrick wrote a poem.

THE GUSTS – LOCH LUBNAIG

I saw it coming.
First the wave it made along the surface
I saw it running
Along the water of the Loch
Scattering shining shards of light
Across the length of the water.

Then I heard it whispering.
In the waving branches
I heard it murmuring
In the pine trees that stood
Close by the side of the path
Casting their dark blue shadows.

Then I felt it coming.
But still it hadn't reached me
I felt it, shivering,
Holding my breath in anticipation
Of the cold blast
That I couldn't escape.

In my face the icy passing.
A slap-like blow
In an instant leaving,
Leaping on down the valley
As my breath escaped
And the sun shone.

He's right when he says it's not easy, constantly worrying about the gusts of wind that'll slap you, but yes, it's a lot better than the alternative. And for Patrick, for now at least, the sun is shining.

10

Finding Strategies

'It is our attitude at the beginning of a difficult task, which, more than anything else, will affect its successful outcome'

William James

Sunday, 14th June

I've found a lump. It's very small, just by my armpit, and it moves when I press it. I'm lying in bed, constantly feeling around it, racking my brains to try to remember whether being able to move it means cancer or not, whether lack of pain means disease or not. I'm trying to get to sleep but am nauseous. I nudge Paul awake. 'I know it's probably nothing, but can you feel this?' I place his finger on the area, expecting him to hunt around for a while, only to suggest it's in my imagination. It's not. 'Yup, I've got it,' he says. The following day I ring the hospital and leave a message with the breast cancer nurses. Nothing. I email, the day after. 'I have a lump – it's tiny, pea-shaped, left-hand side – Paul could feel it too – it doesn't feel like part of the implant and I'd like it checked, please.' I'm sure they'll get back to me with an appointment. Meanwhile, Seth's got exams, Evie has an endless succession of play dates, Paul's wrestling with work issues, there are optician's appointments, summer fetes, birthdays to buy for, enough distractions to pull me back from too much introspection. Nothing has changed – and yet everything has. Life goes on while I wait.

How does the brain deal with practical necessities while also managing an emotional trauma? I'm in the middle of a plethora of recordings for another Radio 4 series I'm doing called *How to Have a Better Brain.* The brain is said to be plastic – not literally, of course, it's mainly fat and water, with around a hundred billion nerve cells or neurons and a hundred thousand miles of blood vessels. There's much we don't know about this complex organ with the consistency of jelly, but we *do* know it can be rewired and we can alter its chemistry. When we learn something new, our brain undergoes physical changes, with new connections formed between neurons. It means it keeps developing, well into middle age and beyond. I want to find out how we can help our brain repair itself and remain resilient, and the neuroscience I learn researching the series helps me further understand how those who have been through adversity survive and thrive. Every time I meet someone who's been through a physical trauma that becomes psychological or vice versa, I'm plundering them for information about how they are, how they cope, what works and what doesn't.

Today, it's Scilla White's turn. I'm having lunch with her and her daughter Catherine at their home in North London and we're in the kitchen, making a healthy salad with tuna, pine nuts, beans and lettuce. Scilla's a former consultant psychiatrist and she's bright and funny, telling me about the four online word games she's in the middle of, with her three adult daughters and a friend in the village. 'I'm winning in all of them at the moment,' she says, triumphantly. 'I'm competitive, and we're quite capable of swearing at each other if someone plays all their letters out.' 'On the board?' I ask. 'No, no!' she laughs. 'Although, actually . . .'

The reason for the meal bursting with goodness and the online games, is the same one that means the walls of her house have big boards full of notes on them, telling her what she's doing that day. Scilla is beginning to lose herself. The woman with a sharp intellect, who's well used to dealing with people's mental health battles, is now fighting one of her own. Bit by bit, Scilla is finding it more difficult to lay down new memories, to remember where she's been, or who she's seen, or what's been said, and it's making her disorientated and confused. For a woman who has always been in control, with a brain fizzing with knowledge, that challenges her sense of self and threatens her identity. The food, the games, the boards, they're part of a complex series of strategies to try to prevent it all slipping away.

Her formal diagnosis is 'mild cognitive impairment (amnesic type)' or accelerated memory loss. It's more than just forgetting where she put her keys, or getting to the top of the stairs and wondering why she's there; this is something bigger, more ominous. It means there are vast chunks of her life that Scilla can't hold onto. Her daughter, Dr Catherine Loveday, first spotted the signs of mental deterioration when her mum started getting lost in places that were familiar. Catherine's a neuropsychologist and an expert on the ageing brain at the University of Westminster and that's where we first met, while I was doing my MSc in Psychology. I thought she'd be a valuable contributor to this Radio 4 series, and it was only when we were talking about what might go in the programmes that she revealed she'd given her mum a series of cognitive tests after she realized she was losing her way. The results showed Scilla was better than 95 per cent of other people her age in tasks like planning, reasoning and attention. On memory, though, she was worse than 99 per cent of her peers. It particularly affects her sense of direction, which is why she won't go far when she takes the dog for a walk. It's a bit of her brain, the hippocampus, that area partly responsible for memory, which is showing signs of cell loss, in keeping with research that suggests navigation skills are tied up with memory. The 'internal compass' has gone awry too, so it's not just remembering the route but knowing which way to turn; she has to rely on the GPS on her phone instead.

Mother and daughter are now using the combined knowledge of a lifetime in psychiatry and psychology in an effort to halt any further decline. 'Memory is so important for our sense of self,' Catherine tells me, 'so we're doing every evidence-based thing we can to keep it. Mum still has her old memories stored, like pages in a library full of books. What we're doing now is making sure those books don't get burnt down. That she can still get to them before it's too late.' They fear she may go on to develop Alzheimer's, and that's a concern many of us can understand. One in three of us over the age of sixty-five will get dementia. It's not surprising Catherine and her mother are doing everything, every moment of the day, to try to stop this memory loss from getting any worse.

Catherine thinks that a big factor in her mum's memory loss is the chronic stress of caring for her very sick second husband. A heavy drinker, he was also 'an extremely demanding, possessive and controlling person'. He died five years ago when his lungs and kidneys failed, and Catherine says that although he was a good man with many qualities, he became more difficult as his illness took hold. It took its toll on her mum. 'I think what she went through with my stepdad was very traumatic and that's what's led her to be so stressed.'

The extended period of anxiety before and after his death meant high and constant levels of the stress hormone, cortisol, which damages the hippocampus. It kills the cells there and Catherine points to evidence that suggests high levels of stress in an earlier period of life can lead to Alzheimer's. Now, having cared for and lost her husband, Scilla is facing 'a new trauma, that of having a significant cognitive difficulty, having always been a very bright person'. That's what her mum finds so frustrating and Catherine compares it to having a brilliant piece of machinery where a part of it doesn't operate properly. 'She's expecting her mind to work, but one component is just so slow that she can't find what she needs in her brain. We can imagine it like waking up after an anaesthetic, when you feel your head's full of cotton wool and you can't think straight.'

It's that daily trauma and anxiety that I see them both trying to manage. It's a struggle for Scilla, yes, but Catherine is shaken by it too. She says it's 'very, very hard' when important conversations seem to 'disappear into the ether'. Relationships rely on shared memories, 'the kids' achievements, or something difficult that's happened, but I speak to her a week later and she can't remember anything about it,' she says. Her mother's memory loss goes even deeper, threatening not just Scilla's sense of self, but her daughter's too. 'There's something about your parents that feels like a real foundation and you never expect it's going to change. Throughout my whole life, my mum's always seemed so in control, on top of everything and knowledgeable, and when everything else is going at such a pace, that's what helps to ground you. When you see that changing it's very unsettling. She is the rock on which I stand and that's the bit that's crumbling. That's hard for me.'

Mother and daughter share some important character traits that are helping them both get through this. They are pragmatic and, when they realized there was a problem, immediately put tactics in place to try to stop her memory failing further. Another characteristic is never losing hope. Catherine says her mum is 'pathologically optimistic . . . she's resilient, she's a fighter'. It's not always easy. If she's tired, or particularly stressed, or if she has too much on, that's when her memory becomes compromised further and Catherine can see her feeling 'as if she's falling apart'. Scilla says it's like going into 'a dark space' and when that happens, everything else is affected too. If she's trying to manage too much, she'll get stressed, and the more stressed she gets, the more she forgets; the more she forgets, the more anxious she becomes and so on. When she feels herself going into that space, she just steps back, gives herself time, forces herself to deal with the anxiety, starts using a few coping strategies. If she doesn't, it 'makes things a hundred times worse'.

That means trying some relaxation techniques, going to church, going for a walk, whatever it takes to remove her from the chaos and convince her that 'I'm not going completely doolally'.

The first thing she does is try to reduce her 'cognitive load', and Catherine says that's the number one thing anyone, at any age, can do to try to improve how they're functioning. Cognitive load is anything that takes up processing space. If we're trying to juggle too many things, it's encroaching on our ability to think straight. Step back, take time, do less and give priority to the important things. Our processing speed slows down after the age of about thirty, so it's something that affects most of us, especially anyone who's going through psychological or physical trauma. Getting the balance right between being busy – which stimulates our brain and gives us respite from thinking about it all the time – and yet not getting too overtired, is one that's difficult to strike. 'You need a little bit of brain space to process the traumatic part of it, but not so much that you end up stuck in it,' says Catherine.

This sort of cognitive rehabilitation is close to Catherine's heart. She got her PhD after spending many years working with older people, testing their brains regularly, trying to investigate what was happening to them. Now she says, 'I realize that the thing I've been doing for the past twenty-five years is worth something. The positive bit of this is that I can do something to help Mum. My knowledge has been important to her and it's given our relationship a real focus.'

All that bonding, all that understanding about what tactics and strategies might work, seems to be having an effect. Scilla has had brain scans and assessments over the past few years and the results are in line with that very first series of tests, four years ago. The memory part is shrunk, a lot more than it should be for her age, but the rest of it is fine, she hasn't deteriorated further. It's frustrating that so many new experiences and conversations still slip through her fingers, but she remains positive in the face of daily adversity. 'It's easier said than done and I know people get really low,' Catherine says, 'but in this instance, it's the worst thing you can do because you need to be proactive, you need that positive energy.'

Scilla says crosswords and other word games 'get my brain working, they challenge me'. It keeps her mind active and the social element of playing friends online and connecting with others reduces her sense of isolation and loneliness. That's just as important, if not more so, than the games themselves. Sometimes, if she's got four or five games on the go, she'll save them until bedtime so she can finish them and 'it sends me to sleep with a sense of . . . I've done it!' she laughs. The vision makes me chuckle, too. 'I can just see you, late at night, playing Scrabble on your computer, swearing at all your mates in the village,' I say. 'Yes, I do,' she giggles.

Night-time has a particular routine to it. Scilla writes in her diary about her day, where she went and who she was with. She reads a little out to me: 'I woke and got up at six thirty, tidied the kitchen and had breakfast, walked up to Sainsbury's. Mimi my dog sniffed at the bag of a man coming out. I apologized and he said his own dog would have done the same.' We laugh again. I'm privileged. None of her daughters has been allowed to look at what she's written. She has five of these books now, full of days and moments and trivialities. Full of Scilla.

Catherine says this works because sleep helps cement memories. 'They so easily slip away, so by writing this regular diary, it means that, just before bed, Mum is having to relive the day. It's not someone delivering those memories to her and saying "This is what happened", either – these are her words, these are the things that are important to her. And if Mum's memory does get a lot worse, she's got her own history to look back on.'

Another key to her well-being is music. Scilla helps run a local church choir and gets great joy from it. 'It's the pleasure of getting together, sharing feelings and wishes,' she says. 'I leave the world behind me, it just lifts me into a different sphere.' She's always sung, listened to and engaged with music. 'It's giving voice to something, I'm expressing part of my own soul,' she says. Catherine says research suggests that music stimulates the emotional part of the mind. 'If you look at brain images of people when they're listening to, or involved in, music, almost all of it is active.' It's also helping with her mum's organizational skills, and recent studies show that learning music may enhance general cognition too. Musical memory is often the last to fade if we're affected by conditions like dementia, and if it can boost our mood, make us lose ourselves for a while and bind us to other people, then perhaps it's not surprising that it's used as a therapy for depression too. A study into patients with traumatic brain injury suggests their emotions improved after listening to music, and they were more socially engaged and motivated. The research says the difference in mood was so significant that both patients and their families noticed a difference; it even goes on to recommend that music therapists could work alongside psychologists, when dealing with people with brain injuries.[1]

Certainly Catherine believes that music is beneficial to all of us. When we're going through something challenging or traumatic, it may be even more crucial, in ways we are still yet to properly understand. 'Prolonged stress is completely toxic to the brain,' she says, 'and we need to find any ways we can to reduce that.'

When I talk to Scilla about that period of her life when she was caring for her husband, her demeanour changes and it's clear that it was a period of acute distress for her, when she couldn't access the things she loved. 'He was not an easy person to deal with and I was very isolated and extremely stressed, without any way out of it,' she says. 'One of the things is to always recognize that stress, to find support mechanisms, and that's where relaxation comes in, that's where friends come in, that's where exercise comes in – all sorts of things that allow you to unwind the coil that's inside you. The fact is, I didn't have a very easy way of doing it when my husband was so poorly, it just took me over, I was wound up like a coil and I don't like to . . .' She stops and looks down. 'The stress is building up just talking about it,' she tells me.

'Then don't,' I say, 'I'm sorry.'

'No, no, that's all right,' Scilla replies, shaking her head. 'It's just one of the factors of stress is that when you're in the midst of it, you can no longer see that there's a way out of it.' I ask her whether her life is now about giving herself the tools to get out of it. 'Yes, very much so, and that's where music has been important, exercise has been important, getting out in the fresh air, just a walk in the garden when I'm stressed, it makes a huge, huge difference.'

Food is part of the package too and that's why our lunch is packed with good things. If Scilla has too much sugar, things become 'much more chaotic'. Catherine smiles at her mum as we begin to tuck into our tuna-pinenut-beetroot salad. 'You probably don't want me to tell this story,' she starts, 'but that Christmas a couple of years ago, we'd planned a big day and Mum forgot what time she'd put the turkey in the oven and no one had any idea when it'd gone in either. Around Christmas, there's chocolates and sweets and everything is out of routine and the combination of things meant Mum's memory was probably at its worst.' Scilla starts to laugh. 'And when we got to it, it wasn't cooked, so we had to go to all sorts of lengths to joint it and put it in the microwave!'

Cognitive function is entirely dependent on glucose levels because a fifth of the body's intake of sugar and energy goes directly to the brain. Too much can destroy cells over a period of time, so this salad will keep sugar levels stable, without the peaks and troughs. If Scilla's routine is out of kilter, her memory is further affected, so it's important that she eats well. The trouble is that following well-loved recipes that she once knew off by heart is no longer possible. 'I get halfway through the cooking and forget what I've put in, I have to be very, very organized about it; I have to get it all out and put it all in front of me and I have to have the recipe because I can no longer rely on my brain to say, "Two teaspoons of bicarbonate of soda," and that might make a huge difference to how the pastry turns out.'

It seems like such a small thing, but it's indicative of a wider problem. I ask her how hard it is, forgetting things that were once part of her. 'Very. The sort of things that I used to take for granted. It takes twice as long to do anything and it is very frustrating to find that your memory doesn't do what you would like it to do. In organizational skills, I'm not as good as I was. There are certainly things that I've put in place to try and help me, I have memory boards all over the kitchen. But I also have to remind myself to take a shopping list and, if I've forgotten it, I haven't a clue what I'm meant to be getting. I'll end up with three of something I didn't need and none of something I did. That's totally frustrating, particularly with the shops three and a half miles away.'

Catherine says it's like writing in the sand and then the sea comes in and it's all gone again. Unless it's written down, cemented in somewhere, all those memories will be lost for ever.

After lunch, we take Mimi for a walk around the park. Scilla wears a small camera around her neck, called an Autographer, and it automatically takes pictures, depending on how it's set up, so either fifty, a hundred, or two hundred photos an hour. When she gets home, she loads those images into the computer and, like rereading her sleep diary, it embeds the day in her mind. If she didn't have that piece of kit, she wouldn't remember many of the details of where we went and what we said. The walking really boosts her mood, too. 'You must admit, walking like this, in the sunshine – it does you good, doesn't it?' she says. I ask her what happens when she doesn't do it and she talks about 'going into that dark space again'.

She's frightened about her mental state, however upbeat she tries to be. As a psychiatrist, she understands better than most that it's declining. I ask her what she fears most. 'My independence is very, very important and my sense of being in charge of what happens to me is also very, very important. Even though I've got three lovely daughters who I'm sure try to keep me as independent as I can be, the fear of not being independent is very, very great.' She puts such a strong stress on the word 'very' every time she says it. Her determination is clear.

She talks about what matters to her now: 'The mental stimulation and still to be able to have questions asked of you and still answer them, to be able to read the paper and make my own decisions.' I thank her for answering such a difficult question and Scilla smiles ruefully at me. 'It's a question that most people ask themselves at some point. Thank you for making me answer it.'

Mother, daughter and dog head home, chatting away about things Scilla will struggle to recall tomorrow, but things she'll try to remember with every strategy she can use. We end the day with laughs and hugs and squares of dark chocolate. This remarkable, funny, clever woman is holding on to who she is, with every piece of energy and knowledge that she's got. She's found her own way of coping with her daily adversity. 'It's not going to go away,' she says, 'and the only way to go on with life *is* to go on with it – and to *get* on with it. It does make a difference, just fighting for something,' she says. 'It's worth not rolling over, and if you fight for it and make some progress, or even halve the decline, you know you're winning.'

With that, I pick up my bags to leave and Scilla turns to the computer. She *is* winning at the moment and she'll do everything she possibly can, not to let that slip away.

11

Finding Growth

'Real growth often happens outside of where we intend it to, in the interstitial spaces – what Dr Seuss calls "the waiting place"'

Bruce Mau

Wednesday, 1st July

Sometimes, just as you think you're 'winning' something can come along to trip you up. I'm going in to see the breast cancer nurse about the lump. The tiny, almost-missable, could-be-something, probably-nothing, lump. Sitting in the waiting room, I'm feeling fraudulent and then stop myself. Worry is worry. When I had surgery to remove the cancer, they told me they took everything they could see and feel. They also said tiny groups of malignant cells might still be there and they often can't be found by the screening tests or by manipulation. Even if the nurse discovers something and even if it's benign, those cells may be lurking undetected elsewhere. This is about living with the knowledge that I can't control any of that, I just have to ride it out. There's no right or wrong way to feel about it, it just is.

*

The psychologist I've been seeing talks about strapping a seat belt on when we know we need it. It's about being emotionally prepared, acknowledging that things might get tough again and understanding what works to support us through it. If this is going to be a rough crossing, how do we protect ourselves? We are all problem solvers at heart, but often there are no clear answers. The nature of suffering and why it happens remains annoyingly mysterious. We may ask, 'Why me? Or what would have happened if . . .?' but we're unlikely to get much lasting satisfaction from that. This so-called 'brooding rumination' focuses on self-blame, guilt or repeatedly asking unanswerable questions. In breast cancer patients, it's associated with stress, anxiety and depression, and can lead to a decreased quality of life, a poorer clinical outcome and increased risk of mortality.[1]

Inevitably, there will be lots of negative emotions after trauma, they happen automatically, and these intrusive thoughts are an important part of working through the trauma. Research suggests, though, that most people graduate from brooding rumination to a more constructive, honest focus, adapting to the new situation by planning and making decisions about how to move on.[2] Growth comes from a struggle with crisis and it's often interrupted by further fear or the repetition of a distressing event (Is it a lump? Is the cancer returning? What happens if it does?). Recognizing these thoughts, not letting them overwhelm us but moving to planning, action and decision (I'll book an appointment, there's nothing I can do until then, worrying will not make it easier), means having a more constructive dialogue with ourselves.

We can't fight feelings of vulnerability, but we can recognize and accept them while trying to take care of ourselves through them. It takes courage to do this and it's not comfortable, but accepting this fragility, sitting and listening to it while understanding that it's likely to pass, is more constructive than trying to push it away or 'fix' it. Research also shows that breast cancer survivors who had a more optimistic, accepting and less avoidant outlook during their treatment, have a better quality of life up to thirteen years afterwards.[3] Even while facing an uncertain future, they saw some benefits emerging from their cancer experience – such as an enhanced sense of meaning in life, a deepening of relationships or a change in priorities.[4] To do this, though, to allow these vulnerable feelings, we need some effective coping strategies.

Scilla was employing a lot of them to deal with the daily trauma of her memories slipping away. The walking, the music, the diet, the diary, the online games with her daughters; she's found ways that stop her going into the 'dark space'. For Patrick, it's talking things through, reflecting on reasons why he may get anxious again, and writing poetry. For Stuart, it's having a clearer line between work and home, it's engaging in activities like going to football with his son, things that he wouldn't have invested so much time in, before his accident and breakdown. For Trude and Floella it's about hope, never giving up during harsh times and, now, about education, using their experience to help, guide and nourish others. Compassion is something I've noticed in all the people that have shared their stories, an increased kindness both to themselves and to others. They were lucky to find care and love while going through their trauma, though. I know adversity can feel like a very isolating place.

Many people find their partners and friends help, although occasionally it seems as if their support wanes after a while. Perhaps they assume that you are back to 'normal' because you look fine; maybe you've returned to work and there's a desire to have the 'old' you back, too. The one that wasn't hurt and bruised and suffering. It's hard to understand that, while you may look the same physically and emotionally, there may be a long way to go. That can lead to frustration and confusion – the initial enthusiasm they showed may burn out prematurely, even if you still need their support.[5] It's sometimes hard to ask for it too, especially if, on some days, you look like you're coping and then suddenly, you're not. I know in my case, Paul needs a very clear signal when I want help and if I'm busy being strong and brave, I don't give it. Then I'll collapse, suddenly, and it takes us both by surprise.

What will get us through is an understanding of how we ask for that help, as well as remaining aware of how our emotions are affecting us and accepting that it's a hard way to develop and change. When I speak to Stuart Hughes, my colleague who lost his leg in Iraq and then went on to develop post-traumatic stress disorder, he talks of 'enforced growth . . . hard-fought growth'. He says he's 'very, very, very vulnerable and scared I'm going to crash again'. Vulnerability and fragility never go away. 'Like anyone who has a mental health problem, what happens if it comes back? I'm not comfortable with it at all, I'm still really scared of it, but that's probably good, because maybe it'll make it less likely.' I know what he means. He sees himself as someone who has a mental health problem, I see myself as someone with cancer. Although neither of us is defined by it, it's now part of our identity and who we are. It's frightening to think of either returning, but perhaps he's right, maybe that fear gives us the edge to make us more aware of how to strengthen ourselves if it does come back. If a wave of adversity threatens to overwhelm, perhaps we'll see it coming and start using strategies to protect ourselves. If we don't and it knocks us over, we can either stay face down in the surf, gasping for air, or we can rise, unsteadily, recognizing the pain and fear and, with great courage, try to stand up again.

I thought that tiny, pea-shaped lump would threaten my recovery. When Shirley, the breast cancer nurse, felt it, she smiled and said, 'That's just part of the implant. Be off with you.' Both she and I are glad we checked. It'll be a long time before I can trust my body. It's a struggle to find the new 'normal', but cancer has brought some positives into my life, just as Stuart's losses have helped redefine what matters to him. He's 'been through this thing and survived' and his identity has shifted. He believes he's wiser, that there's more meaning to life, he's engaging differently with his family and friends, he's more compassionate and takes on more responsibility for others. Thinking about the impermanence of life gave him focus and also made him more fragile, and I understand that too.

Patrick also thinks he's different since his breakdown: 'There was a point in my life where I was in denial about my own fears and vulnerabilities and I would also push everyone else's away. Oh, you know, "Get on with it. Stiff upper lip and all that." And actually it's a shit way to live, it is just rubbish! It's much nicer if you can identify with people, you can have a better conversation with them if you can understand what they are, what their challenges are and what their difficulties are. And part of that, of course, is admitting your own failings and your own shortcomings and your own fears, and I've had to do that, I haven't had any choice. But that's been a great thing for me. That's been a big thing, you know, it's made me happy.' There is strength and compassion in that vulnerability. It's a part of Stuart, a part of Patrick, a part of me.

For all the kindness and compassion we try to show to ourselves and others, for all the recognition of our failings, shortcomings and fears, for all the strategies that can help us cope and get through trauma and thrive, sometimes there's no happy ending. I'm acutely aware that my form of cancer is treatable. That's not the same for a lot of people, like my aunty and my mum, who both lost their lives to the disease. It's hard to see the positives in these and similar scenarios, difficult to imagine how you would 'grow' after being given a terminal diagnosis. However, some feel the full force of such a diagnosis changes their view of the life that's left. The neurologist Oliver Sacks said he felt 'intensely alive' when he came 'face to face with dying'. He wanted to write, travel, deepen friendships, and achieve 'new levels of understanding and insight', with time too, for fun and silliness.[6]

When my mum couldn't move from the corner of the sofa,

when her heavy legs were swollen by steroid treatment and her bone-crushing weariness prevented her standing, I'd paint her toenails bright pink, so at least she felt her feet looked nice. One day, the nail varnish bottle spilt, glooping its contents all over the light beige woollen carpet. Frantically, I began to clean it up. She laughed, shaking her head. 'It really doesn't matter, I don't like this carpet anyway! Sit beside me, tell me about how the kids are.' She would never have reacted like that in the past, but she'd come to terms with her situation more easily than her family, and the small stuff became an irrelevance. Hug them close, she thought, laugh with them while you can, don't sweat over the little things. Would she have said she'd 'grown' in those last weeks? She didn't say. I know that, although the changes to her body were enormously frustrating, she developed an intensity of thinking about the importance of other matters. I'd just had a baby, my fourth child and a daughter after three sons. 'You enjoy her, don't you?' she said, smiling. 'There's nothing quite like the relationship between a mother and daughter. I'm so happy she's here. Remember to spend time with them all, enjoy them all, don't work too hard.'

Some will argue that growing or thriving in the context of terrible circumstances is illusory, that you are somehow 'justifying' the trauma, searching for any light in a life that's suddenly gone very dark. These psychologists call it 'the cognitive adaptation theory',[7] suggesting that any post-traumatic growth is a result of our brains adapting to the horrific reality. They say because almost all the research on growth is self-reported, there's a danger that it's a retrospective construct, that we need to feel we have progressed, believing, as the psychologist George Bonanno suggests, that 'I am better now, so I must have grown.'[8]

But others say the *perception* of viewing life differently is beneficial in its own right. If someone believes they have developed a deeper spirituality or their relationships have strengthened as a result of their struggle with trauma, is that 'growth'? And if so, who are we to deny it? Also, as there's no agreed measurement of illusion or self-deception in growth psychology, no one can test whether you are deluding yourself or whether there's been actual change. Even in the most traumatic of circumstances, you cannot disprove that someone has grown, if they believe it themselves.[9]

Any reminder of our mortality may spur us on to look at the meaning in the life we have left, which can lead to reports of positive change,[10] but it's important to remember that our relationship with, and reaction to, illness will differ greatly from one person to another. The same event will generate a sense of crisis for some, but not others, and we'll interpret any distress and benefit in separate ways. Those who see it as a serious health threat and are more actively engaged in dealing with it are more likely to find benefits in that experience,[11] but it takes time, because it's very back and forth and often it feels like you've stalled or are regressing. Never feel under pressure to minimize your distress because you 'should' be better. It is painstaking, tortuous work trying to rebuild life after loss, and a degree of distress is inevitable as you struggle with it. When just keeping going seems enough, any perception of getting better can take years to realize.

The research into whether our personality, age, gender and marital status make a difference in our reactions to trauma is complex and contradictory, so it's difficult to isolate any of these factors as influencing growth. More research is needed, along with long-term study designs so scientists can truly measure its extent.

What is known is that growth, thriving and a new-found sense of confidence and strength are commonly reported among those who've experienced what seem like the most terrible circumstances, and that certain factors help encourage it. They include, among other things, the ability to talk about the trauma with others who understand, and being able to reflect on its effect, to begin processing the raw emotion and plan coping strategies.

Perhaps the more we learn about an illness or a loss and the more information we can arm ourselves with about what we are going through, the easier it is to deal with. In the hunt for how bad the breast cancer is and whether it'll return, I had tissue taken out and analysed, a lump felt and dismissed, and I have a test result outstanding. I'm still waiting to know whether I have BRCA1 or BRCA2. It's that altered gene that keeps on giving, greatly increasing your risk of breast and ovarian cancer, even if you've had something off or out.

The acronym just stands for Breast Cancer 1 and Breast Cancer 2. A bit like Dr Seuss's Thing One and Thing Two, with their blue Afro hair and red jumpsuits, causing mischief in the house. We know when the Cat in the Hat says, 'these Things will not bite you, they want to have fun', that they'll actually go on to cause massive destruction.

This is such a destructive mutation. If you have the BRCA1 gene, your lifetime risk of developing breast cancer is between 60 per cent and 90 per cent. It's between 40 per cent and 60 per cent for ovarian cancer.[12] Men can also carry the gene and are at risk of breast cancer, and prostate too. Happy little chappies.

My brilliant, bright, sparky, fun friend Alison, the former editor of *BBC Breakfast*, had the gene. Throughout her cancer diagnosis and treatment, she continued to work, remaining dedicated to the team and to making the show sing and win – which it did. She kept her illness from most people, especially management, worried that they might not think her fit enough to continue the job she loved. Only when her hair fell out during chemotherapy did she say anything.

I would occasionally visit some of the radiotherapy and chemotherapy sessions with Alison after the programme had finished, and afterwards, we'd go out to lunch and get riotously drunk, laughing hysterically about some ridiculous piece of BBC gossip. She hated the drugs she was on; the steroids that made her gain weight, the chemo that made her feel sick. Having a large glass of white wine and a giggle with friends meant she could tolerate, at least temporarily, all the crap that comes with cancer.

Here's a small glimpse into our email lives, the Editor and the Presenter. The friends.

November 2011

Thinking of you. Are you taking your pills and have you got a date for your scan?

Sx

I'm not . . . They're still sitting tantalizing on my table in the flat! I'm trying Chinese herbs first.

I should find out a date tomorrow. I'll let you know. You OK?

Ax

Don't be bathing in shark fin. Mate came up in horrible rash. Am fine – talk soon.

Sx

February 2012

Stonking figures again! 1.61 vs. 0.73. I'm off filming in Wales pretending it's June for the Jubilee. Contactable on mobile if you need anything.

Sx

Oh no! I'll miss you. Have fun!! . . . Waiting at clinic place in Harley St to discuss ovary removal. I'm going to ask if he can whip them out tomorrow and get it over with!! Yes, awesome figures. Brilliant all week!

Ax

Good luck – try to rest.

Sx

I'm fine. Doctor was wonderful. Said the op is a walk in the park. Not remotely difficult or traumatic. I'll be back at work the next day. Hurrah!! Xx

Ax

March 2012

I'm gutted but I can't be at the lovely Television and Radio Industries Club Awards with you to cheer our/your (inevitable?) success. Sadly, I can't escape the straitjacket of treatment despite my pleas to the contrary! Good luck!!

Ax

I won best reporter/presenter. We toasted Alison but the bubbly was flat. I had a trophy but she had made the show what it was.

April 2012

Hello lovely!!! I keep seeing you on my TV and missing you. Are you OK? I'm doing fine – desperately hacked off and tired and bored but had some scans last week which showed the cancer has all but gone, which is a fab first step. I'm in London today for more tests and might even venture into the office tomorrow, although the waves of pity are almost too much to bear!! I'd love to see you – my chemo dose is being reduced from this week so I'm told I'll start to feel better. If that's the case, we could get together in the next couple of weeks or so?

Lots of love xxx

Fab – so glad things are looking up. What a gruesome time for you. Let's meet.

Sx

July 2012

> Hey sweetheart. I only just recovered your lovely card last week after finding a pile of post hidden away by my cleaner. It made me want to cry!! I'm so sorry I've not been in touch – I kept holding out, hoping I could suggest lunch dates and then ended up in hospital over and over again. I've had so many infections, dodgy blood and transfusions, that I've lost count. Happily, I finish this round of chemo next Tuesday and then move on to something much, much easier. Hurrah!!
>
> Anyway, how are you? I can't wait to see you and Bill together on Friday. I'm planning to come and hang out there as soon as I can. Next week ideally. I guess lunch during the [Olympic] games is a little tricky? But even seeing you down there would be lovely. I'll let you know when I'm around? Xxxx

> Ah, lovely Alison – I can't tell you how happy I am to hear things are OK!
>
> It'd be lovely to catch up, just let me know when you're free and feeling stronger.
>
> Much love
>
> Sx

We continue with a few get-togethers, but they become less frequent. Alison was often in hospital for treatment and trying to manage a programme, too.

On 2 July 2013, she died.

I was asked to add a tribute to the BBC News website. This is what I wrote:

> Alison was funny, positive, vibrant and strong. She never once complained about her illness, preferring instead to sit outside and celebrate life over a glass of wine. She was a brilliant and inspirational colleague and a true and loyal friend. The loss to her family and those who loved her, is incalculable.

Alison left behind her husband, Martin, and two sons, Jack and Tommy. While she was always trying to minimize the seriousness of her situation at work, she was preparing her family at home for a future without her. Yes, eight in ten women diagnosed with breast cancer now live a decade or more, but thousands, like Alison, don't make it. She was optimistic, energetic and indomitable, and there were times when she was also furious, fearful and frustrated. Two years on, here I am. A very different path, a very different treatment, but perhaps, some shared emotions. I understand the feeling of finding some solid ground – only for something to re-emerge to fell you. That pea-sized lump that moved when I touched it was cancer again, I was sure.

Yet, it was felt and dismissed. There'll be others. You're on heightened alert all the time. I remember Alison showing me a small, raised lump on her forehead; she was worried it was another tumour. It wasn't and she laughed about her 'paranoia'. 'It was probably just a zit!' she said.

I know now how she must have felt, when every new lump and bump feels threatening. But Alison seemed to deal with all those switches in emotion, the scares magnified, the underlying fears, with hope, honesty and humour. Rereading our emails shows how she tackled one medical obstacle at a time, without letting it overwhelm her, trying to focus on her family, friends and work instead. She lived for the day-to-day, and if that day felt brutal, she'd share it, talk about it, but quickly move on to other things in life – a holiday, Christmas, the boys' sports trials.

Like me, she was lucky to have family and friends around her, and that may not be the same for everyone. But that spirit of hope, of not letting a situation drown us and of finding comfort away from trauma, is there, if we know how best to encourage and support it. Perhaps we can accept our vulnerabilities, know our strengths and weaknesses, try not to avoid emotion, and look for the meaning in the life we have, even if it seems to have changed beyond recognition.

I spoke to lots of people who went through extraordinary loss, trauma and illness. Their coping strategies and experiences, together with an understanding of the science around fear and how to manage it, helped bolster me, as I hope it will you. I know how challenging that can be, though, during the uncertain times.

I had the BRCA test months ago on 28 April, a blood sample that'll decide what happens next.

Now, as Dr Seuss would say, I'm in the Waiting Place, 'waiting around for a Yes or a No . . . Waiting for the fish to bite . . .

Whatever the results say, whenever I get them, there still seem to be so few answers as to why breast cancer strikes or whether, after treatment, it'll return and, if it does, with what severity. The odds are certainly better now than they've ever been. Survival rates in the UK have risen by 50 per cent since the 1970s because of an increase in screening and a greater understanding of treatments, but nearly twelve thousand people still die from it each year. There are so many factors, both known and unknown, that can lead to the disease hitting any one of us. The National Health Service suggests they include: increasing age, hormonal influences, lifestyle, genetic factors, environmental factors, and chance. Chance! That's wide enough to be meaningless.

The NHS says only a very small proportion of breast cancers happen due to a strong inherited factor. Certain clues include, it says, several cases of it in the family, young ages of diagnosis and a family history of ovarian cancer as well as breast. I'm told the pattern in my family suggests the possibility of the altered gene and that's why I need the test.

The science of it is this:

One copy of each pair of genes is inherited from our mother and one copy from our father. If one parent has an altered copy of a BRCA1 or BRCA2 gene there is a 50 per cent chance they'll pass on the altered copy and a 50 per cent chance they'll pass on the normal one. If a child inherits the altered copy, there's an increased risk of developing cancer as an adult and they'll have the same 50 per cent chance of passing it on to each of their children.

It's never just a test that affects you. It affects you and your children, your siblings and theirs. If I've inherited it from my mother, my brothers are 50 per cent likely to inherit it, too. As they are identical twins, their result is the same. If we all carry it, each of our children has a chance of having it, too. Breast screening for 'a BRCA candidate' doesn't start until thirty – so my daughter and niece will not be screened until they hit their third decade. Of course, it's not just women, because men carry it as well so it can hit our sons. These mutated genes – these bloody things – are affecting generations and generations and going on for ever. If we have them, it changes everything, for all of us.

Everyone is just waiting.

Tuesday, 7th July

Eleven weeks of waiting around for a Yes or a No and, sitting at my computer, an email pings in:

Dear Sian

I now have the result of your genetic test.

I will be in the office all day tomorrow and all day Friday, so please feel free to telephone me at a time convenient to you. If neither day works, let me know and I can give you a time to call next week.

My heart is beating in my stomach. Why there? I call the genetic counsellor and the phone rings and rings. I leave a message, bright and cheery. 'Hi there! You called, do call back, any time, I'm here by my phone.' I feel woozy. This will determine months of surgery – or not. A greater risk of the cancer coming back. Or not. My young daughter and son and their children, and my older two, having the mutation. Or not. Please call back. I rang immediately after getting your email. The results are probably in front of you, on your desk or on your computer. You know my future and my children's future, their children's future. My brothers' future, their children's future. God, this goes on and on. It's like some crazy 1970s cartoon where I have a gamma-ray gun and I fire it out and all the people I love get hit. Ring, please. Don't say you've sent the email and have gone to lunch. That you know what I don't, while you're having a sandwich in the hospital canteen. Right. I'm ringing again . . .

Her secretary says she's in a clinic and not out until a quarter past five. It's now a quarter past one. Can't be urgent, can it? I can't have it, otherwise she'd have rung, yes? Watch it, I've been there before, misinterpreting a letter, a smile, an incline of the head, thinking they must mean I don't have cancer when – whoops! There go your social antennae – I did.

So, if I have to wait for hours, I'll distract myself. Breathe, calm. My son Alex is downstairs, I'll make him lunch, put the washing out, be normal. Normal, with or without mutations. It's either lurking in the nuclei of my cells, allowing those potential cancer cells to slip through and thrive. Or not. Safe, or not. Diseased, or not. Ring back.

I have lunch with Alex and we talk about BBC 'Top Gear' and the train strike later this week. I mention the frustration of waiting. 'She's glossed over your uncertainty because she doesn't know what it means to you, that's all. Let it go for a bit.' So sound, my boy. I wish I had his calm, his ability to float, his refusal to give in to stress. Proud Mum, yes, but I think he'll make a lovely doctor, I really do.

It's a quarter to six. She didn't call.

Wednesday, 8th July

Out running with my friend, the last mile home, wheezing uphill and the phone rings. 'It's genetics here, I have positive news. You don't have the gene mutation BRCA1 or BRCA2. You have no greater risk of cancer recurrence than any other woman who's had it already.'

I thank her and hang up. Relief. And then a pang of guilt for having been so cross yesterday waiting for the results; there will have been other women waiting for that call, whose news was very different. I hug my friend. Can I celebrate, then? Is now the time I count my blessings and move on? The threat never seems to go, even after good news – I've had cancer and I feel it could raise its ugly head as soon as I take my eye off the ball; if I become less vigilant, or when I have the audacity to raise a toast to seeing the back of it.

For the time being, though, I count my lucky stars. Alison lived with this mutation and it eventually let her down by letting the cancer in, even when she thought she had it conquered. There will be so many others out there now, living with it, undergoing harsh treatment, blasting and killing cells, worrying about every subsequent lump and bump and what they might signify. Not quite a celebration, then. More a reflection on how the spin of a wheel can dictate your fate. 'Genetics and bad luck' was how the surgeon framed my cancer diagnosis. Today, the genetics at least seem to be on my side.

12

Breathe

'No passion so effectually robs the mind of all of its powers of acting and reasoning as fear'

Edmund Burke, *A Philosophical Enquiry into the Origin of Our Ideas of the Sublime and Beautiful*

July is full of lumps and bumps. I'm back on TV this month as the returning host of BBC1's *Sunday Morning Live.* Every week, for the next six months, I'll be tied up with scripting and researching a weekly show. I'm excited, anxious and unsure about how I'll be. We've done a non-transmission 'pilot', a run-through on the set, and it was hopeless. I watched the DVD of the recording and although I look the same (a little rounder, perhaps) and sound the same, there's something missing. I was not 'on my game', I let the guests talk over one another, didn't have the level of knowledge I should, was too laid-back. Was it the lack of adrenalin, knowing that this would never be broadcast, or something more fundamental? Some change in character? The ground has shifted and the million or so viewers who watch the show will have no idea why. Can I slot back into the old me or is this slightly more removed version the one I'm left with?

A friend asks how I feel about going back into TV. 'I want to control it, rather than it controlling me,' I say. It can become obsessive, eating into all aspects of your life. It sucks up your time, it dominates your thoughts and it can turn you into a pleading bundle of neuroses – 'Please watch my show, please like me!' When viewers do, you're 'popular' and 'respected', your worth measured in audience share and column inches. What happens when those same viewers turn away or turn off? When those same presenters who've been courting the spotlight and tracked by the paparazzi are suddenly dropped? As the pack moves on to someone new, they're often left making increasingly louder noises just to be heard. I watched it happen as a producer and thought, 'I do not want to be like them, I will not be someone that's sucked into narcissism and neediness, defined by who I am on the television.'

When I was offered an anchor's job, I accepted, knowing I could retreat behind the glass and be a producer again at any time. I've now spent more broadcasting time in front of the microphone than I have producing behind it. It's a privileged position to be at the heart of ever-changing events and that's what makes it addictive. No two days are the same; it's an adrenalin ride where you're a baby-step from disaster, teetering on the edge of the career precipice. When I first started presenting, I had an overwhelming desire to swear on air to see what would happen, an impish excitement about saying something that would stop everything, instantly. It's like standing on a platform as the train hurtles towards you, thinking, 'I could just step out now and everything would change.' I didn't swear, although plenty of guests did. Dame Helen Mirren said 'shit' on *BBC Breakfast* first thing in the morning, a comedian insulted a top singing star with a brain tumour, we've fallen off air, had convulsive giggles that contort the face and leave you unable to talk. Lots of train wrecks over the years.

It's such an exciting job. Bruising too, on occasion. You forget the audience is judging you and a bad reaction on social media can leave you battered, or you can feel wretched after a poor review. When I joined a relaunched Radio 4 show, *Saturday Live*, as the new co-presenter with the Reverend Richard Coles, we had a somewhat difficult debut interviewing the Seventies pop megastar David Cassidy. A schoolgirl crush of mine, he was described by a journalist writing her weekly radio column as 'a death-defying, medal-winning, uninterruptable bore'. The headline of that piece screamed 'Hop along Cassidy and take Williams with you'. Turns out Cassidy was not the only problem with the show; I was 'ill-suited' to it, I wasn't 'quirky' enough. It went on: 'I'm not sure where her personality is located. Possibly in her dressing table. Perhaps she only gets it out on special occasions, like a posh brooch.' I really thought I'd struggle to do the next show after that. Pathetic really, when I look back now. It was a personal opinion in a well-written piece and the listening figures were continuing to grow anyway. But at the time, it felt as if that columnist had come to my house and slapped me round the face. Or sat on my shoulder as I broadcast, shouting, 'You're crap! You're crap!'

And I'm about to do it all again in a matter of days. Perhaps that's the distance I saw in my eyes during the pilot. Trauma makes you see the vacuity of things. The author Iris Murdoch described it as our 'fat, relentless ego' – we pack our lives with event and drama until the real drama comes to remind us that the rest is just logistics. Part of recovery is in the questioning that comes with the trauma. It is very hard to do this without judging yourself, being unforgiving and harsh.

After my mum died and I went back to presenting, the successive months were spent constantly questioning life and work. At the time, I was doing a lot of careers talks in universities and wrote this, not for publication, just to vent:

When I meet young women who want advice about how to 'make it' in television, they usually fall into two distinct categories: those that want to be presenters and those that want to be journalists. The ones that want to be presenters have always been the ones at school who were good at drama; pretty, popular, very sure of themselves, who have already perfected the beaming smile. They want to be on TV. The ones that want to be journalists aren't so sure of themselves. They hope their brain, not their looks, will get them there. Hard graft, get your feet dirty, earn the respect of your colleagues, then you can sit in front of the camera with some degree of authority, I tell them. Those are the ones I mentor. And then, bit by bit, what I tell them is undermined. In the press, another woman presenter is collecting a Rear of the Year award or talking about how embarrassed they are at being 'forced' to wear tiny, revealing outfits for a TV charity show.

It's demeaning. I can't compete and I don't want to feel like I have to try. I do not want women news presenters to be placed in some sort of beauty league. Where the only articles you're asked to do are 'Me and My Wardrobe'. Where your popularity is judged on how many bloggers fancy you, how many celebrity up-skirt moments find their way onto YouTube.

I feel so strongly that the women on TV, especially in news and current affairs, should be people the young look up to, knowing that they've got there because they've worked hard and have a decent track record in journalism. That, yes, they can have fun – but not at the expense of diminishing or reducing everything they've done to whether they 'should give up short skirts and disappoint their male fans'. Can we redress the balance and if so, how?

Mum died in November and when I returned to the *BBC Breakfast* sofa soon afterwards, it was as someone who'd been hollowed out. Someone tense, brittle, hurt and sad.

Here's a small part of what I wrote then.

14th January 2010

Get back to work with Bill [my co-presenter], after a week off in the snow, trying to get my health back and put a bit of weight on after a horrible end of year and the first email to ping in from a viewer is this:

> Just to let you both know you were not missed. Your replacements did it far better than both of you. Jane

21st January

Wore brighter colours this week after last week's comments from some in the audience which said I looked depressing. Have to dress appropriately for the news and I rather thought two hundred thousand people dying in an earthquake in Haiti merited a more sombre approach and dress code. Wore purple today – the colour of mourning. Got a text saying, 'Why does Sian think orange hair goes with mauve?' Can't win.

3rd February

Here's another email. From a viewer called Tom:

> Sian Williams is clearly a good interviewer, as her savaging of Prime Minister Gordon Brown shows, but she's mumsy and completely lacking in sex appeal.

Bit worried about all these messages – Sian's looking old/gaunt/ thin. So come home and despite good audience figures and everyone in management being lovely, decide I really should give it up, am getting too old, not glamorous enough. As if to add weight (ha!) to my theory that it's time to go, I google myself. Oh, the horror. Here's how one conversation goes:

Bill Turnbull and Sian Williams on *BBC Breakfast*:

– Is it just me? I find these two utterly unbearable as presenters. I don't know how they get on in real life, but on screen I cannot stand their contrived banter and fake laughing.

– Nothing wrong with Bill Turnbull IMO, however Sian Williams is slowly morphing into Nancy Reagan.

– The Lovely Sian (TM) 'slowly morphing into Nancy Reagan'?! How very dare you?! I laughed lots this morning . . . The Lovely Sian (TM) has got a bit spikier since she came back from maternity, but she's still a real favourite. They're a TV Dream Team for me . . .

– Oh come now, she is looking a bit too scrawny these days. She's got that 'Ooh I've just had a whole lettuce leaf for breakfast' look.

– Yes, and is it just me, but I noticed a while ago that, depending on which way she sits, her head sometimes looks way too big for her body. For a time, it was really noticeable and made her look deformed.

Enough! Enough!

So I go out and buy some clothes. Bright ones. And eat lots. And try to get myself into the frame of mind that says – sod this! I'm not going to read it, or listen to it, I'm just going to go on and do my best because I'm being distracted from doing my job properly.

5th February

This from the audience complaints and comments log:

> I am fed up with Sian Williams and Bill Turnbull and their methods of presenting the programme. They seem to argue a great deal and it is in a rather childish manner.
>
> I was unhappy at the way one of your female presenters angled her head as she was speaking. It looked very subservient and it was off-putting.

16th February

Oh my word. Have we set the cat among the pigeons? Ray Gosling, 'veteran local broadcaster', comes on the show to talk about killing his gay lover by smothering his face with a pillow. He had AIDs and says they had made a pact. It felt confessional and sensationalist. We couldn't ask him any details about the incident, because there may be a police investigation, so it meant we couldn't say, 'Don't you realize this is murder?' We danced around the interview, really. It was more than twenty years ago, he says the doctor seemed to accept he'd done it, but the police will still want to talk to him. He spoke directly to Bill during the interview, not me. Used his name, not mine. Shook his hand, not mine. Maybe I appeared unsympathetic? The viewers were divided. Some called him a murderer and said we were endorsing his actions, others applauded him. (He was later found to be lying and was sentenced for wasting police time.) After the programme, one of the deputy editors said, 'Let's not be judgemental, I don't suppose we can understand what it's like to watch someone you love die a horrible death.' 'Yes, I can,' I said. 'Three months ago, I held my mum's hand for five days and watched her dying a horrible death (and for the record, never once thought about ending it sooner for her). Hated the whole thing.'

Tomorrow I will make my questions short and to the point. And I will wear trousers so I can move around freely and not worry about people looking up my skirt. I will go back to being a grown-up who reads the news, rather than this light-headed, uncomfortable-looking, fumbling woman that I saw before me who – as one viewer said this morning – has the body of a twelve-year-old.

So that was six years ago and I want to hold out my hand to that woman and say 'Escape. If you are feeling like this every day, something has gone wrong. You are still traumatized by the death of your mother. You haven't allowed yourself to grieve. Take time off, if only to reconfigure who you are and what you want. Try not to punish yourself daily. Try not to be suffocated by the vacuity of life – it will get better, you will get better.'

And yet – similar feelings are threatening to bubble up now. Stay strong, I keep telling myself, provide a distance if it helps, ignore the reactions if they threaten to wound. This way might not work, it might feel similar to before, when you went back early and ended up being hollow and self-flagellating, because you weren't ready.

Grief and loss do this to us. They render us vulnerable, so threats that used to be manageable become less so. It's tempting to put the original traumatic experience in a box, sealed shut, at the back of our brain so we can get on with our 'old' life. We have things to do, families to run, work to attend to. And yet it's vital to reflect on what's happened and to acknowledge that we are still recovering and we can still be knocked back. Trauma opens us up to questions about our life, our work, and our place in the world, our sense of self and our relationships. A shift in perception is not a bad thing, it can, eventually, be positive. But how we manage that process is crucial.

Fifty years ago, Professor Richard Lazarus defined stress as an individual's perception of their inability to cope with the demands of an external situation, which could have a detrimental effect on their health and well-being.[1] Years later, Lazarus acknowledged it was also an important and inevitable part of daily life, but it's how we interpret those stressors that determines how we cope with everyday hassles. 'A stressful encounter should be viewed as a dynamic, unfolding process, not as a static, unitary event,' he wrote. 'Life would be dull and unsatisfying without some degree of stress, and boredom is stressful too.'[2]

Elevated and continual stress, though, can become a threat to our physical and emotional welfare. A traumatic event provokes high, sustained levels of stress and, as we've seen, whether it's the loss of our health or someone we love, that can put our identity and our stability at risk. Here's how the World Heath Organization defines that traumatic event: 'a stressful event or situation . . . of an exceptionally threatening or catastrophic nature, which is likely to cause pervasive distress in almost anyone'.[3]

After an especially stressful incident, there's thought to be a critical period of increased brain plasticity, when new neurons are firing and wiring together. That can result in long-lasting change, like acute stress disorders, because even if the initial trauma has gone, the after-effects continue to resonate, affecting the very structure of your brain, manipulating your thinking and emotions. Think of a war veteran, returning home to civilian life, hearing a car backfiring and throwing himself to the floor. His brain has reminded him of gunfire, it alerts him to a threat and he reacts, instinctively. Logic hasn't got a hope. It's an automatic response – fight, flight or freeze – and is extremely difficult to overcome. You can do it though – you can rewire your brain so that the automatic response to fear or stress is replaced by something more rational. Your brain can be instantly responsive in real danger, while not being 'hyper-vigilant'.

The part of the brain that reacts to intense emotional states such as fear is called the amygdala. The name comes from the Greek word for almond – like its shape. Normally, the amygdala is very useful, alerting us to threat. It's the same response that prompts a deer to freeze when it sees a predator and then run for the hills. When we were hunters and fighters ourselves, it was very useful. It is now, too. If we slam on the brakes when a child runs into the road, we do it without thinking. Mostly, though, our everyday threats come in different, non-life-threatening forms – missing a train, losing out on a job or delivering a presentation. Yet we experience a rush in hormones that causes the amygdala to work in the same way. That's why we sometimes feel we want to run away from stressful situations, why we can react aggressively when things don't quite go to plan, why we can clam up when asked to speak in front of our peers: it's that primal response – fight, flight, freeze.

The amygdala – that almond-shaped bit – works together with another small part of the brain, the hippocampus. It's Greek again, based on the word for sea horse because that's what it's said to look like. The hippocampus is largely responsible for facts, figures and memories. So, when you miss that train and the amygdala starts doing its thing, the hippocampus may remind you that there's another one in ten minutes, that it's not the guard's fault, that next time, you'll try to be punctual. The sea-horse shape in our brain helps remind us that although we missed out on the job, we are still of value, or that while our colleagues are waiting for us to speak, we've been in this situation before and know we can gather our thoughts to deliver the presentation.

When we have been in excessively stressful situations, the unthinking, instant, reactive part of our brain goes into overdrive – Quick! Fight, flight, freeze! That reaction can be triggered again, in similar though less stressful situations, because the instinctive part of us registers some kind of threat. The surge of adrenalin prompts physical or physiological changes (sweating, trembling, muddled thinking) and a feeling of what's called hyper or hypo arousal – too much, or too little arousal – leading to an urge to fight, or submit.[4] There's a physical state called 'tonic immobility' too – that's the freeze response activated by sudden fright. Our focus narrows onto the threat – which means there's less flexible thinking and little or no processing. Those neurons have fired together and wired together. It takes a while for the hippocampus to kick in to remind us this isn't the same experience. Sometimes, it doesn't. The amygdala takes over and suppresses the rational, replacing it with threat. The sea horse doesn't stand a chance.

I get a real understanding of how this affects my thinking during an experiment at the Behavioural and Clinical Neuroscience Institute at the University of Cambridge. Dr Annette Bruhl is going to test the effects of stress and anxiety for the Radio 4 series on the brain. She runs through a series of questions before she tells me what she's going to do to me. Am I stressed? No. Do I have an abnormal heart rate? No. Have I ever had panic attacks? That accelerated heart rate, sweating, confusion and fear thing? Not that I can remember.

Dr Bruhl is a psychiatrist who is interested in anxiety disorders. She's doing a series of experiments designed to try to understand how stress changes our memory and decision-making processes. I'm one of her guinea pigs. Her hypothesis is that people with anxiety perform very differently when they are stressed; they can't stop worrying, they can't distract themselves and they can't perform well. She'll put me in that state deliberately, during which I'll do some cognitive tests on a computer, trying to spot numerical patterns in a series of numbers flashing up on the screen in front of me, putting objects in the right boxes, matching pairs, that sort of thing. Dr Bruhl explains that she'll put a gas mask on me and I'll receive a mixture of oxygen and carbon dioxide. Inhaling more CO_2 than usual will provoke anxiety – it is, she says, 'intended to cause distress' and I'll feel like I'm struggling for breath. My heartbeat will be recorded with an ECG, my blood pressure monitored, too. If I think I'm in danger, I need to let her know and she'll stop. She then tells me what to expect. During a panic attack, you shift from the higher, thinking part of your brain, to an automatic, reflexive one. Your breathing increases, from an average of 9 to 16 breaths per minute, to up to 27 breaths per minute. You experience one or more or the following: numbness, a dry mouth, tingling, and the feeling of being light-headed. 'What's the worst that can happen?' I ask Dr Bruhl. 'If I don't give you enough gas?' she asks quizzically. 'Suffocation,' she replies, without smiling.

She turns the gas on. It's horrible. The compression over my face and the strange oxygen and CO_2 mix begin to give me a headache, then slight dizziness. I start to breathe faster, begin to sweat. After ten minutes, I'm confused, I can't do the tests and I'm frightened, I want to tear the mask off and escape. 'How much longer?' I mumble through the mask. 'Six minutes.' Oh, this is ghastly, I'm nauseous, woozy, scared, constantly pleading for it to end. Do the test. Concentrate. In, out, in, out.

'Why can't I breathe?' I gasp. 'Why can't I do this? Come on, brain!'

Dr Bruhl calmly answers from the back of the room. 'It's your brain under stress.' Where's the air? They're depriving me of air. Paranoid. I'm going to faint. Or die. It takes me back to every terrifying place I've been to before. Collapsing into unconsciousness after a marathon, losing four pints of blood after delivering Seth, waking up in a hospital bed after my breasts had been cut off. This was a medically induced panic attack, which was reviving my previous terrors and memories; the feelings of dread were all so familiar and daunting. As in all the other situations, I tried to calm myself. Slow, steady, you won't die here, Sian, not today. It doesn't work.

When the doctor takes the mask off, my head slumps onto the desk. She's got her results. My very small part in the growing scientific literature on how acute stress affects our brain. I look at my friend and producer, Dixi. I trust her implicitly and she makes me laugh. Today, I'm cross.

'I hated that,' I say. 'I've been in difficult situations for work but never one like that.'

'Sorry, sweetheart,' she says. 'It makes good radio, though.'

Our body and brain function differently when we are stressed. First, here's how the body reacts. The breathlessness, tingling and sweats are caused by an accelerated heart rate. My normal blood pressure at rest was measured before the gas and it was 92 over 60. With gas and the ensuing panic attack, it soared to 144 over 83. My heart rate was 51 before the gas; while I was experiencing extreme anxiety inhaling the carbon dioxide and oxygen mix, it went up to 82. Here's how the brain responds to the body in panic. My total error rate on the tests, designed to measure learning, attention, reaction speed, strategic thinking and accuracy, went up by more than 30 per cent when I was inhaling gas. The anxiety meant my brain was in a state where it couldn't process information effectively, so was making many more mistakes than when I was calmer.

What is interesting is that in one of the tests, the one designed to examine my spatial working memory, my errors were fewer. It could be because that part of the memory is about processing what we see. In a threatening situation, we need that bit to work effectively. If something is galloping towards us, for example, and we need to escape, the spatial working memory is accessed – what's around me? Where can I escape to? On other measures, though, such as attention, the results were catastrophic. Annette explains that the brain is designed under extreme stress to think: 'There is something behind me, run, and this is enough.' The other parts of brain-processing are not as relevant in such a threatening situation. The thing, of course, is that often when we experience intense anxiety, we are not running from something that's going to kill us. Stress can make us think we are, rendering us unable to think clearly, so we have to actively switch on our attention, decision-making and memory functions and try to override the panic.

Is it any wonder that our minds are so out of kilter after trauma? That, under acute stress, our decision-making is so impaired? If we know that under highly stressed situations our memory is dramatically affected, what strategies can we use to calm us?

I ask Annette if there was anything I could have done to diminish the feeling of panic. 'Good question,' she says. 'Possibly.' (Ever the scientist, nothing conclusive, yet.) 'We know people who are relaxed at the beginning respond less strongly to acute stress testing. A colleague of mine in Southampton looks at the influence of meditation training and suggests that it helps diminish the subjective responses of anxiety and fear.' She says research is investigating whether the memory can be protected from the effects of stress by training it to respond differently. Meditation or mindfulness training may be a way to do that. She talks about soldiers, going into war zones where they are highly stressed: 'We know many come back and they are not healthy afterwards, they suffer from PTSD, so if we could find ways to protect them, this would be great.' No, they are not healthy afterwards and yes, it would be great to find ways to protect everyone from the effects of acute stress – not just the soldiers and the journalists, those groups that we have studied, but also the cancer patients, the bereaved, the mentally ill, the physically sick.

When Annette mentions meditation, it chimes with research I've done, too. Whether you use that definition, or call it mindfulness, or maybe even think of it as controlled, conscious relaxation, they all rely on steadying the breath. Chronic stress often makes us breathe more shallowly and tense our muscles. One quick way of changing that is stretching and breathing deeply, slowing your heart rate and activating the neurochemicals that tame your amygdala and calm you down. If we can focus attention by reflecting on what's happening and standing back from it rather than being 'in' it, then that distance will help with those subjective feelings of fear and panic. Acknowledge the emotion. In my case I was saying to myself, 'You're frightened, but there's no threat. You've been told this can stop and you are getting all the oxygen you need. Stand back and observe yourself doing this test, without judgement. Breathe more slowly, breathe deeply.' The problem was I could not breathe deeply because, when I tried, I just got more CO_2 – increasing the panic. I couldn't utilize all the techniques that I knew would work. I couldn't use my breathing.

I did use the breath when I was heading under the scanner and they were about to give me a deep injection in my breast without anaesthetic. I used it when the effects of the morphine were wearing off. I used it on my hospital bed when pain and distress threatened to overwhelm and, as simple as it is, it works. I have one man to thank for helping me understand the value of that and I met him more than four years ago. His words then meant nothing. I heard them and ignored them. His words now carry me through one of the most challenging periods of my life.

13

Be Happy

'You will never be happy if you continue to search for what happiness consists of. You will never live, if you are looking for the meaning of life'

Albert Camus

The man who taught me to breathe is sitting in the audience, in a beautiful eighteenth-century church hall in London, with a group of people who all want to make me happy. They want to make everyone happy. There's a row of journalists right at the front of this crowd looking up at me, pens hovering over their notebooks. They don't look happy.

It's 11th April 2011. 'Good afternoon!' I say cheerily. 'We're all here for the launch of a new charity, Action for Happiness, and I'm honoured to be asked to be part of today's event.'

Honoured and slightly wary, if I'm honest. I'm hosting this event not because I'm the cheeriest person around but because the BBC got involved in trying to define happiness a couple of months previously. We selected a few volunteers, got them to rate how they were feeling on a scale from one to ten and then asked them to follow a few simple exercises to see whether their mood improved. The experiment raised many questions. What exactly *is* happiness? How do you define it? The *Oxford English Dictionary* says to be happy is to be 'lucky, fortunate, contented with one's lot'. Is that state of mind measurable? The government thought so at the time, asking its Office for National Statistics to pose hundreds of thousands of people a series of questions to try to measure their well-being. If we can define what happiness is and think we can measure it, can we also then 'produce' it or improve it? How might we become happier as individuals and as a society? Can we move up the international happiness charts? Will we finally be able say we are as happy as Bhutan, for example, where every policy is related to 'gross national happiness'?

As I look around the room, the hacks are still sceptical, scribbling away, thinking to themselves, 'Yeah, let's all be happy. This is motherhood and apple-pie stuff.' Those behind this new charity, Action for Happiness, are nodding, vigorously. They are leading economists, psychologists and educationalists and firmly believe there are ways to make society happier.

I plough on: 'Those here have been studying happiness and today will tell you about practical ways to try to make our society a better one; a more contented one, a more cohesive one. The overall theme of today is: "Building a happier society together". And that "together" bit is important. It's not about individuals striving to better their own lives; it's helping others to improve their "well-being".'

I introduce Andy Puddicombe. Andy's a former Buddhist monk who's been meditating since he was eleven. He's the founder of a company called Headspace, which aims to demystify meditation, and he's going to take the audience through a few moments of mindfulness.

Andy asks everyone to breathe slowly. The supporters close their eyes. The reporters look around. 'I'm not doing it,' they're thinking, 'you're not getting me doing this nonsense.' Andy's voice is soothing. I'm on the stage and close my eyes, then after a while, squint one of them open, hoping no one will see. The hacks are still looking around. The others are concentrating. Andy's talking. Counting breaths, visualizing light, slowing things down. When the peace is suddenly and determinedly shattered by a mobile phone ring-tone, he smiles and continues until the ten minutes are up.

Next, I welcome one of the founders of Action for Happiness, Lord Layard, professor at the London School of Economics. Richard Layard is a force of nature. One of the world's leading economists and a member of the House of Lords, he's done a huge amount to raise the profile of mental health. A book he wrote more than a decade ago – *Happiness: Lessons from a New Science*,[1] which emphasized how happiness can influence society for the better – has since been translated into twenty languages. Even now, he's still arguing for change, calling for treatment for those who can't get access to mental health support, pushing the government to spend more, arguing that economies will benefit if those who suffer depression and anxiety are helped, telling ministers they should judge success not by economic growth, but by the growth of happiness, with a focus on improving well-being and relationships rather than income.

This word 'happy' is a tricky one, though. The so-called father of 'positive psychology', Dr Martin Seligman, the man behind resilience training in the US military, wrote a book called *Authentic Happiness*. Now he says he dislikes the title immensely; apparently his publisher believed they'd sell more books with those words on the cover. Dr Seligman doesn't like *authentic* because 'it's a close relative of the overused term "self" in a world of overblown selves', or *happiness* because 'the modern ear immediately hears "happy" to mean buoyant mood, merriment, good cheer and smiling. Just as annoyingly, the title saddled me with that awful smiley face whenever positive psychology made the news.'[2]

Dr Seligman disagrees with his 'good friend and teacher', Lord Layard, about trying to increase happiness, saying it brings to mind 'cheerfulness', which many people struggle with, especially in difficult times. We are not all optimists, capable of seeing the glass half-full, but does that mean we are failing to be happy? Far better than concentrating on our mood is to focus on positive emotions, he says, together with engagement, or absorption in a task and having a sense of 'flow'. Also, to get the most out of life, we need a degree of meaning in it, a sense of interest and purpose, we need to accomplish something, to be kind. Dr Seligman uses the word 'flourishing' instead, suggesting it encompasses all of the above: positive emotions, engagement, meaning, interest, purpose, plus other measures like self-esteem, resilience, optimism, vitality and so on.[3]

Whatever definition of well-being you use, what I want to know is how can you be happy, how can you feel you're flourishing, if you're suffering loss, or grief?

I didn't get the answers then, but I do end the day truly believing I will strive for happiness. We all take the literature home, with tips and tools on how to be happy. It's similar to the 'online workbook' that we'd offered viewers a few months ago in that 'Happiness Challenge' on the BBC, which was backed by the charity. Our happiness is determined by attitudes and choices, rather than our circumstances, it says. It lists ten actions that make for a happier life, including doing things for others, connecting and socializing, being active and so on.

We reduce the ten actions to three main ones for our film on *BBC Breakfast.* Three's a good number. The Greeks used three actors in their classical plays; philosophers and writers often use an unspoken 'rule of three' to get their point across, and we can hold that amount more easily in our working, or 'short-term', memory. If we can remember tasks, we're more likely to try them. The first of the three is being mindful; in other words, doing less and noticing more. The second is being grateful, or remembering the good things. And the third is being kind, doing things for others. Yes, I think. How hard is all that? I'll start tomorrow. Three things. Be mindful, be grateful, be kind.

*

In the morning, I pick up the newspapers and see the coverage of the event. Here are some of the headlines: 'Action for Happiness movement launches with free hugs and love', 'Is there any more to this than Hullo Clouds, Hullo Sky?' 'This idea of happiness makes me queasy'.

The editorials continue the theme: 'Being unhappy does not put you further down the karmic food chain or make you less worthwhile. It's guilt-tripping by positivists.' The launch, says one, feels 'akin to a happy cult'. It was 'earnest self-improvement', just going along with a 'modern obsession'. I wonder how the charity will react. An optimistic, smiley email pings into my inbox. 'You were absolutely wonderful and helped create a perfect atmosphere, upbeat and enjoyable but allowing for much needed serious discussion and scepticism.' There was plenty of that, yes. Here's the interesting thing, though. Despite the coverage, or maybe because of it, that day, the newly launched Action for Happiness website collapses under the weight of traffic. To date, the members of the movement number around thirty thousand in a hundred countries.

Whatever we call positive emotion, we are all striving for 'better', aren't we? There's a biological need to reach upwards, like that potato tuber stretching towards the sun. We need growth and we're biologically programmed for it. After trauma, we want to move towards light and warmth. In fact, even without the adversity, it's what we strive for. The *idea* behind wanting to be happy, or wanting to flourish, is one we can all understand, even if we know what hard work it is to get there. Maybe happiness is a by-product rather than a goal. Maybe, while working towards something better, we will stumble upon it, if only briefly. Even if it's transitory, does it matter, as long as we continue to feel as though we are thriving and flourishing? As long as it's on our own terms – no one else's – and we feel 'better' and are being kinder to ourselves?

Of those three things – be mindful, be grateful, be kind – the first intrigues me. Andy Puddicombe is excited about his new app, also called Headspace, and at the launch, I tell him I've never been able to do the whole mindfulness thing. I mention that I bought a meditation CD with good intentions and as I listened to it in my bedroom, I was thinking, 'If they can just speed this up, I can be out of here and put a wash on.' Andy gives me his card. 'Let me help,' he says. I smile and put it away and then pin it up on the noticeboard in my kitchen, where it sits, ignored, for years. I don't ask him for help, at least, not then. It's the last time I hear his voice for four years.

The next time I hear him, I'm going under the scanner just before my double mastectomy. That app he made is now playing through my headphones, convincing me to slow down my breathing. His is the voice that helps me through those long, morphine-induced, sleepless nights, after they'd taken my breasts away. I emailed him recently to say thank you. I remind him of the launch of the charity and then say, 'You have been helpful in a BIG way. You will never know how much.' That app he created must have taken off. In 2011 he was based in North London. He replies from Los Angeles, where he now lives with his family. 'I remember that launch well, and a mobile phone going off in the middle of the meditation.' And once again, he offers any help he can. I've let the mindfulness thing slacken off recently. The thing is, when I have the motivation to engage in it, like during or after trauma, I try it. Then as I recover and life speeds up, I forget to slow back down. Since the operation, I've gone from 'stop', to 'OK, now breathe', to 'go really, really fast'.

Every time I see the research behind mindfulness, I swear to do it properly. The year after the Action for Happiness launch, we ran another series of short films on the BBC looking at 'the science behind the silence'. Six large, randomized trials suggest mindfulness can halve the rate of relapse in depression and has a positive effect, we say. 'Within a few days, certainly weeks, your mind will become incredibly calm,' intones our soothing voice-over. I haven't got the time, I think. I'll be fixing supper, tidying the lounge, clearing the stuff-to-do pile on the table and the stuff-to-take-upstairs pile on the stairs. Danny Penman, a doctor who's written a guide to 'finding peace in a frantic world', says encouragingly, 'Just ten to twenty minutes will have a very deep and meaningful effect and response. The more you meditate, the more time you spend being serene. You will find your life is an awful lot easier.' I look at Bill, my co-presenter. 'Right,' we promise viewers, 'we're going to do it.' We don't.

Mindfulness links physiology, the mechanisms of the mind, with psychology, the examination of the consciousness that exists there. The concept is ancient, stretching back to Buddhist practice two and a half thousand years ago, and it's about being 'present', not allowing thoughts, especially negative ones, to take hold and dominate. I like the thoughts of a nineteenth-century American physiologist, psychologist and philosopher, William James, who argued that 'relaxation' was key to improving the state of the individual and the nation. 'To wrestle with a bad feeling only pins our attention on it and keeps it still fastened in the mind,'[4] he said. That, to me, is the point of mindfulness: to try to stop pinning those bad feelings to our mind.

They were fastened on very tightly a couple of years later when I gave mindfulness another try. The BBC had just decided to move the *Breakfast* studios from London to Salford and the timing couldn't have been worse. My son was just about to start his A levels, my dad was on his own in Eastbourne after the death of my mum, and my husband had a full-time job in the capital. I went up to see the planned new offices, my Manchester-based best friend was trying to convince me to live near her, and I was desperate to please Alison, my editor, who was bending over backwards to accommodate me ('Come later, after Alex has finished his exams, work a three-day week,' she urged). Yet I knew I wouldn't forgive myself if I put my career before the rest of the family. It wouldn't be fair on my son, my dad, my husband. I loved this show that I'd presented for eleven years, the team was wonderful, our viewers were loyal and we'd doubled our audience. It was going well, but it was the right decision to say no, however persuasive the arguments.

As all the kerfuffle about the move was beginning to die down, I went to see Joss, who was then working in India. I took a notebook for the long journey and on the first page I wrote a Dr Seuss quote: 'Don't cry because it's over. Smile because it happened.' After seeing Joss for a few days, I booked into a yoga and meditation retreat, three hours' drive from Goa. It was monsoon season, so the hotel was cheap and the journey was hot, damp and mosquito-ridden. When I arrived, the manager told me I'd come to a place where I could let my thoughts 'breathe'. 'What if I don't like them?' I asked. 'Allow yourself to be comfortable with them,' she replied, insisting I'll take something positive from my stay.

It didn't start well. I wrote in my diary: 'There's little lonelier than sitting in a room full of couples when you're eating by yourself.' They all seemed beatific; it must be all that yoga and meditation, I thought. I missed home. I felt I'd made a mistake in coming. I didn't want to let my thoughts breathe if it would let the bad ones out. The jet-lag meant little sleep and I was wired. I wrote that I was 'on high alert for something, heaven knows what. Chill. C-h-i-l-l. Zen out, live in the moment, etc.' I did some yoga in one of the hotel's scratchy white outfits with some very fit, older German women. The teacher, a tiny, bird-like yogi, urged us to have a 'gentle smile! Gentle smile!' I found myself looking at the clock. 'It'd be good to think this is something I'd do at home,' I wrote later, 'but it seems a little – what? – wasteful? Selfish? To spend an hour and a half stretching?' The thoughts remained pinned.

After I took the decision to leave *BBC Breakfast* when it moved, some suggested it was because I didn't like 'The North'. As that's where I started as a journalist, with seven years in Liverpool and Manchester, it hurt. I wrote: 'Why do I feel judged – condemned – for a decision taken which I know, for our family, is the right one? Other people's judgement. It'll be the death of me unless I sort it out.'

I cried, I did yoga and meditation, I painted, I walked on the beach. I bought a 'family yoga book' (even in paradise, there's a souvenir shop). Encouraged to develop a mantra, I came up with: 'I resolve to find full happiness with my family.' One diary entry says: 'Yoga is marvellous! It really does lift the spirits! I am going to start yoga again when I get back.' (I didn't.)

It was a fascinating, disturbing, revealing few days. I resolved to change. Again. I wrote some resolutions: 'Find reserves of bravery on your own, even when things feel threatening. I want us to live by the sea, the vastness puts it all in perspective. Everything matters, but "nothing matters frightfully" (as Paul's mum would say). Ignore the ephemeral, concentrate on family. I am comfortable with the truth, I'm doing the right thing at the right time for the right reasons.' Then this last one: 'Yoga and meditation work. But they are tough and they don't come easily to me. It'll involve practice, but I believe it to be rewarding. I must continue at home, find a space, enjoy it, not feel guilty about taking time out to do it.'

Here I am, a couple of years later, still making promises to myself that prove hard to keep. OK, so I don't do the yoga. I did the mindfulness and am about to start again. Really. We did move closer to the sea. I know I can be brave on my own. I do concentrate on family and try to ignore the chatter, although I'm still distracted by the opinions of others. At the time I wrote: 'I know my strengths. I'm caring, a good mother (usually) and have an incredible husband and amazing children. Life is full of change. Learn, grow, accept.' Learn, grow, accept.

The thing is, many journalists have such butterfly minds. 'Hmm, that's interesting,' we say when speaking to experts. 'Give me the headline, précis it, make it simple.' Then we're off onto another subject.

In the midst of my psychology degree, I wrested my attention back to the tricky topic of mindfulness and got together with another mature graduate and journalist, Clare Reynolds, to research and present a paper on it. If we could see the science behind whether it changes the brain structure, we'd understand why so many advocate it (and as we've both lapsed, maybe even try it again). After a few months, we presented our work to our tutors and the rest of the students with the title: 'Stress correlates with structural changes in the amygdala.' Catchy. Remember that induced panic attack? That happened when my amygdala, the part of the brain that detects stress, was working overtime. It's the same in those who are hyper-vigilant, and it's why people with post-traumatic stress disorders have more active amygdalae than others. While its known function is to detect stressful stimuli, there's less scientific consensus about whether all that stress makes nerve cells fire, prompting the amygdala to grow larger. Also, as most research on individuals takes a 'snapshot' or 'cross-sectional' approach, it's difficult to see what difference continued mindfulness makes to the brain in the longer term. Many of the studies we look at just use an eight-week mindfulness-based stress-reduction program (MBSR). Participants are asked to fill out a stress survey before going on the course. Afterwards, they complete it again. The research suggests that most believe that their stress levels have dropped because of the mindfulness, but as it's 'self-report', you're relying on what your participants tell you, rather than testing whether it's the course itself that's made a difference to their stress levels, or other factors like diet, exercise, a change of job, or the enjoyment of socializing with others during the sessions.

We decided to look at a study that examined the structure of the brain using imaging technology, to see if mindfulness made any anatomical difference. It's a small study, just a couple of dozen people, and there are limitations, but those who had completed the course and reported lower stress levels had less grey matter in the right amygdala too. In other words, it was less active. The part of the brain that we know responds to threat was not being stimulated as much.[5] We cross-checked the results with five other studies that said more or less the same thing.

It's important to note here that research does not suggest the mindfulness course *caused* stress levels to drop, although there was a relationship, or correlation, between the two. 'Cause' is something that produces an effect and you'd need to screen out every other lifestyle and environmental effect to prove that it was the mindfulness that did it – an extremely difficult thing to do. We need much larger, longer-term studies – and perhaps you can never hope to screen out all the other compounding factors. Even so, the research seems quite persuasive. If your amygdala is behaving erratically and you can't switch off, if you are in a state where you're looking out for the next threat and don't know where it's coming from, it's worth a try, isn't it? Even for those of us with butterfly minds.

In fact, maybe we can follow Scilla's example and boil it down to the essentials. She tells me: 'Recently I've been consciously trying to so some mindfulness meditation, usually in the mornings when I'm still quite fresh and the world hasn't started to get to me. I try to remove myself from everything, apart from emptying my brain and letting it go, and I find I do gain a tremendous amount from that.' I ask her how she learnt and she tells me she's self-taught, from a book. She tried it when she was a psychiatrist in some group sessions, but it didn't work as well, although she knew it helped some of her clients. Now, it's all about 'putting the thoughts and worries about the day away and allowing my brain to empty'. She gets an egg-timer out and, here she starts to laugh, 'I sit on a big ball and I consciously relax bits of my body until the egg timer tells me I've done it. I find it very useful. I also find that, having learnt to do it in a very structured way, when I go to bed at night and I'm lying down, I do something similar in the way I breathe and I fall off to sleep much more easily for doing it. It improves the way I go to sleep, but it also improves how I go into the day, being more relaxed.'

It sounds so straightforward and achievable. Maybe if we just thought of it as 'relaxing with an open mind, letting thoughts come and go and not pinning them to our brain', it'd be easier for people like me to take up and stick to. Dr Catherine Loveday, Scilla's daughter, says it's about directing our attention. By practising mindfulness, she says, we are using 'part of the brain that enables us to daydream and is important in consolidating memories. You're not switching off, you're actually exercising a different part of the brain. It requires a significant amount of your executive function to say, "I'm not going to listen to this, I'm going to direct my attention elsewhere."' Executive function covers brain processes like working memory, reasoning, decision-making and planning. When we are relaxing, quietening our mind, we are not closing it down, far from it: 'Your brain is actually incredibly active when we are in that state, when you see functional imaging studies, there's this particular network, a "default mode" network of neurons that are active when you're in that day-dreaming, relaxed, meditative state and it's a very important activity for the brain.'

Good for our brains, good for our mental health – it's not surprising so much research money is going into mindfulness and why academics are encouraging schools to take it up. In fact, more than six million pounds has been invested by the UK's largest charitable research organization, the Wellcome Trust, in a project to see whether it can help stop depression and anxiety and build a more resilient brain in teenagers. It will follow seven thousand adolescent brains and report back in 2022.

*

I call Andy Puddicombe at his new home in California. We chat about his online mindfulness course and I say that a profile of him in today's paper has the headline 'From monk to multi-millionaire'. He laughs. 'I see that kind of stuff and my wife says – OK, where's the money, do you have a bank account that I don't know about?' Since we last spoke, four million people have downloaded his courses and he thinks that one hundred million is achievable, even if it takes a long time. He's excited about the number of people doing it, he says, not the amount in his bank account. It's all about the 'social mission' that has taken off because 'there's a change in the way people think about looking after the health of their mind and it's a really nice thing to be involved with'.

Andy tells me his own trauma was the way into this. When he was in his twenties, a drunk driver crashed into a group of his friends, killing two of them. A couple of months later, his stepsister died. He thought, 'I don't know how to deal with this. It was a quarter century crisis, a calling or something, I didn't want to live my life as I saw it being played out for other people, I didn't want to have a career, I wanted to be a Buddhist monk, it felt like the only sane and rational thing to do. For my family, it was the least rational and sane, but if there's no other clear road ahead and that seems like the only way to go, it's a surprisingly easy decision to make.' Andy spent ten years training as a monk, focusing on teachings that have existed for hundreds of years. What did you learn from that decade? I ask. 'Kindness,' he replies, instantly. 'If I had to pick one word from the ten years that resonated, then kindness to myself and kindness to other people. Just being more interested in the happiness of others and less obsessed with chasing happiness for myself. Ironically, when we do that, we find happiness anyway. I always thought happiness existed somewhere outside of myself. I think my journey as a monk taught me it was here all along and it's found by focusing on the happiness of others, rather than on our own happiness.'

There's that word again, 'happiness'. Andy says it's found through being kind rather than being a pursuit in itself. He calls it 'the goal-less path'. The reason there's no goal is because our focus is on living in the present and observing our reactions to what's happening to us, rather than chasing something in the future or worrying about something in the past. Also, it's not so much what happens to us in life, it's the way we relate to it. Andy likens it to being in a traffic jam: 'We're beeping the horn and we're looking ahead and trying to work out what's going on, thinking about being late, and we're caught up in this maelstrom of the mind and we are creating a world inside it; we are creating, in that moment, an experience that is incredibly painful. But we can be in the same traffic jam, on the same stretch of road, and the radio's on, the music's playing, we're looking out of the window at the fields next to us and we're quite content. Now, we have no more time pressure than we had in the other situation; we are, to all intents and purposes, in exactly the same situation – and yet our mind on that day is choosing, for whatever reason, to relate to that experience differently.'

How we think about and react to circumstances is how we *choose* to perceive and relate to the experience. 'We all have these thoughts in everyday life and some we see as being a little crazy and we think – nah – and we let it go. We already have that ability, it's not like this is some kind of new-fangled skill that we've never really confronted in our mind before, it's just a discipline around training it. So when thoughts arise and they start jumping ahead or start going back, we could see them and say, OK, well it's not that helpful. That idea of perspective and relating to the world around us and taking positive steps to stay in the here and now, rather than creating a world which either once existed or has yet to exist, well, I find it hard to think of a more valuable pursuit in life, given that we experience our entire life through our mind. Be present.'

Why then, if I know this, I say, why don't I do it? Why do I start practising mindfulness when I'm faced with trauma or adversity and then put it aside when things start getting better?

'It's desperation. We're faced with the unknown and because we live with a sense of being in control of our life, even though it's a delusion, suddenly, being confronted with the possibility of our imminent departure, that's enough to think – "I'll do anything." Very often, whether it's illness, addiction, anxiety, exhaustion, it's only when we get to that point, when we think, "Right, I'll do anything!" that we think we will even consider doing any of these things.'

Then convince me to do it when things start getting crowded and when the flotsam and jetsam of life begin to coagulate again, I say. Tell me that the moments of clarity that I had in hospital are worth hanging on to. That reflecting, being calm and having a sense of perspective, is worth investing in, and shouldn't be dropped during busy times when you're not confronted with the possibility of 'imminent departure'. Refusing to let go of something stops growth, he says. Let it go, because when we do that, 'we might experience something even greater. But we prevent that from happening because we are trying to hold on to the experience that was once so precious and so helpful in the past. And we all do it, all day long in every aspect of life, but in those bigger moments you feel like, finally, "OK, I get it. I get what this is about, this journey called life, and it feels so special because I've never experienced it in that way before and how can I put it in a box?" Don't try. Let it go. Be present. Greater experiences will come from that.'

Andy equates it to physical exercise. 'We don't wait until we're obese or have a heart attack before we start training our body.' Do it before you get desperate to fix something, then you are better prepared when adversity strikes. He believes society will begin to change its attitude to mindfulness practice. At the moment, 'some people use meditation as an aspirin and some will use it as a vitamin and over time we will move towards a place where we use it in the same way as running to stay fit – where we train the mind because we recognize it benefits our brain and it helps us to feel good and healthy and happy.'

He is good and healthy and happy, but a few years ago, adversity struck again. Andy got testicular cancer. He 'lost a jewel or two in the process', but says he appreciated how big a difference mindfulness can make and how 'precious' having these tools can be during a major life struggle. I ask him whether he felt it was unfair, that despite all those years of deep breathing and being 'in the present', with a clear mind, he got cancer anyway. 'And I raise that,' I add, 'as a green tea drinking runner, with a husband who describes himself as 'a fat bum who drinks double cream and eats Haribo'. Did you, like me, ask why?' He replies that when he was diagnosed 'lots of other people said "that's so unfair", but I didn't have that in my mind. Just look around – there are babies born with extreme disabilities, I watched my parents lose a child. That idea of fair and unfair, that's more a reflection of how we think life *should* be rather than how it *is*. The world doesn't really make sense, that's the truth. You can flip it round: would either of us be here if we hadn't lived like this up to this point? Is it because of that, that we are more resilient? Why do some survive and some don't? It's definitely a surprise – you know that with cancer, I'm sure, Sian. It's a surprise, but if we've done enough meditation and are happy to engage in the practice, you can rest with that surprise, with that shock, rather than jumping ahead and thinking, "This is going to happen" or "It's not fair". We are present and watching it unfold, rather than examining what was, or what might have been or what will be.'

Andy survived the testicular cancer and, subject to check-ups and further tests, he's OK. The experience is part of him, it hasn't come to an end and he doesn't want it to. 'That's one thing that has surprised me about the journey with cancer. I can only speak personally and

I know other people have very different ideas, but I did think there would be an end point and, interestingly, there's not, or there hasn't been for me. It's not that clinically it's reccurring. And psychologically it's not that I'm spending any time thinking about it. Yet when I'm reminded of it by other people, I don't feel like it's something in my past, because it becomes who we are. We are so used to saying, "OK, right, you're treated, you're healed, you're done, take your pills" – and this felt and feels different.'

When Andy was diagnosed, he says, everything was brought into sharp focus. It felt 'deep' and 'amazing'. It sounds controversial and confusing, coming from someone who was told he had cancer, but he's insistent about the benefits to him. 'I'm not wishing it to happen again, but I would go as far as to say I'm actually glad it happened, I really feel it's enriched my life. I don't feel that I was cheated out of life or that it was unfair, I feel like it was a genuine privilege to have experienced it and to have been OK and lived through it to this point. It's added a huge amount and I wouldn't swap it for the world. I wouldn't wish it on anyone else either but I wouldn't swap it for the world.' He recognizes that he is extremely lucky because his cancer was treatable. The reason he thinks it was a 'privilege' to have it, is that it forced him to confront issues he'd been trying to understand for years. 'As a monk I used to spend many, many hours and weeks and months contemplating impermanence, change and death and the intellectual idea of that. But the experience of it is always a little bit different.' He had moved to America just before his cancer was diagnosed and he took eight weeks off work after surgery. 'I walked like John Wayne for a while!' he laughs. 'But to be able to spend that kind of time at this stage of my life, at home, with my wife, I really felt it gave us a chance to settle into our life here. Now, I look at that time and I think, wow, that was probably one of the happiest times of my life. And yet for many people it's like . . . what? But you had cancer! Yet it made sense and it turned it into a really amazing experience.'

Contentment from cancer? As he says, he wouldn't wish it on anyone, but he wouldn't swap it for anything, either. Cancer gave him a different lens through which to see the world, and for that he's grateful. And he's happy.

14

Laugh, Write, Talk

'To truly laugh, you must be able to take your pain, and play with it'

Charlie Chaplin

On the radio there's a woman talking about her new show at the Edinburgh Fringe Festival, where she makes fun of her breast cancer. Beth Vyse had a double mastectomy and was given a five-year 'all clear' recently. That's when doctors tell you there's just as much chance of you getting cancer again as everyone else in the street. Except you're not like everyone else on the street, she says, because the cancer's already hit you. Her comedy focuses on the incongruity of an extreme situation colliding with the mundanity of the NHS – and oh, how I understand that. It's like life-or-death to you, but to the staff, you're just part of their day job. There are absurd moments, living with cancer, as there are with any illness. And just as mindfulness and reflection help guide you towards being healthy and happy, observing the madness in it, the nonsensical nature of it, can be a release too. Laughing about some aspects of my cancer helped me get a lot off my chest, as it were.

Dixi, handing me those ridiculous pink knitted woollen breasts that her nan had made, gave me as much pleasure and as much release from obsessing about what was happening as any therapy did. The other flashes of discordant laughter have been as important. Being asked if I wanted to get my nipples tattooed and, if so, what colour I wanted. Sitting on a bed just before surgery with a doctor drawing round my breasts with a Sharpie pen. Surgeons grabbing handfuls of flesh with delight a few months afterwards, discussing how much they can 'harvest' for reconstruction. Doing the corporate job for the company that makes bras for buxom, ample-breasted women a couple of months after mine were taken away. I have often been struck by the lunacy of all this. It is not always about despair. Sometimes it's pain mixed with incomprehensible laughter, and that's OK. More than OK, that's good, because it helps you grow and thrive. It gives you a breather from all that intense emotion, it lightens the load and provides a sense of humility that punctures your self-absorption for a while.

It's good for the mind too, as Dr Hannah Critchlow from the University of Cambridge tells me. 'If you laugh, then you're exercising the body and also your brain, because you're causing the release of endorphins, the feel-good factors which help lift your mood. You're also increasing the amount of oxygen that's rushing to your brain and your body by exercising your ribs and your intercostal muscles, by having a really good hearty chuckle.' Dr Critchlow has been to some laughter clinics under an oak tree in a park in Cambridge with another neuroscientist and they discovered that laughter switches on different areas of the brain involved in trying to problem-solve; you are actively trying to figure out why things are funny. Also, she says, you are more likely to laugh with people that you like, because you want them to like you back, thus it helps facilitate social bonding and releases oxytocin, helping to combat stress and anxiety. Laughter is good for oxygenation and endorphin release. It stimulates the puzzle and reward areas of the brain, while we work out why it's funny, and it helps socialization and dampens down anxiety. All good things when you are struggling through adversity. Positive humour has a real impact on depression and self-esteem, too. 'The one thing we can all do to help light up our brains,' Dr Critchlow says, 'is to have a good laugh.'

We may not achieve happiness, but we can thrive, we can flourish, we can grow, if we can occasionally laugh at our condition. Doing so feels like a release, as if we're deliberately not letting ourselves wallow in it, but are standing alongside it, being positive, coping, accepting that there's an absurdity to our situation. It helps get us through. I've already talked about the psychiatrist Viktor Frankl who survived the Nazi concentration camps. In his book, *Man's Search for Meaning*, he writes: 'humor was another of the soul's weapons in the fight for self-preservation. It is well known that humor, more than anything else in the human make-up, can afford an aloofness and an ability to rise above any situation, even if only for a few seconds.' It also taps into that idea of trying to gain a bit of mastery back. Frankl wrote: 'forces beyond our control can take away everything you possess except one thing, your freedom to choose how you will respond to the situation.'[1]

If you choose to share humour with those who understand your situation and are going through a similarly difficult time, it binds you together. It acknowledges the adversity but refuses to be weighted by it. Some of our most creative talents turn suffering into wit. I spoke to the comedian Ruby Wax a few years ago, just before she went on a stand-up tour called *Losing It* about her struggles with her mental health. I wanted to know when she realized she was in the midst of depression. 'How do you know if you're falling off a cliff?' I ask her during an interview on *BBC Breakfast*. 'When you can't decide whether to have a manicure or jump off it,' she shoots back.

There's a book called *The Resilient Self* by Drs Steven and Sybil Wolin, where they talk about how individuals survive and rise above adversity by tapping into reserves of creativity and humour to 'turn nothing into something, and something into nothing'.[2] When we can observe adversity, sometimes laugh at ourselves, share it with others, occasionally even reduce it to nothing, we are no longer stuck inside it.

Comedians turn adversity and trauma into humour, musicians turn it into beautiful sound, artists paint with it, writers make poetry and prose with it. We can create with it, mould it, use it, fashion it into something else. It's about using whatever wit, music or art we can find, to express the trauma in a way that may still be raw and vulnerable but means we are no longer imprisoned and defined by it. Perhaps we can come to grips with ourselves without further damage through the writing, sensing and imagining – finding the curious and inexplicable, sometimes even the absurd, in our suffering and making something different. There is no meaning *in* suffering, no real reason as to why it happens, but we can get meaning *from* it and it helps if we can reframe it in some way. Humour, art and writing enable us to do that.

~

> For those who, like me, believe that literature is the ultimate expression of life, if the illness has helped you to write the book in question, people will think you must have been only too happy to welcome the inspired collaborator.
>
> Marcel Proust

The author John Updike, who spent a lifetime writing about the loves and lives of small-town America, suffered throughout his childhood from psoriasis. Updike spent a lot of time indoors, reading. At first, he escaped into books that were full of adventure and mystery, fiction and humour. Then, he began reading authors like the French novelist and essayist, Marcel Proust, who wrote about themes that were more complex, darker, threatening and whose early life echoed his own. 'I began my adolescence reading rapturously,' Updike told an American magazine a few years before he died, 'and somewhere Proust describes the joy of reading when you're young, and that the days best spent seem to be those entirely spent reading a book.'[3] Both men had difficult, diseased childhoods. Proust was a sickly infant, who had chronic allergies and asthma. Those asthma attacks would disrupt his sleep and his allergies meant he spent days and months living in a cork-lined, shuttered bedroom. The illnesses were thieves of his childhood and robbed him of time. Literature provided temporary respite, as it did with John Updike. That Proustian quote Updike was reminded of, is this: 'On no days of our childhood did we live so fully perhaps . . . as those . . . that we spent with a favourite book.'[4] Proust was a perpetual patient, imprisoned in illness, but, as those who study him acknowledge, the suffering and the inspiration from others allowed him the insight to write his monumental novel *À la recherche du temps perdu* (*In Search of Lost Time*) which was published in seven parts between 1913 and 1927.[5]

Childhood trauma helped both Proust and Updike become the key writers of their generations and they often reflected on their illness in their work. Updike wrote an essay called 'At War With My Skin' for *New Yorker* magazine in 1985, where he describes his endless self-examination, his strategies of concealment. How he was constantly moving around the world and chasing the sun because it eased his suffering, how he married a woman who 'forgave' him his psoriasis. Earlier, in 1976, he had fictionalized his condition in a short story called 'From the Journal of a Leper', where the character says, 'this skin is me, I can't get out.'[6] It is him and he can't get out but, like Proust, he seeks to use it, it has a therapeutic value because it contributes to him being a great author. It was, for Updike and Proust, as it has been and is for many, an 'inspired collaborator'.

Franz Kafka was another who turned illness and suffering to good account. He was born into a German-Jewish family in Prague in 1883 and had an unhappy childhood at the hands of an abusive and authoritarian father. In his early twenties, while studying law, he began writing and, at the same time, began to show signs of early lung disease. It was the start of tuberculosis, which would eventually lead to his death at forty-one. Much of his writing was done in a state of fatigue, depression and insomnia, and his essays and short stories are often about being trapped in situations from which he cannot escape. In one of his best-known stories, 'The Metamorphosis', his character Gregor awakes to find himself lying on his back as a beetle, unable to flip himself over. Kafka told his fiancée that the disease was some sort of punishment for who he was: 'I don't believe this illness to be tuberculosis . . . but rather a sign of my general bankruptcy,'[7] he said. He used it, though, turned it into something else, stood outside and observed it.

I most like the words of a great French Renaissance humanist and writer of essays, Michel de Montaigne. He suffered terribly from kidney stones, those hard, lifeless balls of calcium that bury into soft tissue, causing great pain. In the sixteenth century, left untreated, they could kill you, as they did his father. Montaigne wrote about the impact these kidney stones had on him and devoted much of his final essay, 'Of Experience', to what it was like living with them. Attempting to heal himself through language, trying to get some control of his pain, he wrote this:

> Consider how artfully and gently the stone weans you from life and detaches you from the world; not forcing you with tyrannical subjections . . . but by warnings and instructions repeated at intervals, interrupted by long pauses for rest, as if to give you a chance to meditate and repeat its lesson at your leisure. To give you a chance to form a sound judgement and make up your mind to it, like a brave man, it sets before you the lot that is your condition, the good and also the bad . . . if you do not embrace death, then at least you shake hands with it once a month.[8]

*

Shaking hands with death once a month, those warnings of fragility and pain, interrupted by time to rest and meditate on how to deal with it the next time it strikes, is such a powerful way of looking at an affliction, an illness. Some of these authors believed they were more because of their disease than without it. They tell themselves that it's a blessing to have suffered, because it reveals the clarity of life and death to them. Montaigne was exhibiting what many writers before and after him show – that welcoming their suffering is a way of showing resilience, determination and growth. It's a tough thing to do, but as F. Scott Fitzgerald wrote, 'the test of a first-rate intelligence is the ability to hold two opposed ideas in mind at the same time and still retain the ability to function.'[9]

I know what you're thinking. Get away with your Updike, Proust, Kafka and Montaigne, you don't write like them and neither will I. Perhaps you're saying to yourself that you can't express yourself lyrically, or poetically, and turn pain into art. Can I suggest that it really doesn't matter whether it's good or not? When you write and it hurts, you don't do it because someone else is going to read it, you do it because otherwise the words and images will ricochet around your head with no exit. You do it because you want to shout but don't feel you can hurl these ugly things you're feeling at anyone you love. Then shout it onto a page. Do it because, otherwise, what's it all for? Do it because even if there's no meaning *in* suffering, there has to be some meaning *from* it. And do it because one day you'll look back on your words and think, 'Crikey! Was I really feeling that at the time? Glad I didn't say that out loud.' Those writers said it out loud, for public consumption. You don't have to. Write nonsense, spew it out, like I did in my diaries written in a hospital bed and when I limped home. Reading them back, I know that sometimes they ached with pity and fizzed with fury. If I had been writing with you in mind, I might have been more self-conscious, worrying about what you thought, editing myself as I went along. But I wrote because I was in pain and sad and vulnerable and frightened. And I left all that in because I wanted you to know that it's OK to be in a state of bewildered, terrified incomprehension when you encounter trauma.

The brain is hardwired to remember the intense, negative experiences. It takes a lot of effort to rewire that thinking – and writing it down helps. Research suggests that so-called 'written emotional disclosure' can alleviate trauma and improve general psychological health.[10] The writing can be for as little as fifteen minutes over the course of three days, and those who benefit the most tend to be emotional, open, and use thinking, or reflective words.[11] Another study found that women writing about a traumatic event saw a reduction in their depressive symptoms.[12] It's thought this may have something to do with the way we create narratives about what's happening to us. Perhaps translating the experience into language, describing what it's like and putting feelings down on paper, enables us to manage and articulate the chaos. Confronting tough times and converting raw emotion into words can provide distance, clarity, understanding. That's why talking can help, too.

~

> The work of the eyes is done. Go now and do the heart-work on the images imprisoned within you.
>
> Rainer Maria Rilke

Writing, laughing, painting, dancing, singing – whatever it is you do to find a voice for what's going on inside you – sometimes, you may feel the need to say it out loud to someone. I had an emotional 'blip' after attending a course for those interested in helping others with trauma a couple of years ago. It was targeted at senior journalists and we all gathered in a countryside hotel for a few days and swapped experiences about the people we'd met and the challenging experiences we'd encountered. These were reporters who'd seen atrocities in Syria, Iraq and in Northern Ireland; they were battle-scarred and eager to share what they'd learned.

We were all asked to present a piece of our work to the group. I chose a clip of a Radio 4 recording I'd done with PC David Rathband, the policeman who was shot in the face and wounded by gunman Raoul Moat in Northumberland. It was the same section of the interview I used a year later, sharing a stage at King's College London with Julie Nicholson, when we spoke about trauma. On this course, I explained that when I'd met David, I'd been struck by his calmness, his positivity, his wish to engage with life, despite the fact that he was blinded permanently by the attack and some of the shotgun pellets were still embedded in his face. He wanted to talk about what had happened to him, to raise awareness and funds for a charity he'd set up for other injured officers, called the Blue Lamp Foundation, so I suggested to Radio 4 that we record a chat with him. We met in a London hotel, the day before the marathon, which he was running in order to raise funds for the charity.

It's an emotional interview. David describes his endless runs tethered to a sighted police colleague – and how he loathes it. He speaks openly about his visions and nightmares. How the picture inside his head is relentlessly dark and ugly. How Raoul Moat is constantly on his shoulder, no matter how far he goes and how hard he pushes himself. How he feels less of a father and husband because he can do nothing for himself. How his police uniform is still hanging in his wardrobe, yet he doesn't know how and when he might put it on again.

At one point during the hour-long interview he cries and reaches for my hand. He can't see my producer and he isn't aware of the microphone; all he can hear is my voice. I ask whether he's comfortable that such an intimate and personal conversation is to be edited to less than a quarter of its length and broadcast on Radio 4 to more than two million people. He says yes, he wants his story heard, however uncomfortable it feels.

The interview was transmitted, winning plaudits and being acclaimed as one of the 'Best Ever Broadcast Interviews' by the *Radio Times.* Less than a year later, PC David Rathband killed himself.

I played an intense, upsetting clip of him to the other journalists, where he talks about the dark places he goes to in his dreams, to prompt a debate about our roles and responsibilities when we talk to people who are going through a profoundly traumatic experience. News is always looking for the personal story to illustrate a global catastrophe – and the more emotive, the better. There was a brilliant US broadcaster called Studs Terkel who said of his approach: 'there were questions, of course. But they were casual in nature . . . the kind you would ask while having a drink with someone, the kind he would ask you . . . in short it was a conversation. In time, the sluice gates of dammed up hurts and dreams were open.'[13] We need the 'hurts and dreams', so we run up to people who've just lost a loved one, or who've been caught up in a tragedy – whether it's a rail crash or a natural disaster – and shove a microphone under their nose, or point a camera at their face. 'How do you feel?' we ask (or rather we don't, because that sounds crass, so we ask the same question using different words: 'What are your thoughts, now?').

The day David Rathband was discovered hanging in his home, they replayed part of the interview on the BBC. At the time I felt overwhelming guilt and could only hope his family weren't listening. I suspect anyone who's been involved in some way with those who have died have asked themselves the same questions: Did I listen? Could I have helped? In truth, only the person who has taken their own life knows why it felt impossible to live. David was not only recovering from the shooting and coping with disability, he was also experiencing the failure of his marriage after he had an affair. His life was messy and complicated and it was his decision alone to end it.

As I'm talking to the group of journalists, the breath catches in my throat. I abandon the talk, explaining that I'm reacting because it's the first time I've listened back to the tape. When the session ends, one of the counsellors who've come along to tell course attendees what acute stress looks like, takes me outside. 'Let's walk,' she says. It's lashing with horizontal rain; so fierce and cold it stings our cheeks. We march, without speaking, getting wetter and wetter. It's ages before I apologize for my mini-meltdown. Hearing David again and asking myself those questions has loosened the lids of some boxes I wanted to keep well and truly shut. Not so much boxes as packing crates, which have been locked in the attic, stored away for decades, with some nasty experiences as a young adult inside. Crates packed with grief, loss, guilt.

I don't tell the counsellor exactly what's in them, but she suggests I see a clinical psychologist she knows. I tell her I'm fine and don't need to. That it's just a momentary lapse and all will be well.

When I get home, all is not well. I'm detached and flat. I don't talk much and cry without warning or explanation. Paul and I know something is wrong, but I can't articulate what it is. I just say that it's been a 'very heavy' few days, I'm tired, perhaps it's a virus and I'll get better.

The counsellor contacts me a couple of days after the retreat weekend. Her email suggests I'll be feeling emotionally exhausted and will be having doubts about whether to contact the psychologist she suggested, although she thinks it would be helpful. The message ends: 'for now though, be as gentle with yourself as you can & hang in. Things can get better.'

I make the call. A week later, I'm sitting in a small, airless room in North London, my arms crossed, a defensive and unwilling client. 'How long have you been doing this?' I ask, tersely and unnecessarily. She runs through her qualifications. A consultant clinical psychologist who trains, lectures and publishes books on trauma and who sits on various groups and working parties. She says all this with humility and good nature. She shuts me right up.

The next twelve sessions are difficult. She uses some cognitive behavioural therapy (CBT) to retrain my thinking and prevent too many negative thoughts. I know about CBT helping those with trauma from my psychology degree. Research suggests that 50 per cent of those who're treated recover, and that it is as effective as drugs in the short term, and sometimes even more so in the longer term.[14] It works by first identifying types of unhelpful thoughts that sabotage us. There are many cognitive traps or beliefs that stop us living positive lives, or thwart us while we are trying to recover from a trauma. Very often, these thoughts take us back to the acutely stressful event, with the centre of fear, that hypersensitive amygdala again, reacting instantaneously to something that appears to be a similar threat.

My husband remembers a three-week stint in Lebanon, as a TV producer for the BBC's *Newsnight*, during the 1982 Israeli invasion. Because he was young – not yet thirty – he relied on his correspondent, cameraman and sound recordist, who were very experienced, to tell him the difference in the sound made by a shell overhead, and whether it was coming in or going out. He was witnessing the massacre at refugee camps in Sabra and Shatila in West Beirut and was shot at on a number of occasions, so the assignment was a baptism of fire in every sense. A week after he came back, he went on holiday. Sitting on a beach, he heard the sound of a Cobra military helicopter overhead, the same type used by the Israeli Air Force. Paul immediately leapt up and started running in fear. His amygdala was so attuned to threat and the hippocampus (the part that provides context) was so overwhelmed by stress hormones that it couldn't do its job effectively – just as I was incapable of thinking clearly while undergoing that CO_2-induced panic attack at Cambridge University.

In Paul's case, his brain failed to remind him that he wasn't in a war zone now, but on a beach in Malta.

You can interrupt that pattern of thought and circumvent the central nucleus of the amygdala – which has linked the non-threatening stimuli with a threatening one – but it takes effort and determination. In the same way that concentrating on breathing helps slow down your heart rate and provide focus, rethinking the situation by trying to provide context and logic and standing outside it, can quieten the mind too. Eventually, with practice, the new, more positive way of thinking becomes habit, replacing the old, negative, automatic, instinctive response. It's all about activating a part of the brain called the frontal lobe. The frontal lobe helps control attention and emotion, so essentially, it decides what's important and what's not. It works with the hippocampus to establish whether it's right to react and, if not, it 'calms down' the amygdala.

We can all fall victim to these negative thoughts and assumptions that sabotage our thinking and plunge us into negativity. There are a variety of mind-traps lying in wait. 'Catastrophizing' – blowing a setback out of proportion; for example, worrying that one small mistake could cost you your job, even though everything else about your work is up to standard. 'Personalization' – blaming yourself for events beyond your control, assuming others will interpret them as a negative reflection on you. 'Generalization' – when we think we can't succeed and move forward because we've had one or two knock-backs. One mind-trap that I'm particularly prone to is minimizing the positive and exaggerating the negative; I often find myself responding to praise with, 'Oh, anyone can do that'. I also have a tendency to polarize – for example, chastising myself for being 'a terrible mother' because I shout at the kids occasionally, as if everything's got to be black or white, good or bad.

We can restructure our thinking to change the way we feel and consider alternative routes rather than continually falling down the same potholes. CBT can activate the hippocampus, cutting through the negative thoughts and replacing them with more realistic ones. It's a strategy that allows the brain to rewire itself. Each time you put it into practice you're firing up the frontal lobe, decreasing the amygdala activity, creating new neural connections and new patterns of thinking. Over time, you'll learn to change how you are feeling.

How do you do this, though? We can start by looking for alternatives to those negative mind-traps. If you feel snubbed, rather than assuming it's because that person doesn't like you, think about whether they were simply too busy, too stressed, or just failed to see you. Was that mistake at work due to lack of ability on your part, or could it be that there might be other factors involved? If you feel stuck in a situation, try to take a step back and find different ways of looking at where you are and how you feel. What opportunities can you grab to get you out of a depressive hole – will it help if you spend time with friends, go for a walk, lift your spirits with a bit of singing or writing?

Try to imagine your situation and your feelings from another point of view. What might we say to a friend in a similar position? I bet we'd be kinder to them than we are to ourselves. Finally, ask this: What's the worst that could happen? How likely is it? And how would I cope if it did?

We have to really work at reassessing our thinking because often, when we're in a dark space, it's hard to find any light or think differently. Start with focus, using some attention, to activate and engage those frontal lobes. Notice the negative thoughts and think about how to change them; it helps put us outside them and work on them. It takes a good deal of practice, all this focus and attention, but it can stop us being sabotaged by our own destructive negativity.

It was suggested that I try 'eye movement desensitization and reprocessing' (EMDR), a treatment developed by Dr Francine Shapiro in 1989, after she was diagnosed with cancer. She noticed that when she was frightened her eyes would move back and forth, a bit like they do during some REM sleep when we do most of our 'active' dreaming and when difficult and traumatic experiences are being sorted through, so the brain can try to make sense of them.[15] Some psychologists use EMDR when they believe an event or events have been 'inadequately processed'; it involves recalling the distressing event while the counsellor moves a finger from side to side in front of our eyes. It's meant to help those suffering from post-traumatic stress disorder. Firstly, I didn't think I had PTSD. Secondly, this finger-waggling approach alerted my 'psycho-babble' response system. Alarm bells were going off all over the place. During the sessions, whenever it was mentioned, I kept putting it off. Whenever my counsellor suggested EMDR, I deferred – 'Maybe next time.' I did some research on the therapy and found it had mixed reviews, but a study that assessed rape victims who'd received the treatment concluded that EMDR had some efficacy, and it was a recommended trauma treatment according to the International Society of Stress Studies practice guidelines. Still – moving fingers before the eyes? Reliving the experience? How's that going to deal with the traumas in the packing cases in the attic?

Eventually I agree to try it. The psychologist sits opposite me and holds her finger in front of my eyes – uh-oh, here we go. She begins asking questions, asking me to remember disturbing memories and how I felt, for about fifteen to thirty seconds at a time. It's stop and start. I cry and feel weak. She asks me to rate my distress, on a scale of 1 to 7. She asks me to replace the negative memory with a positive thought, to try to be kinder to myself, not to judge my reactions. It's horrible.

She sends me an email a few days later, asking whether I'd 'recovered from the EMDR session'. I reply: 'That night I woke up screaming – saying I couldn't get out, and it took a while for Paul to calm me down. The night after, I didn't have waking-up nightmares, but did have ones that I'm not aware of waking from. I think I'm OK now, though disturbed sleep . . . is that normal?' She writes back that it is normal, although it's difficult to predict whether an individual will experience that particular side effect. During sleep the mind is subconsciously processing the events of the day, without the same cognitive and emotional defences kicking in. She says I need to do more 'processing'. I'm doing the processing, that's for sure. It's still horrible, I still have the nightmares and I tense every time I walk into her treatment room, but I finish the twelve weeks of CBT and EMDR and I can think about traumatic events now in a more detached way, without feeling the pain and emotion that hit me when I first lifted the lids and looked inside.

Remember Patrick, who returned to London after a seven-year tour of duty in and out of Baghdad and who had a panic attack on the London Underground that took him back to Iraq, triggering post-traumatic stress disorder? He had three years of therapy, including EMDR and CBT. He's not 'cured' of PTSD, but he knows how to stop the panic attacks, he knows how to explore the 'labyrinthine sewers' of his mind. It's not easy, as he told me, but it's better than the alternative.

I was offered therapy after the double mastectomy and took it, gladly. I'm lucky and I've being seeing a wonderful psychologist with experience with women with breast cancer. Every time we meet, I feel her words resonate for all those going through adversity and I write down anything that I think might help at a later stage, or when another difficult and challenging event happens. Perhaps they'll help you, too. Don't worry if they don't chime with you now, they may do later. If you have someone you love who is going through something horrible and you want to offer support but don't know how, hang on to these thoughts, in case they're of value.

Ask yourself some questions about how you feel now. If you got up tomorrow and felt better, what would need to happen? What would you notice? What help would actually be helpful? Try not to use words like 'I should' and 'I shouldn't', because they are judgemental. Let yourself off the hook and be kind. Recovery and growth are not linear, so if you have setbacks, reflect on them and rest awhile. Focus on those life issues which have priority; it might be the emotional, the physical, the treatment decisions or whether to return to work. Try to get clarity and help when wrestling with them, from those you trust. They may not know how to help you, so tell them, throw them a lifeline and let them know what'll be useful to you. That may be saying, 'I feel under pressure and I feel I have to pretend I'm OK, when I'm not. It's a step too far to do *that*, but *this* feels OK, is that possible?' Find your voice and listen to it, life will never be the same again and you are changed, so explore new ways of managing and coping.

I often ask my therapist what people will think, when they know I've got cancer. How will I be seen and judged? 'If it's negative and horrible, if people are harsh, how do I find a way of dealing with it?' I say. 'Teflon yourself,' she replies. 'If you receive nasty comments, then find a way to hand it back to them, it's their issue, not yours.' She asks whether I'm the one judging myself, rather than being judged, and asks that CBT question: What's the worst that can happen? Your body has changed, you don't have to be perfect, is the thought of being public with your illness too much? How can you manage that, and who and what can help? She suggests it's about having internal conversations, refining thoughts, going back and forth sometimes, being mindful to protect yourself. It doesn't happen overnight.

The hardest thing for most cancer patients, the psychologist says, is when treatment is at an end. The 'getting through' mode is replaced with the aftermath. You're out of synch with other people, because you've been in a fog of treatment and a state of 'survival' arousal and when you come out of that, it feels different. 'You don't want to upset people, but they want you back,' she says. Only, it's the old 'you' they want, the one before all this happened. And that old you has gone away.

Talking has been helpful. These therapies can take less than sixteen sessions and more than half of those who undertake them recover, in many cases permanently.[16] Breast cancer patients at this hospital where I've been having treatment are lucky to have them as part of our NHS treatment. I know lots of people are not in a similar system and may not be offered help. Many doctors can't offer psychological therapy, and services are still very patchy across the UK. Antidepressants, though, are handed out frequently. In 2014, more than 57 million prescriptions for antidepressants were issued in England – the highest number ever and up 97 per cent on a decade before.[17] It seems unjust, doesn't it? These talking therapies are shown to be effective and their use can cut down on further costs – to the NHS and the wider economy – of mental health issues going untreated. If, in some instances, they're better than drugs, or might work well alongside them, isn't it strange not to offer that help to more people?

Until they are widely available, we need to share our knowledge of what works. Preventative strategies before and after trauma may stop us needing therapy. Understanding what tactics work in combatting negative thinking and knowing when to deploy them is crucial, as is knowing what makes us happy, how to laugh and when to reflect and breathe. Having someone we trust, and can talk to, is immensely supportive. Practically, having decent rest, food and the energy to get up and move, will also help in surviving and thriving (I'll focus on those in the next chapter).

The philosopher Ludwig Wittgenstein who I studied in psychology would urge his pupils to 'go the bloody hard way'. He also admitted that it's tough to do. 'But it is, if possible, still more difficult to think or try to think really honestly about your life and other people's lives. And the trouble is that thinking about these things is not thrilling, but often downright nasty. And when it's nasty, it's most important.'[18]

Well, we are, aren't we? We are all going the 'bloody hard way' and it's often 'downright nasty'. If that's when it's most important, let's try to fill our backpacks with whatever sustenance we need, put the right boots on and reach for the support to help us go forward.

15

Sleep, Eat

'O sleep! O gentle sleep!
Nature's soft nurse, how have I frighted thee,
That thou no more wilt weigh my eyelids down
And steep my senses in forgetfulness?'

William Shakespeare, *Henry IV Part 2*

When we are 'frighted' it disrupts our sleep and, perhaps more than anything else, affects how we deal with trauma and adversity. After surgery and then recovering at home, there were long nights where I'd lie awake in desperate frustration. When I read my diary back, there were vivid, nightmarish visions, and I'd written that 'I dream when I sleep, of walking through crowded places with bloodied bandages.'

I've spoken to many people who've been through difficult times and they always talk about how hard it is for them to sleep properly. Patrick, who had post-traumatic stress disorder, spent a few months when he couldn't sleep for more than two hours. He'd rise after another sweat-drenched night of tossing and turning, feeling 'completely broken'. For Stuart, who lost his leg and then suffered a breakdown, it was remarkably similar. In the past, he says, he could 'sleep like a baby', but suddenly he 'would lie awake all night having panic attacks, then try and get up for work in the morning and present a good front, and you can't do that. The harder it was to sleep, the more stressed I got about it, the more tired I got, the more anxious I became.' This went on, with Stuart hoping 'it would just stop, that I'd just come out of it, but it didn't, it got worse and worse and worse and worse and worse, and then after two weeks of barely getting more than an hour's sleep a night, it was time to press the nuclear button and go into hospital'.

Are there ways of coping with a lack of sleep that will help us before we have to press the 'nuclear button'? Professor Barbara Sahakian, a world-renowned researcher in the fields of neurology and psychiatry, based at the University of Cambridge, tells me that 'sleep is probably the most dramatic cognitive enhancer that we know of'. How, then, can we make sure we get that dramatic enhancement to our brains and the restful sleep we need, in a time of acute stress? In our relentless, wide-awake, mobile-by-the-bed society, so many people already struggle with it; more than ten million prescriptions for sleeping pills are issued each year in England. I took them once, when rest eluded me during a morphine-induced night in my hospital bed.

I know what shift work can do to your sleeping patterns, even when adversity isn't thrown into the mix. My father was a journalist who worked nights, my mother worked antisocial hours as an intensive care nurse, and I've worked shifts for most of my adult life too, including more than a decade of getting up at 4 a.m. for *BBC Breakfast*. I've been aware of the increasing evidence that the health of shift workers can be at risk from constantly disrupting these natural circadian rhythms. Some people are more vulnerable to lack of sleep than others; 10 per cent of the population are quite happy and healthy on very little sleep, but most of us find it debilitating not getting the restorative rest we need, because it affects our mental health and our well-being. We need a flexible mind during the day, to deal with the unexpected, to plan, to communicate well, to concentrate and give our attention to something. These are the 'executive functioning' skills, which are controlled by the prefrontal cortex. This part of the brain is sensitive to stress and sleep deprivation, which can leave our thinking clouded.[1]

When we are distressed by something, we can get into a state of being 'hyper-aroused', which results in the autonomic nervous system (ANS) being thrown out of balance by the strain on us, physically and mentally. Sleep should be a time when we 'let go', and that's incompatible with this hyper-vigilant state, when the amygdala, the fear-and-threat response area of the brain, is on high alert, disturbing our sleeping and waking patterns.[2] Once these patterns of rest and recovery are disrupted, the chances of us becoming even more ill increase. As Stuart and Patrick found, it's a vicious cycle. The less you sleep, the more anxious you become about it, the more those stress hormones circulate, the harder it is to drop off. The bad news is that, during a tricky time, our sleep patterns are often thrown out of kilter. The good news is that we can rewire our brains and establish new neural connections to change this, if we adapt our sleep 'habits and hygiene'.

These changes can be hugely beneficial to our mental health and well-being. A few years ago, I recorded a two-part TV documentary on sleep for the BBC called *Goodnight Britain*. In the course of it, I met two women who'd suffered with insomnia for most of their lives and had reached a point where both they and their families were at the end of their tether. Gwen Young, a book-keeper in her fifties from Peebles in Scotland, told me that she'd been living on three to four hours' sleep a night for more than thirty years; that's three decades of restlessness and going through the day feeling wretched. She'd tried everything: lavender, books, bath, relaxation tapes, meditation – and nothing worked. For her, bed was not a place of comfort and rest; it was so unwelcoming she likened it to 'a bed of thistles'. Her inability to sleep was having an impact on Gwen's mood, her health and her relationship with her husband – they hadn't shared a bed in more than twenty years.

We wired her up to a polysomnogram – a device to record brain waves, oxygen levels, the heart rate and breathing, as well as eye and leg movements. As soon as her eyes closed, she was monitored by two of the UK's leading sleep experts: neurologist Dr Kirstie Anderson and psychologist Dr Jason Ellis. When they looked at the test results, they could see that Gwen was only getting tiny snatches of rest throughout the night. Our cameras showed her falling asleep on the sofa in the lounge; she then wakes and wanders off to her room, only to find she can't get back to sleep again.

In order to transform those four disrupted hours into a continuous block, the experts banned Gwen from dozing in the lounge and told her she must stay awake until 2 a.m. She could then go to bed – but she would have to get up at 6 a.m. The plan was to make Gwen so tired that when her head hit the pillow, her body would want to rest. Initially, she found it impossible and kept dozing off in the living room. The experts then shifted her bedtime to midnight. After two weeks, she started to get six hours of proper rest. A month after that, she'd cracked it. Gwen was going to bed earlier, getting up later – and husband and wife were back in the double bed that they hadn't shared for two decades. All in all, it was a drastic way of tackling the problem, but as a result Gwen was getting better sleep, feeling less stressed, was healthier and finally waking up next to the man she loved.

Sheila Boughey, the other woman struggling with insomnia, was in her forties and worked as a town councillor. She told me she was sleeping less than three hours a night. Still wide awake when the rest of her family went to bed at 10.30 p.m., she would take her computer into her room and busy herself on emails and eBay. Her dog, Boo, slept on her bed while her husband was banished to a different room. To occupy her when she woke in the night, she kept a knitting basket in her bedroom. On nights when she couldn't get any rest at all, she'd nip downstairs to the kitchen for a bit of nocturnal baking: cupcakes, Victoria sponges, scones – you name it. The kids were always thrilled when they came down of a morning and saw what she'd made, but Sheila's night hours were so full that her body clock had completely forgotten when to wind down.

She was told to de-clutter her room, take out the computer, the TV, the knitting and the dog, and not turn in before midnight. Deprived of distractions and under strict instructions not to look at the laptop after 11 p.m., she started to feel drowsy much earlier than usual. What's interesting, though, is that tests showed Sheila was one of those individuals who can survive on less than seven hours' sleep, because when she finally did drop off she would instantly fall into deep, nourishing rest. All the same, she gave up baking, knitting and sending emails at night, and reported that she was sleeping much longer than the previous three hours a night and was much happier for it – although her children missed coming down to freshly baked buns for breakfast.

It underlines an important point for all of us about how much better we can feel if we have proper 'sleep hygiene' in our bedrooms and more regular habits. Following a similar routine every night can ensure more nourishing sleep. Going to bed and waking up at the same time each day, not falling asleep away from the bedroom, and avoiding long daytime naps – these are all proven methods for getting more of the restful sleep we need.

Think of sleep as a way of putting our brains on standby; those early stages of rest, with slow-wave activity, are crucial to the brain's recovery from its day's work. Too little sleep hampers that recovery and hinders cerebral function. Too much can be almost as bad, with one study suggesting there's a relationship between mortality rates and daily, habitual sleep in healthy adults that goes beyond eight hours.[3] Teenagers do need lots of sleep – eight to ten hours – but the rest of us don't need quite as much. Less than five and we may not be as sharp mentally; more than ten and we can feel jet-lagged.

Regular sleep patterns tend to be disrupted when we are anxious or dealing with something difficult. Sleep issues are among many of the symptoms for stress-related disorders[4] and are especially common if we're experiencing anxiety or depression, as we saw with Patrick and Stuart. Stress raises our levels of hormones like adrenalin (epinephrine) and neurotransmitters such as noradrenalin (norepinephrine). These act as stimulants, carrying signals to different parts of the brain during the day, helping us stay alert, giving us that surge in energy, to allow us to react quickly, to slam the brakes on in the car, or run from something frightening. We don't need it at night and neither do we want too much cortisol – the other stress hormone designed to keep us vigilant. They all need to subside in the evening, but if we're worrying too much about how many hours of sleep we're getting, or thinking through traumatic experiences, our brains will be working hard, our heart rate will go up and our stress hormones will be circulating. Let go, if you can. Take the pressure off, perhaps don't try too hard to sleep and accept that this will be a period when you feel out of sorts. Breathe, observe, be gentle on yourself.

There are other ways you can help. We know physical activity can lead to better sleep, as long as we do it at least three hours before going to bed, otherwise, we're in that hyper-aroused state again. Give yourself enough time to slow down, before you lie down. Caffeine sometimes wires us too, stimulating adrenalin and preventing sleep. Another stimulant that can keep us awake is alcohol. Although, initially, it can lead to drowsiness, when the alcohol works its way through the system and the initial sugar high drops in the early hours, we wake up.

I mentioned cortisol and why it needs to be low during the night, so we are not on high alert. This stress hormone affects every cell in our body and if there's too much of it over an extended period, day *and* night, it undermines our well-being, our memory and other brain functions, too. But cortisol can actively make us feel better as well, promoting good health, energizing us and priming and prepping the body and mind. It's all about its variability and having peaks and troughs of it throughout the day. A good strong burst when we wake makes us much more responsive later on. It's called your 'cortisol awakening response,' and I was asked to be part of a study at the University of Westminster, led by Dr Angela Clow who's been studying it for more than twenty years. She tells me: 'At night when we're asleep, our cortisol needs to be low otherwise we will have a restless night, but when we wake up – wham! – we have a burst of cortisol and then over the rest of the day, it falls down again.' It's a vital biological signal that helps keep other parts of the body functioning, and Dr Clow says, 'if that's not working properly, you're not going to feel as healthy and you are more prone to illness'.

Bearing in mind that many of us who're going through a particularly anxious time might have high, flat levels of cortisol most of the time, how can we help our levels get back to being healthy and varied? Dr Clow agrees about exercise earlier on in the day helping you sleep and then giving you a greater cortisol awakening response when you wake up. She also says people who smoke have a smaller response, so cigarettes affect it. Drinking alcohol 'deadens the brain and makes it less responsive to the challenges and expectations of the day ahead' too, she says. She suggests ditching the lie-ins, as well, because the later you sleep in, the more sluggish your cortisol response. That's why we often feel worse after we've had more hours in bed than usual.

Light is crucial. If your moods feel lower during the winter than the summer, or you suffer from Seasonal Affective Disorder, it's often because you are not getting enough light, or you are getting the 'wrong' sort for particular times of day. Your cortisol awakening response is much greater in the summer than the winter because it responds to gradually increasing, early morning light, the sort we get in the lighter months. Similarly, exposure to light during the night can affect our hormones, inhibiting the night-time hormone melatonin and promoting production of that daytime one, cortisol. We know high levels will disrupt our sleep, so Dr Clow's advice is to make rooms 'dark when you're asleep but, ideally, have gradually increasing light for about half an hour before you wake up, like a natural dawn. It helps to prime your brain so that when you wake up – whoosh – your cortisol responds.' Dawn-simulation clocks, using light which comes on gradually, seem to work for many, because even though you are not conscious of that light, it still penetrates through closed eyelids, alerting your brain.

A note on electronic devices here, because even their small 'standby' lights can penetrate those eyelids and tell the brain it's daytime. Also, if you're on a mobile device or computer late into the evening, you are exposing yourself to a certain kind of light, designed to wake you up, as Dr Clow tells me: 'Natural morning light is blue, evening light is more red than blue and our brain receptors respond to blue light in the morning. Electronic devices naturally emit blue light which is going to be giving your brain all the wrong signals, so your brain is not being primed to go to sleep, it's being primed to stay awake.'

I do a test, with and without an eye mask, to see the effect morning light has on my brain for the rest of the day. One morning, I wake to gradually increasing light. I instantly chew on a wad of cotton and do the same every fifteen minutes for an hour. The researchers take those swabs away to test how much cortisol is in my saliva. Later that afternoon I'm given a series of cognitive tests, designed to challenge my spatial awareness, attention switching, concentration and other tasks. A week later, I collect another set of saliva samples to measure my cortisol awakening response, but this time after I've slept in an eye mask. Then I do the same tests again. The results back up the researchers' hypothesis: I do better on the tests – especially the attention-switching ones, the ones that affect our ability to multi-task and make decisions – when I wake to gradually increasing morning light, rather than when I wake in darkness.

Dr Clow emphasizes how important this is to our health and well-being: 'If you wake up properly, it can affect the whole of your day, I've absolutely no doubt about that.' She envisages a future where, if we can't produce a good cortisol awakening response because of mental health problems, for example, we can take something that'll do it for us. 'That's something I dream about in the future which would make a real difference to people's lives.'

Until then, we can try to encourage that good strong burst of cortisol with artificial, gradually increasing light. We can come off our electronic devices a few hours before bed. We can sleep in a dark room, with no extraneous light. We can go to bed neither too full nor too hungry, without alcohol or sugar to keep us awake and in a cool bedroom with no distractions. We can try to have the same routine every night, not going to bed too late and not sleeping in either.

So many of us struggle with it, I know. When I go to bed, thoughts often circle around my head like the moths that invade our home. Flap, flap, flap . . . Will they change the copy I've written for that newspaper? Have I organized the kids for next week? What topics will we do on my TV show this Sunday? What's for breakfast? How will the Radio 4 series go down? Why does my chest still hurt? Why is this song going round and round in my brain? (It was 'Many Rivers to Cross' by UB40 the last time I was struggling for sleep.) Wow, I need to start doing mindfulness again, I always say to myself. I try the breathing, try the warm yellow light visualization and yet that soundtrack is still running – change the tune! – and the questions are still coming – Should I run tomorrow? Will it rain?

Relax. A few bad nights will not kill us. Try to follow the sleep habit and hygiene rules. There are some other positive things we can do to make our sleep work well for us in troubled times, too. Dr Hannah Critchlow, the neuroscientist from Cambridge University, tells me that when we learn something new during the day, a connection forms in our brain between one nerve cell and another. When we sleep, that connection becomes strengthened and more stable. It becomes a memory, one that's reinforced with rest, during the night. That's why it's particularly helpful to think about the more positive moments of the day before bed, rather than difficult ones. 'Because sleep helps to reinforce memories,' says Dr Critchlow, 'then one thing that's really important is not to revisit any traumatic thoughts just before you go to bed. Don't dwell on anything negative that may have happened recently because sleeping directly after that will reinforce the memory of that traumatic event . . . and will also strengthen the emotion of fear that's attached to it.'

She suggests that if we can think of something positive, however difficult a time we are going through, then that will be the memory that's cemented in our mind, rather than the negative one. Dr Critchlow says this is important for everyone, not just those going through trauma. 'Think of the three things that we are grateful for in that day, so whether it's the sun being out and a big blue sky or meeting with your friends for lunchtime and having a nice time – that will help to reinforce that positive memory when we sleep.'

She recommends a 'gratitude diary' which we write before we drop off. Scilla has accelerated memory loss, and writing her diary helps consolidate the day's moments for her and gives her a better, more positive attitude when she wakes up. She relives her day, revisiting the things she's done – and she's seen how it helps to lay down and cement all those positive thoughts.

Also, she consciously relaxes in bed, using breathing techniques rather like mindfulness exercises. When she talks me through it, I can see her anxiety diminishing. She describes taking a 'deep breath in and as it goes out slowly, I'm feeling the relaxation starting from my shoulders and going down the rest of my body . . . and if I'm very clever and very patient I can get it going down to the tips of my toes – and then I go 'ahhhh . . .' (she exhales deeply) 'and let it out. And then I stop and then I go . . .' (inhales a big breath) 'and as I breathe in I think "My shoulders are all achy, just relax them and let it go, let's unlock these fingers . . . just relax . . ." Oh, if I'm not careful, I'll fall asleep!'

Try everything, until you find what works for you. Let me know, because we are all searching for a better night's rest. Until then, good luck and sweet dreams.

~

Let us cultivate our garden.
Voltaire

Just after I was diagnosed with cancer, I was in one of those soft-play areas that smell of chips and parental desperation. The Christmas holidays were almost over, the sleet was hammering down outside while the kids screamed inside, and I decided to sit at a table near the chaotic scramble of over-heated children and focus on what was about to happen. I needed A Plan.

I was already on the hospital conveyor belt and the only part of my life I seemed to have any control over was trying to build up my strength to get me through the double mastectomy in a week's time.

I grabbed a menu from the café, full of hot dogs and fizzy drinks on the front. On the back, I wrote an ambitious title – 'Eating for Strength'. The day before, I'd spoken to Stephanie Ridley, a nutritionist I'd met during my psychology studies, and asked for some last-minute advice pre- and post-surgery.

Here is some of it, with a proviso. You may remember my

wheat-free, dairy-free, sugar-free, alcohol-free month, which ended in France when I stuffed my face with pasta, ate buckets of muesli and topped everything off with mini ice-creams and half a jar of chocolate spread – all within two hours! I am the last one to suggest giving everything up. Denying yourself the things you love can make you miserable and obsessive. My mum tried every diet from grapefruit and egg to cabbage soup, and it messed with her metabolism, made her grumpy; then when she went back to eating 'normally', she became heavier than when she'd started. Diets (generally) don't work. Denial is (always) horrible. When you are low, punishing yourself over what you've eaten will make you sink further into pitiful, food-based self-loathing. We've all done it. Instead, during this time, try to give yourself a bit of space and be as forgiving as you can. Food that's fatty and sugary can be wonderful and our brains respond accordingly, releasing this lovely chemical called dopamine, in the nucleus accumbens, or the 'reward' centre of the brain. Eating the food we like lights up these reward pathways, which is why we get feelings of pleasure from eating it.

The issue here is that too much of it can mess with the health of our digestive system and damage the protective bacteria. There are more than a hundred trillion microbes in our gut, ten times more than there are human cells, and it's the balance of these microbes that's so important, because they are interconnected with your brain by a system called the 'gut–brain axis'. Throughout history, the stomach has often been called our 'second brain', and we need to eat a varied and healthy diet in order to keep those microbes in synch and working together in a balanced fashion. That'll support our thinking, too. Eating foods we like makes us feel good, but eating foods that we can digest well helps our mental faculties work better, which is vital if we are dealing with any trauma, stress or adversity. There's a lot of scientific research on this at the moment, including a study from McMaster University in Canada, which suggests there's a link between stress and the microbes living naturally in the intestines. It's lab research involving mice at the moment – like many studies – and more work needs to be done to see if it applies to humans, but the authors say that bacteria in the stomach play a key role in anxiety and depression. Mice who were deliberately stressed, after separation from their mothers, showed poor gut health with abnormal levels of the stress hormone corticosterone, which is produced in the adrenal glands and responds to fear conditioning. The research is, as I say, on rodents, not humans, but the authors say that in the future, therapies could be developed that target intestinal microbes, benefiting patients with psychiatric illness.[5]

In the meantime, how can we make sure that if we are stressed, it doesn't adversely affect our 'second brain', the stomach, and lead to further anxiety and depression? Taking probiotics, the ones in natural yoghurt, seems to work for some, but early research into prebiotics suggests these might be even more effective. *Pre*biotics are like food for the 'good' bacteria – they're dietary fibres, which the bacteria break down and then use to multiply, outnumbering the 'bad' bacteria. They're found in raw onions and leeks, dandelion leaves, Jerusalem artichokes, chicory, bananas and garlic. You'd have to eat a lot of that kind of food to make a real difference – more than a pound of bananas or a quarter-pound of raw onions, and they can make you gassy, so many people take a supplement instead. Researchers in Oxford took a group of subjects to see if prebiotics made a difference to their mood. They first tested them on their perceived levels of stress. They were then divided into two groups, with one taking prebiotics and the other a placebo for three weeks, in a random, double-blind trial (so no one, including the researchers, knew who was getting what). At the end of twenty-one days, the participants were given positive and negative information to see how they processed it. So they were shown faces, emotional and descriptive words, and given a memory test. Those who'd taken the prebiotics paid more attention to the positive information and showed less anxiety when given the negative information. They had less of the stress hormone cortisol in their system, too. The suggestion here was that the increase in 'good' bacteria had a positive effect on mood and anxiety. And the stability of mood and emotion from those who'd taken the prebiotics and had higher levels of those good bacteria was similar to that of individuals who had taken antidepressants or anti-anxiety medication.[6]

A healthy stomach means a better brain and, with the digestive tract containing more than half our immune cells, it's vital we try to keep it functioning as smoothly as possible during challenging times. The trouble is that, if we're ill, or after surgery, we're often given high-strength antibiotics. *Anti* means 'against' in Greek and *bios* means 'life'; it's as if these pills are literally life-killing, wiping out both 'good' and 'bad' bacteria. We have to recultivate our stomach to make sure the protective ones flourish after taking them. The fuel for the pathogenic, or 'bad', bacteria, is sugar. Foods high in sugar – not just the granulated stuff but refined carbohydrates like white bread and pasta – make the so-called 'damaged flora' in our stomachs much worse. The more you eat, the more the sugar-loving bacteria multiply, the more your brain is told to sustain those levels and the more sweet and processed food you crave.

How you break the cycle seems relatively easy. Firstly, try to avoid sugar for a while. If the good/bad gut bacteria and the effect on anxiety and mood aren't enough of an incentive, then think about this too: a diet high in sugar accelerates ageing because it has an adverse effect on protein, toughening up molecules. The older you get, the less able you are to absorb sugar and the more protein you need. But excess glucose will stop that protein moving freely, blocking membranes in the body and slowing down the communication between the nerve cells in the brain.

I discover how food can affect your thinking when I have that lovely tuna-beetroot-seed-salad lunch with Scilla White and her daughter, Dr Catherine Loveday. They believe high levels of sugar are toxic to the brain and can cause additional stress, killing the very cells the brain needs to survive. Mother and daughter, with a combined wealth of knowledge of psychiatry and psychology, believe there is a clear correlation between sugar intake and poor memory function and increased stress response. Scilla forgot to put the turkey in the oven at Christmas because, they believe, she'd eaten too many sweets and chocolates and it had affected her thinking.

They have replaced foods that Scilla used to eat with things that won't spike her blood sugar levels. Now she eats grains, avoiding overly processed wheat-based foods and replacing them with oats, rye and barley. Her diet includes pulses – beans, lentils and chick-peas – that help stabilize the levels. She tries to avoid high-sugar fruit like bananas and mangoes, as delicious as they are, and goes for those with a lower sugar content, such as blueberries, blackberries, blackcurrants, cherries, plums, apples and pears, again, to avoid those sugar spikes.

Society has tended to avoid fats in our quest to be slim and, as we now know, this is wrong. More than half of our brain cells are made of fat, so it's really important that we don't eradicate them from our diet. Oily fish, nuts and seeds all contain the essential fatty acids that help form membranes around our brain cells and they are key for brain development. As we can't make these fatty acids ourselves, eating them is the only way of getting them into our bodies. There's a huge amount of evidence around benefits to the brain of essential fatty acids and scientists have criticized much of it, because they believe some of the initial studies were not robust enough. However, these fats are generally good for us and the latest research suggests they're especially important for pregnant women and newborns. The jury is out on other groups and whether taking Omega 3 oil will directly lead to positive moods, as some studies suggest, but frankly, until there's more long-term research into its effects on the brain, you may as well use these foods as part of a healthy, varied diet. Avoid trans-fats, also known as hydrogenated fats, which are used for frying or as an ingredient in processed foods like biscuits and cakes, because they can increase your risk of heart disease. In recent years many food manufacturers in the UK have removed them from their products, but check on the label anyway.

That's fat and sugar dealt with. Here are a few more tips that may help with blood sugar stability and a healthy stomach and brain after a stressful time. Eating protein with every meal and snack will help with cell renewal to support the rebuilding of the immune system, especially after surgery. Foods like meat, poultry, fish, eggs, raw nuts and seeds, beans and lentils are all good sources. If we are chronically stressed, we can feel fatigued and that can mean our iron levels are low. Iron is a component of haemoglobin, which carries oxygen to our cells for energy production, so eating iron-rich foods will help boost that. Lentils, dark green vegetables, olives and beans are all iron-rich, and having them with foods containing vitamin C, like tomatoes, kale, broccoli and leeks, enhances the iron absorption. Try to avoid coffee because caffeine hinders it. Adrenal glands, which are compromised by stress, need extra support during this time and the mineral magnesium helps. It's also involved in the conduction of nerve impulses, regulating a receptor in a part of the brain important for memory, and some research suggests a magnesium deficiency contributes to irritability, nervousness and depression.[7] It's found in dark green vegetables, wheat and oat bran, brown rice, cashews, almonds and halibut. The vitamins B5 and B6 help with adrenal function too, and lots of foods have them: avocado, eggs, broccoli, new potatoes, cod, halibut, spinach, tuna and seeds, to name but a few.

Stress often has an impact on our eating and sleeping habits, creating a perfect storm of an unhappy stomach, fatigue and no energy to sort out either. To get a good night's sleep, try not to go to bed either too hungry or too full, and eat a supper that includes complex carbohydrates, like wholemeal pasta or brown rice. The protein serving at night can be much smaller than during the day because it's harder to digest. Some foods are rich in L-tryptophan, an amino acid that converts to the chemical messenger, or neurotransmitter, serotonin. Unlike some of the other neurotransmitters that help stimulate the brain, serotonin is thought to act as a mood stabilizer. It maintains balance and also activates the release of a hormone, melatonin, which regulates the body clock and our sleep cycle. Think of melatonin as being at one end of a see-saw with cortisol at the other – while one helps us rest, the other wakes us. As one goes up, the other goes down. If either is disrupted – say, if we're too stressed, with high cortisol levels – then our melatonin levels will be too low to get a decent night's sleep. Food affects that balance, as well. As L-tryptophan can improve restful sleep, mood and calmness, our evening meal could include some foods that contain it, like turkey, milk, bananas, soya beans and wholewheat foods. Eating too much protein with our evening meal, though, can affect the amount of L-tryptophan we absorb, because it contains a lot of other amino acids and the brain's barrier only allows a certain amount through at any one time. Perhaps give the brain a break before bed and eat less of it.

Is your head spinning yet? Sorry. Basically, the main thing is to nurture and nourish the body and brain as best you can during this time, using whatever advice you find here, to help stabilize your moods. Sleep can make an enormous difference to our mental health if we make quite small changes to improve it. Regular bedtimes, waking to gradual light, moving electronic gadgets from the room where you're sleeping and going to bed having eaten foods that encourage rest, are all a good start. A healthy, balanced diet will settle the stomach and calm your mind. Both work as a foundation on which to build.

Nothing, though, is worth caging the mind in further stress, fear and anxiety. Sleeping and eating are friends that help support us through trauma. If they turn into enemies, something frightening, where you hate yourself for what you've eaten, or get frustrated by how little you've slept, then it's working against your recovery. Constantly lurching from green-juicer to pie-eater, with all the blame and shame that accompany the latter, will elevate stress levels further. You may, like me, have 'A Plan'. You may, like me, deviate from it spectacularly and subsequently spend hours self-flagellating, because you're 'weak' or 'not doing it properly'. Last night I ate half a box of chocolates, one after the other, and went to bed on a guilty sugar rush. It's hard to stand back and try to let the judgement go, telling yourself it's not a pattern, just a blip. Understanding what works and gently steering ourselves back can help. I often think of those three tips that we know help us to thrive: be mindful, be grateful, be kind. Remind yourself of those and add the other three that support us during adversity: learn, grow, accept.

16

Move

'You may encounter many defeats, but you must not be defeated. In fact, it may be necessary to encounter the defeats, so you can know who you are, what you can rise from, how you can still come out of it'

Maya Angelou

Six months after I left hospital, with two bottles attached to me draining my bodily fluid and with a frustrating inability to open doors or comb my hair, I was lacing up my old trainers to head out on a run with my ultra-fit neighbour, Caroline, who's trying to knock me back into shape. She's run through deserts, up mountains, thinks nothing of a Sunday sixteen-miler. As an athlete, she sees pain as part of the deal. You push through it, because it makes you stronger. We do 'hill repeats'; running up the same incline and then down again, ten times. I watch her lithe body in shorts and a vest top, power effortlessly away from me up the hill as I shuffle behind, looking to the floor, cursing. It hurts. Nothing to do with the surgery, just being heavier and hauling an unconditioned, unwilling body up a slope when what it really wants to do is have a nice sit down. Yes, there are a few twinges in the chest area, pectorals pulling, tendons stretching, breasts complaining – that's inevitable. It won't wash as an excuse, either to me or to her, but I mention it anyway, just in case it lets me off the hook.

It doesn't.

I've run since I was a teenager. I was never in contention for team games because I was so small, and inevitably, the last to be picked. 'Oh, OK, Sian then,' one of the more solid captains of the hockey team would say with a shrug of the shoulders, rather resentfully accepting the runt of the litter. Running was the thing I could do on my own, with no one to compete against. It cleared my head and stopped me from going bonkers when I was getting up at 4 a.m. to present a breakfast show, with all the myopic egotism that can create. It's a very levelling thing, running. I'm not particularly fast and I always moan about the first kilometre, it never comes easy. I remember on one fun run in 2008, having spent months training, I was lapped in one hour fourteen minutes by a reality star, Nikki Grahame from *Big Brother*, who told me she'd popped on a pair of plimsolls to 'jog round for a laugh, because I've never done it before'.

The team on *BBC Breakfast* once agreed to do a triathlon, to raise awareness for a charity. Two of my colleagues took the cycling and swimming and I opted for the run. It was 10k and as I pushed through the finishing tape, feeling tired and very ready to stop, I gratefully accepted the medal. 'How does it feel to be one of the elite runners?' someone said. Elite? Me? I don't think so. It turned out I'd completed one lap, not two. So I handed the medal back and, face burning with shame, returned to complete the course. How's that as a metaphor for cancer? Just when you think that you've finished, when you're ready to accept a medal for getting through it, some bugger forces you to go round again . . .

I thought I'd never run again after my first marathon experience in New York in 2001. It started with high hopes and good spirits and ended with me strapped to a bed at the city hospital, unable to speak.

Here's how I remember it. In the early hours of a November morning, thousands of us were gathering near the start line in New Jersey. It was humid and all the advice at the time was to keep hydrated, so I was chugging down bottles of water as I waited. My running partner was my then-husband, Neale. A marathon veteran, he was strong and powerful and sweaty (he won't mind me saying), and once we set off, he would pick up a cup of water at every mile marker to replace fluid, as did I. The race was amazing and the atmosphere incredible. Just two months after the 9/11 attack on the Twin Towers, this was New York's way of saying, 'we're back in business'. The streets were lined with fire and police crews, saluting the runners who'd come from all over the world, and we clapped them back. I've never experienced anything like it. The solidarity and compassion, the intensity of emotion, made it unforgettable.

The race was hard, much harder than I'd trained for. I kept drinking water, thinking I was dehydrated, but became progressively slower, which must have been frustrating for Neale as we'd trained to finish under four hours. The enormous support along the route kept me going, seeing my boys in Central Park with their home-made banner, 'Go Mum!', and hearing the local spectators trying to call out my name on my bib, 'Go . . . Si-anne?' But we were missing our four-hour target and were heading towards five. My legs were leaden and my head was tightening with pain. It was as if someone had attached a vice to my brain and was slowly turning the handle, compressing all the soft tissue.

As soon as I crossed the finish line, I collapsed. Paramedics rushed forward but I couldn't speak to them properly, all the words were coming out wrong. 'What's her mother tongue? Is she Eastern European? We can't understand her!' they said to Neale. My hearing started to go, followed by sight, feeling and consciousness.

I woke up in a hospital bed, curtains drawn, attached to white, bleeping machines. As I started ripping the tubes out, disorientated and fearful, the doctors came running. They explained I'd drunk so much that I'd diluted the essential salts in my blood and my brain had swollen, cutting off non-essential functions. It's called 'hyponatraemic encephalopathy' or water intoxication, and is potentially life-threatening. This brain-swelling, or 'cerebral oedema', causes vomiting, headache, confusion, coma and seizures. While I had most of those, I was lucky – my liver, heart, lungs and brain function were all checked and they were fine. I still couldn't move or talk, though. It was as if my tongue had doubled in size. I couldn't organize my thoughts even if I'd had something in my brain to articulate. It lasted a day or so and no one except my then-husband and the hospital staff knew. The boys had been told that I'd fainted and they were young enough to be distracted by hash browns in a typical American diner and the promise of new toys from FAO Schwartz. After a few days, we all went home and I swore I'd never run a marathon again.

More than a decade later and I began contemplating another marathon. I chose New York as the venue, thinking it would be cathartic to excise the memory of that Kafkaesque moment when I woke up terrified, alone and tied down. The training was hard, but each step put me further away from the hospital bed and showed me that the experience need not be repeated. I had to prove to myself that, just because a life-threatening event happened once, it didn't mean it would happen again.

Overcoming the fear of that experience recurring was key and it took effort. It's hard to find the willpower to get you back up and out after one of life's challenges knocks you down. It means having to change patterns of thinking and become more flexible, which takes deliberate engagement with uncomfortable thoughts. My thinking was initially set by that marathon horror; I believed running long distances was too risky and I would fail again. Rethinking that took a lot of energy, not just during the running but in training, when I was trying to rewire my thinking, stopping the automatic, negative thoughts and replacing them with something else. Using tricks from cognitive behavioural therapy (CBT) can help with that, as we've seen.

Brains change and grow in response to challenge, but in order for that to happen we need to replace rigid patterns of thinking with more flexible ones. We are less likely to grow if we believe that a knock-back is a failure, or represents the end of something, or will be repeated. Of course we *may* fail, and our experience *may* be repeated, but if we allow ourselves to be prevented from doing something because we're consumed by fear, we're doomed to stay where we are. We can't develop unless we get back up and try. If we worry too much about the worst that can happen, it might as well have occurred anyway. Be present, watch life unfold, be flexible and expect change. Change can be good and is often beneficial. If we're rooted in the past or terrified about what's coming next, we'll be stuck fast.

When I signed up for the marathon, I set up a website to raise money for the charity that looked after my mum: Macmillan Cancer Support. I knew I wanted to get enough to pay them back for some of the care they'd given her and I set a target of £10,000. Once people started pledging donations, I was committed to running those 26.4 miles come hell or high water. It helped me persevere and persist in the face of a stiff challenge.

But there are often hurdles and bumps in the road. Having found donors to back me, done the training, bought new running gear, I thought I was good to go. Then the day before we set off for New York, news came through that a hurricane was heading for the city. The race organizers announced: 'Runners should come, the race will go ahead, we won't be defeated.' Twenty thousand international athletes heeded their advice, but by the time we got there it was obvious that New York was struggling to cope with the devastation caused by the winds. In some parts of the city, there was no electricity or water. We checked into our hotel and as I picked up my runner's bib, I passed the Fox News building with its ticker tape broadcasting the latest news: 'Race sponsors criticized for giving bottled water to runners when New Yorkers have none.' That night we went out for pasta. As I tucked into my tagliatelle, I read the caption flashing up on the TV overhead: 'Marathon cancelled due to Hurricane Sandy' – a decision that should have been made as soon as the storm hit.

Some of us decided to run the twenty-six miles around Central Park anyway, and medals were handed out but it felt as though we hadn't earned them. I did a couple of news reports on the hurricane for the BBC before heading home weighed down by the feeling that I'd failed. I'd set out with a goal and I hadn't reached it. It was a knock-back – and frankly, talking to the New Yorkers who had to live without water and power for days on end, a small one – but it left me determined to run somewhere to justify the money that people had pledged.

So, a few months later I took my place on another start line – this time, at the London Marathon. I finished in four hours and twenty minutes; a respectable time and a decent amount of cash for Macmillan, a fantastic charity and one that would end up supporting me when I was diagnosed with breast cancer, just over a year later.

I'll sign up for a race to raise money for them again when these operations are over. I might manage that, what with these hill repeats and my ultra-runner neighbour, pushing me on. The furthest we've done is eight miles and it's tough, so I try to distract myself with puffy, gasping chat, finding excuses for my lack of fitness, wondering out loud when it'll feel easier. As we run through a Kentish vineyard, Caroline asks how the scars look. 'Fading, rather puckered still. Here – they look like this,' I say, stopping to pull up my T-shirt so she can examine the oddity of it. She peers, curiously, at the two small balloons on my chest. We look up and there are three men, staring with open mouths, their hosepipes suddenly unattended, spewing water over the vines. 'Morning!' we say cheerily, straightening up, starting to run again. 'Gives them something to talk about over their tea,' I say, unabashed. Any mystique or sexuality, any delicious unctuousness I ever had, is gone. My chest is interesting, a curiosity, nothing more.

It is a challenge getting out to huff and puff around these hills. When I look back to where I was in January, I know I'm doing OK because the goals keep shifting. Then, they were to move from the bed to the bathroom and to raise my arms above my head. Now they're different: run a bit further, try to keep the body fit, in case the cancer strikes again. I won't tell you it's easy, because it's not; some months, I don't run at all. But, to reinforce what my colleague Patrick said about recovering from trauma, it's much better than the alternative.

In his effort to overcome the post-traumatic stress disorder brought on by his time in Iraq, Patrick found that exercise helped – but he had to reframe it. He had been fit before his crisis but during it, he began to look at exercise in a very rigid way. He set himself the goal of training for a half-marathon because he felt it would help him deal with his distress, then he pushed and pushed. 'It was all about getting a better time, improving my personal best.' He didn't have days off and he didn't allow himself any down time or flexibility. It became an unhealthy distraction, a stressor that prevented him from dealing with his trauma. Exercise was detrimental to his health because neither his body nor his mind was able to recover. He was unable to sleep, but would still get up the following day and punish his already tired body, so the psychological effects of exercise were not allowed to work. Now, he still enters races occasionally but it's 'much more about the enjoyment'; the focus is on getting something positive from it. He does a broader range of activities too: 'I cycle a bit, swim a bit, walk a bit. So you know, I feel very good about the benefits of exercise but it's not in the same obsessive, rigid, focused way. It's just for its own sake. And that is a huge benefit, that's a better way to live, definitely. And a better way to exercise, I get injured less.'

A number of things that Patrick says about exercise strike me, because they are underpinned by research. It's not beneficial, psychologically, if you are forced, or are forcing yourself, to exercise. Your self-regulation goes to pot and you are more likely to end up tired, resentful and reaching for a doughnut afterwards. The way we define exercise needs to change, too. Maybe thinking of it as physical activity, rather than exercise, will make it seem more doable when we are feeling low. Patrick does a bit of everything he fancies. For you, it might be gardening on the allotment, dancing, or walking the dog. It doesn't really matter what you do, as long as you do something. It doesn't matter whether it's twenty minutes or an hour, or how hard you push yourself. Or even where you do it. Simply moving, regularly, like we used to before we had lifts to take us up the stairs or cars to carry us a short distance rather than walk. It makes a huge difference to our well-being and to our brain, even if it seems our mind is fighting against it.

Most days I'm waging an internal war on activity. My sane, rational, know-all-the-arguments, cognitive brain says I will feel better afterwards. Look at all the studies. Not just studies, but studies of studies. Meta-studies. Exercise jump-starts development in the brain. We know that it releases endorphins and serotonin, both of which help elevate your mood, and that it lowers blood pressure and increases oxygen intake, allowing you to feel alert yet calm. We know it and I've researched it, and yet the logical part of my brain battles with my irrational, emotional, instinctive brain, which doesn't want to be alert and calm. It wants to crawl back to bed, eat biscuits, watch TV and get more frustrated by my slothful self. The brain after trauma will often not want to do anything, let alone lace up a pair of trainers or walking boots.

*

Here's the evidence, given on the understanding that sometimes it'll resonate and other times it won't. For the times that it won't, I've asked a couple of experts for advice on motivation.

The science is quite clear. As Patrick discovered, if you suffer from anxiety, exercise can help to minimize it. Most of the meta-analysis, those studies of studies, says there are real benefits to it, across many areas. I learn about the potential of exercise to boost our thinking while recording my series for Radio 4, *How to Have a Better Brain*. Dr Alan Gow, from Heriot-Watt University, is collaborating on a long-term study based at the University of Edinburgh, which is trying to discover what part physical activity plays in protecting our mental abilities as we age. Their assessments take many lifestyle factors into account, and the evidence so far suggests a relationship between being physically active and brain health — those who were more active did better on tests of general cognitive ability and processing speed.

Here's what they don't yet know, though. How long do we have to exercise for? How intense should it be? How frequently should we do it? Which type, aerobic or strength training'? These are all key questions and there's research out there, but none of it is conclusive. So for the time being there's no individual prescription; no one can yet say: Do a bit more of this, for this long, in this way. The advice is that you should always include some strength and muscle training with aerobic training, but, as ever, we could do with more research.

What we *do* know is that even simple things, like walking more, has benefits. OK, we don't know exactly when, how often and for how long. There's generic advice about doing 150 minutes a week and good indicators to say this works to make you feel better both in body and mind, contributing to a more positive mental state, but there's much more to discover. Plus, a lot of the research being carried out is still in the early stages where scientists are studying mice in laboratories rather than humans, so it's too soon to say whether models that work for rodents will do the same for us.

The concrete science is there, though. Dr Gow tells me that the speed of our thought and general reasoning appears to be better in those who are more active. He, too, calls it physical activity, rather than exercise, because he says the latter suggests something planned and purposeful. Saying we'll do more physical activity somehow feels more manageable, something we can accommodate into our day, becoming part of the way we live. He says the research project in Edinburgh, led by Professor Ian Deary and conducted over decades, suggests that 'the people who do more of this activity have slightly higher grey matter volume and less damage to white matter'. The grey matter in the brain processes information like memory and learning. The white matter is the connective tissue that 'wires' the brain together. Those who do physical activity have fewer lesions here or damage to the connections between nerve cells, which disrupt the passage of information partially or completely.

To put it bluntly — those who are more active seem to have less shrinkage in their brain. The mechanism underlying *why* the brain shrinks less when you move more is still to be understood. But in other studies, those who increased the amount they walked saw improvements to their brain structures in just six months. Of course, diet might be important, as is socialization, and lots of other lifestyle factors affect our brain health too, but Dr Gow says that the general evidence in favour of physical activity being beneficial is perhaps more consistent and more robust than the other influences. He's insistent that we shouldn't be discouraged from other activities that are socially and intellectually stimulating, but exercise tops the list of things we can do to improve our mind.

'Exercise and physical activity seem to be beneficial, not just for people's cognitive abilities and cognitive health but for cardiovascular disease, cancer, diabetes. So if people were choosing to do one thing for a health benefit, exercise is up there,' he says. What happens if you really don't want to do it, or feel you can't? He replies with a smile· 'If you're doing nothing, then doing something will be better than that, and if you're already doing something, then doing a bit more will be a bit better still.'

Dr Gow knows how hard it is to motivate us: 'People think, "I know I should take more exercise, but it's really difficult, isn't it?" We need to let them know it doesn't have to be a really intensive, hard gym workout, for example. It can be as simple as walking a little more, taking the stairs, perhaps even standing a bit more, things that get your heart and lungs working. The quick summary: if you are doing something, great, you probably could do more. If you're not doing anything, don't worry, because the evidence suggests that even people who become a bit more active much later on in life may see some benefits in terms of effects on the brain.' He means effects on memory, reasoning skills, planning, changing from one task to another; the management-type or 'executive' processes in the brain that tend to be disrupted as we get older, or indeed, after a traumatic event. Even if those effects are small, physical activity is yet another thing that can help our brain.

Dr Gow goes on to list the other ways it can help us, like the relationship with better sleeping patterns and reductions in chronic stress. 'While my focus is on the ageing brain, there are studies that link physical activity with better outcomes, not just in terms of anxiety, but positive feelings of self-worth, focus and various aspects of mental health that may benefit from it.'

Being more physically active makes the heart work more effectively, which means more oxygen and nutrients will be pumped around the body. In the brain, this promotes growth and development in many areas: in the blood vessels, in the little gaps between cells where communication happens, in the nerve cells themselves. As Dr Gow says, one of the ways physical activity might benefit the brain is by directly affecting grey matter, either in protecting the existing nerve cells or even promoting the development of new ones.

There's other research that points to this activity affecting our neurochemical levels, the hormones, neurotransmitters and other chemicals that help promote wellbeing.

When neurotransmitters send out their chemical messages, it sparks the nerve cells, or neurons, to communicate with one another across a gap called a synapse. There's a saying, 'neurons that fire together, wire together' – in other words, when the brain recognizes a new experience, the neurons fire and the connections are strengthened, making it easier to replicate that experience. That's why the more you do something – like practising on an instrument or using a new language – the better you get at it; and the same is true of physical activities. The more neuronal activity, the more the synapses fire, the greater and more established the connections. When they fail to fire, we forget and the information is lost.

There are dozens of chemical messengers in the brain, each with its own role; two that play a particularly important role in the firing of the synapses are glutamate, which triggers brain activity, and gamma-aminobutyric acid (GABA), which calms it. Many anti-anxiety drugs work by enhancing the effects of GABA, but it can be stimulated without pharmaceuticals, and exercise is one of the key ways to do it. It's the same with that other neurotransmitter, serotonin, which we hear a lot about in relation to depression and anxiety. When levels are low, it can really affect our mood; if our body is moving and needs to fuel muscles, serotonin levels will rise. Exercising outdoors increases levels further still, because serotonin reacts to daylight. Even on a cloudy day, levels achieved outside can be greater than those achieved indoors.'[1]

Serotonin gets a boost from another biological wonder that helps to enhance memory and promotes growth in a part of our brain responsible for learning, context and mood. This wonder is a rather mighty protein, one of the many neurotrophins which help promote the development, survival and growth of nerve cells, or `neurogenesis'. Some evidence suggests these proteins can increase when people are more physically active. The studies indicate that exercise encourages the brain to produce more of a key neurotrophin called BDNF, which stands for 'brain derived neurotrophic factor'. It's important for those recovering from trauma because this BDNF development takes place in a region of the hippocampus associated with learning, memory and depression. Research suggests that those with depression have lower levels of BDNF and that acute stress produces hormones that decrease it still further.[2] Most studies use animals including mice, but there are a few studies with human subjects. One took place in Ireland, using two groups of students to test the theory that aerobic exercise increases the levels of BDNF and improves the function of the hippocampus.[3] Both groups were asked to take a memory test. Then one group did some cycling, while the other remained sedentary. Afterwards, they did another test. Those who had exercised showed significant improvement in the test, those who had not, did not. Blood samples were taken and that protein BDNF, responsible for the health of nerve cells, was higher in the cyclists than in those who sat quietly.[4]

BDNF is a complex protein and there are some studies that are contradictory, but research suggests it increases with the short-term use of antidepressants.[5] If this is the case, and if links between BDNF and exercise have been known for about a decade, can't we try to raise our levels more naturally by physical activity?[6] It doesn't matter at what age you start either; what matters is that you keep it up. A study from University College in London looked at people who were 36 years old, then they studied them again at 43 and finally at 53. Those who were physically active at 36 and 43 showed less cognitive decline as they got older. The people who were physically active to begin with and then were *not* active at 43, didn't see the benefit of that earlier activity. But the people who took up physical activity between 36 and 43 still had that benefit years later.[7] There might be critical periods of our life when exercise is important and it can certainly help after trauma, especially if we're prone to persistent sadness. Another piece of research looked at women over 50 with depression, and found that those who walked between 150 and 200 minutes a week felt better physically and emotionally, and that it helped with their depressive symptoms.[8]

The UK's health watchdog, the National Institute for Health and Care Excellence (NICE), has examined the various methods that can be used to treat mild clinical depression and found evidence that exercise is more effective than antidepressants, largely because with drugs 'the risk-benefit ratio is poor'. (In cases where there's a history of moderate or severe depression, or if the depression lasts for a long time, typically around two years, NICE found a stronger case for the use of drugs.)[9] In the meantime, there's the physical activity. The science says it works and if you speak to anyone who's beginning to walk their way out of adversity, they will tell you how much it helps.

Begin slowly and remember where you are on the path to recovery. If you are dealing with a physical or mental trauma, your body will be focused on healing, so try not to stress it further by doing too much. Start small. Set your goals so they are measurable and achievable. Mine was to walk to the bathroom, then to the top of the road, then a jog and many, many months later, my first eight-mile run. Often, I slip back. At the moment, waiting for more surgery and struggling with a heavy cold, I'm not running at all, although I am trying to walk as much as possible. Yes, it's hard and every additional challenge is harder than the last, but that's because you're growing stronger and you are taking on more. You and your body will adapt. I remember something Trude, who lost her parents in the Holocaust, said to me about the capacity of the body and mind to change: 'All animals have the potential of adaptation,' she said, 'and we adapt as best we can to the circumstances — the better we adapt, the better our lives. The less we adapt, the more likely we are to sink.'

17

Live

'She is clothed in strength and dignity, and she laughs without fear of the future'

Proverbs 31:25

I'm weeping all over my laptop (again). I've been tweeting about this new Radio 4 series I've been making. It's a mix of crunchy science, some of which I've told you about, together with some lovely case studies. Lots of listeners have been in touch since the first episode went out (about how physical activity can help boost the brain), letting me know what they think of it. Someone tweeted that 'many cancer patients walk to stave off side effects from treatment, especially stiff joints'. 'Yes,' I reply, 'it also helps with low moods.' I'm thinking not of my desperate, panting runs up Kent hills, but rather those early, solitary walks through wintry fields, down to the reservoir. It was a struggle to get over the stiles because I couldn't put any pressure on my arms (the surgery had involved moving and cutting the chest muscles), so those walks were hard, but each time I felt a little stronger and each time I walked a little further.

Yes, exercise is good for stiff joints and low moods. If I hadn't walked, I'd have gone mad. When I finally made it down to the water's edge, I looked across the vast expanse, totally alone, with no one and nothing in sight except some nesting birds and a beautiful view, and I felt such pride and joy to have made it, I stayed there until the light dimmed – and then I had a slight panic about the long walk home and who would be there to pull off my wellies.

I look to see who sent that tweet and it's a lingerie company. Why would they be interested in cancer? I search the name, Millie Lingerie, and find they're looking for kick-start funding to develop prototype bras for women who have breast cancer. On the website is a short video featuring a woman called Sue Pringle. Sue calls herself a 'twice survivor of breast cancer'; in one of her blog entries she recalls how it felt going into a changing room six weeks after surgery to try on a new bra for a charity ball she was attending. The bra-fitter worried that it was too soon after the operation. Sue writes: 'I was medically glued back together, free of dressings and any risk of infection, but for a brief moment I felt like an untouchable, as she said I was a "risk" and I should come back a few weeks later.' She ended up buying a bra to get her through the ball, but it wasn't designed for her. A few months later she returned to the shop, only to have another miserable experience: 'It was when I'd paid for bras for my two girls who'd shopped with me (they'd been awash with choice, prettiness and colour), and walked away from the till, that the tears came.'

Now, I'm in floods myself and I try to donate but the website won't let me, so I email asking how I can do so. The kick-starter campaign has closed but Sue says she'd like my support in other ways. It makes me giggle, a lingerie maker asking for support. Yes, I'll do that. Every time someone with breast cancer wears a bra, they're reminded of their disease. It needs to be soft because many of us have scars that hurt if they're rubbed, or have tubes leading into temporary implants with 'ports' or buttons jutting out under the skin, which some doctors position right under your bra strap. I've still got them, those implants, the plastic tubes, the 'ports', and it's a daily reminder of what's happened, I'm aware of them all the time. It's very hard to find something lovely when you are feeling at your most unlovely. Like Sue, I know how a bra-fitting can reduce you to tears. In my case it was in the changing room of a large department store when I first went for my fitting. I apologized to the fitter before I undressed about what I looked like, my chest was pretty brutalized and I didn't want to shock her. She was sweet with sad eyes and her kindness made me dig my nails into my hand so I wouldn't start blubbing and embarrassing myself. The small kindnesses at that stage, like touching a hand and showing you care, are a huge comfort. I hope she knows what it meant to me at the time, as she was busily squirrelling away, trying to find something that wasn't too ugly and ludicrous for me to wear, knowing that it mattered, for so many reasons, caring. Lots of women don't have 'expanders' as they're called, or temporary implants, because the varying nature of breast cancer means many of us have different treatments. Some have lumpectomies, which is the partial removal of breast tissue, or single or bilateral mastectomies, which is the loss of one or both breasts. There are a huge number of different breast reconstructions, too, with some choosing not to have one, using prosthetics instead. Even if they are 'remade', it's not like a straightforward cosmetic boob job. Sometimes it involves multiple surgical operations. They won't feel the same as before, either, because they often have no feeling – the nerves are taken away with the breast tissue. They won't bounce, so they'll feel like oranges, or balloons, depending on what size you were before.

Finding something that suits women and, more than that, makes them feel feminine again, is a huge challenge and I admire Sue for taking on the task. I want to know more about her, so she gives me her number and I call. I'm not going to tell her about me.

Sue and I chat about her initial diagnosis. Like mine, it was ductal carcinoma in situ (DCIS), but she had a lumpectomy, then a single mastectomy, followed by hormone therapy once a month for two years, the impact of which was 'massive and messy' and put her into the menopause 'literally overnight'. She didn't have chemotherapy or radiotherapy and felt disconcerted by that, needing constant reassurances from her medical team that it was the best decision for her. 'I doubted whether it was the right thing and had to put my faith in them. It was only when I went to a support group and met other ladies and found they also had a full head of hair – I remember seeing another lady with a bob and thinking, "Oh, it's not just me, it is all right!" It's the strangest feeling, there's a definite uncertainty.'

Sue says during diagnosis and treatment it felt as if 'a carpet had been whipped out from under my feet and I fell over'.

Friends react differently, some helpful and some not so. Sue says, 'There is a line that's drawn in the sand in people's minds where they think, "Oh, great, you're fine now" and that's because they *want* you to be fine and they *need* you to be fine and they just think, "You're out of clinic and you're all sorted. Tickety-boo." It isn't like that. It's part of my life, every day.' So she walked away from a lot of friendships that weren't helpful, when people were 'clumsy' or tried to make light of it, telling her she was fine and strong and admirable. The language that accompanies cancer infuriates Sue, as it does me. All this talk of 'strength' and 'bravery', Sue says she wanted to scream, '"No, I'm not! – I'm struggling with this and I don't have a choice! Please don't tell me I'm strong." There's an implication that the minute you have a diagnosis, you become a superhuman, because you're doing "all this". And you have no choice, you have to get on with it.'

After the first diagnosis, Sue stopped working, became a school governor, spent more time with the children. Then as she got better, she took a full-time job, a management role, which came with daily commuting and chronic stress. The pace got faster, the job got harder and her sleep became more disrupted. She found a little lump, on top of her reconstruction. Her medical team 'think it could have been as simple as one rogue cell that'd been sitting there, dormant, in the chest wall and it decided to have a party because I was under a lot of pressure. I think stress is a massive, massive drive to what happens to our immune system.'

More surgery and a five-year course of a different hormone treatment, a 'nasty, nasty drug' that, once again, is knocking the wind out of her, making her joints ache. I ask her what helps. 'I walk, I swim, I practise yoga – and if I don't, I soon know it. I feel ten years older physically and I feel weary, I feel unable to cope with life some days, it affects my mood quite significantly.' What doesn't help is when she slips back into her old patterns of thinking. 'There's always the temptation for anyone who's had cancer, to think, "I should be normal, I should be getting on with things" and I try not to use the words "should" and "ought to" any more, because they're so judgemental.' Does that sound familiar?

It's taxing, living with breast cancer. 'It's a mental effort, just keeping it at bay and keeping it in a place where I feel I can live with it and to have it in my life without being afraid of it every single day.' Are you afraid every single day? I ask. 'Overtly, no, but somewhere in the recesses of my mind, yes, it's demonstrated by the trips and the triggers that bring it out, it's like the elephant in the room for me, it's always there, omnipresent. I'm very realistic about it, but that residual fear is there and it lurks and it can be the smallest things. Some days I breeze through and other days, it cuts a little bit closer.'

I ask her how she deals with it, on those days when it cuts a little bit closer. 'I take a deep breath and allow those feelings to happen, rather than try and block them. Let them be and accept them. It's very hard and that's the effort I'm talking about. I usually get myself home, or to a quiet place where I can have a cup of tea and reflect inwards. How am I feeling? Why am I feeling this way? And there's a bit of, "Oh, OK, that's what this is, it's not great but it's all right and it'll pass."'

I'm interested in the language Sue uses. Sometimes she says she 'has' cancer, other times that she 'had' it. I know what she means: she feels like a cancer patient when she has to go into hospital for another check-up or for more treatment. She's changed the way she deals with it, though. 'I used to avoid it, occupy myself, keep busy, use displacement tactics, whereas now I'm much more realistic about the fact that actually I *do* feel I have cancer today, I do feel like I'm dealing with the impact of cancer. That's the word I use a lot: the "impact" of cancer. And I am more accepting of it. I get very frustrated by it, though, because there are days when I want to get lots done and sometimes it just doesn't happen, I have to rebalance, re-measure, re-pace, reschedule, all of those things.'

Sue feels she's different and, like me, she notices the cancer has brought into focus the important things in life. For her, it's her two daughters. 'I will always do whatever I can to reassure them. It's not quite a pretence, because there's a reality of some days when they have to see the full impact of it, but I will try to save my best time for them.' The best times are taking the family to a campsite in Cornwall every year where they watch sunsets and eat pasties. It's an 'annual pilgrimage' which is 'messy and wonderful' and she wouldn't have invented it if she hadn't had cancer.

When you have/had cancer, you live with daily reminders, whether it's the pills, or the things you could do and now can't and the things you couldn't do and now can. Sue has a mirror in the bathroom and says, 'I should just take it down, really. I stand there thinking, "Yup, there we are" – because I've got the nipple reconstruction, but I'm all baggy, I've got the bunching from where the lines went in and they took muscle from my back, so I'm a bit battered. The impact doesn't stop, it's there in everything I do, so I drive down to Cornwall and by the end of the journey my arm aches and then I've got to put a ruddy tent up!'

She's laughing and so am I. I thank her for her honesty and then tell her there was much that she said that I recognize. She pauses, as do I.

'I had a double mastectomy earlier this year,' I say with a gulp.

She gasps. 'Oh my goodness, Sian, oh gosh,' she says. 'Was that elective or diagnosis?'

'Diagnosis.'

'Oh my goodness. Oh. Right. Thank you for sharing that with me.'

My nose is running, my eyes are streaming, my voice sounds snotty, I can barely string a sentence together. 'The things you're saying are so . . . you're the first person I've spoken to who's had what I've had, in seven months . . . oh, I'm sorry.'

'It's a journey of exploration, isn't it?' Sue says. 'It's so inward.'

'But you're using your experience to better the lives of others, it's as simple as that,' I reply.

Sue talks about the bras she's trying to create, going back to that changing-room experience where she wailed and wailed and wailed. I tell her my dressing-room story, where I too tried to hide while trying on these 'bloody ugly bras'. It feels cathartic to talk to someone who really understands, even if I'm the one now wailing.

'Oh bless you,' she says. 'It's very early days, Sian, goodness yes, very early days. I would say it was well over a year before I could look at myself in the mirror and say "Oh! That looks like Sue again!" Because the reflection that was coming back prior to that . . . yes, of course it was me, but I wasn't actually seeing me. The whole of that first year, there are so many depths to probe about who you are and how you feel about yourself – I'm thirteen years on and it *still* happens. There are days when I look at myself and think, "Really? Is that as good as it gets today?" And I probably would have done that anyway at the age of fifty-three, let's be honest! But sometimes there are times you think, "Oh God." A bra is part of that and it can help to, literally, give the lift you need.'

It may seem trifling, a little piece of lingerie. It's not. It's part of our armoury, part of the team of things we rely on to help us feel that bit better on the days when we feel that bit wobbly. And we will. Whatever adversity or trauma we're going through, we need to know the back-up team is there.

Wednesday, 5th August

Exactly seven months to the day since I had my breasts cut off and today, I'm about to board a train to go back to the hospital where it all happened, to see the oncologist, Dr Blackman.

I'm nervous. I suspect he'll be brisk and efficient, managing my fear, just as he tried to many weeks ago when he said yes, some of my disease was high grade, but they used to call what I had 'pre-cancer'. He was the one who said that, ordinarily, I'd have between three and five weeks of radiotherapy but he'd advise against. I suppose he'll examine me today, feel the ridges of the implants, the dips and creases, the tubes leading to the 'ports' that still stick out like large shirt buttons on my bra line. They're so prominent, I'm sure I saw them under the tight dress that I wore for last week's show. I hadn't camouflaged them effectively and I thought they looked like some strange, jutting growths on my ribs.

Two days ago, Paul threw me a casual glance as I was getting dressed and said, encouragingly, 'Almost healed!' I looked down, impassively. 'Really? Hadn't noticed. They're alien to me, not part of my body. I'm disinterested in them, they get in the way, if anything.' I'm ambivalent about reconstruction. I want these fake, salt water-filled bags out, along with the tubes and the ports. What replaces them? Carved-off bits of thigh, back, stomach, shaped into a breast? More surgery, anaesthetic, tubes and wires, tethered again. Stitching together all the minute veins and threads of my internal workings. It's an incredibly complex job, I'm in awe of those who can do it. Maybe they'll whip out what's under my skin and muscle and pop silicone cushions in. Neither seems particularly attractive.

I know a man who had heart failure and his doctors recommended a pacemaker. He decided against it; he didn't want a foreign body inside him, tripping off airport scanners and buggering up his mobile phone signal (if that's what they do). The option is to do nothing, I suppose, take out what's there and leave it all flat. Body of a twelve-year-old, face of a fifty-year-old. Nice. I'd like a shape back, some sense of femininity. I hear of women who choose to have cosmetic implants and they're thrilled, whipping them out to friends, posing in bikinis, being braless and liberated. Is it liberation? Feels like being moulded into an expectation, to me.

I'm in reception. Alex has taken Seth to the park while I'm here. I was up until midnight organizing childcare for the endless summer holidays and I completely flew off the handle at Paul this morning. He'd offered to help a couple of weeks ago, saying he'd be happy to take the kids to his work so I can attend appointments, but when I suggested it last night, I thought he just looked blankly at me. He was probably exhausted but when he went to bed, I was in the kitchen, furiously organizing things, finishing an article for the 'Radio Times' that I'd been given less than a day to write, checking the scripts of the Radio 4 shows I'm doing and sending them to the neuropsychologist who is working on the brain series with me.

So I went to bed in a state of toxic anxiety and fury and woke up pretty much the same way, despite knowing all the science about clearing your head of difficult thoughts so they don't cement themselves while you sleep. That fury was well and truly cemented. Lesson learned.

The waiting room is full, as ever, with people trying to distract themselves from having cancer. Some coughing, some bald, some old, others not. Ages must range from thirty upwards, one woman walking with a stick, pain contorting her body, anxious husband checking her in. A young lad waiting for his mum, maybe. Or just unlucky. What a strange disease, this thing that throws us all together, makes us the same, however bad it is, whatever age we are or background we come from. A homogeneity of human suffering. Couples look weary. A man in front of me, who's just come out of his appointment, goes to the front desk and asks for another in three months. December. I'm three months away from having lived with this, like this, for a year. The tortuous waiting, the never-quite-clear, the threat of more. The flashes of irrational anger, the deliberate wounding, prompted by fear.

As Dr Blackman collects me from reception, he asks kindly, 'Did anyone come with you?'

'No,' I say, 'should they?' I become fearful, suspecting another routine appointment will turn into something different, as it did before, when I was expecting an 'all clear' but heard 'You've got cancer.'

He smiles. 'No.'

We sit in his office and there's a medical student with him. 'Do you mind if she watches?' he says. I don't. It could be my son. A young trainee doctor, full of hope and good health, looking at this middle-aged woman, just one of many they'll see today, who's living with disease. We are medical curiosities, ways to put textbook learning into practice. She'll know my history and diagnosis, what surgery I've had and the treatment we're discussing. She won't know yet how to talk to a patient about the grey areas, the lack of certainty in cancer, the emotion that accompanies it all. Take notes, I think. Listen to what this man will say between the lines. It may be more nuanced than you think. It is.

Dr Blackman repeats his view that I shouldn't need radiotherapy. His belief is that we sometimes over-treat cancer and that no treatment is without risks. You can never take the effects of radiotherapy away, he says. I ask for the numbers, the science and the evidence about cancer recurrence if I choose not to have further treatment.

'I feel it's difficult to say, "Here are the numbers, now you make the decision." There is a certain amount of belief needed,' he says. The numbers are always open to interpretation, or change. I am to trust his 'belief' – and I do. I ask him whether one day soon they'll stop cutting bits of our body off, to treat cancer. Yes, he says, and we'll change chemotherapy and radiotherapy too. They are all blunt tools. Soon we'll be able to target individual cancers.

He examines me and asks if the female medical student can watch. As he traces his fingers along the scars and runs them across the skin, she's watching intently. 'Would you like to feel what it's like?' I ask her. Her face lights up and she looks thrilled yet slightly terrified at the same time. 'Would you mind? Really?' Her voice is that of a teenager who's been given a gift. A slightly scary one, like a bungee jump or a parachute drop. Dr Blackman smiles. 'I'll leave you to it.'

The hands of the student are cold, her fingers delicate. Her touch is light, too light to be able to detect anything if it were there, I think. 'You can press harder,' I say, 'it doesn't hurt.' She focuses intently on each breast, searching around them, feeling the ridges and creases, running fingers over ports and on top of chest muscle. 'It's a long journey,' she says, glancing to catch my eye as she traces the scar lines. 'Yes,' I say, 'sometimes I feel like I'm a warrior and other times . . .' She stops tracing and looks at me, two women separated by a generation, united by a strange understanding. 'You are *a warrior,' she says, definitively.*

Dr Blackman comes back into the room. I get dressed. 'It all feels perfectly healthy,' he says. 'Anything that doesn't feel right, just contact me.' I ask him how I'll know. You probably won't, he replies, so make sure you get advice about whether what you are feeling is right or wrong. It's about living with uncertainty too, he says. 'And living with uncertainty becomes easier. Every day that passes, your chances of the cancer returning are reduced.' He asks me if I think about it every day. I start to well up. 'I do,' I say, 'and I know I'm not entitled to have this concern and anxiety when I look at the others in the waiting room.' He reassures me that it's quite usual, it's only been seven months so it's inevitable that it'll be on my mind, but 'there will come a time when you don't think about it daily. It will be in the past, one day.'

We shake hands and I'm taken in to see my surgeon, Jo Franks. She says I look good – better than when she saw me before, more myself. She asks whether working is making me feel more normal and tells me she loved the yellow dress I wore for the show at the weekend. 'You could see my ports,' I say. 'No you couldn't,' she replies. 'You know they're there, that's all.' She asks me if it feels any better now I'm used to them. 'No,' I reply. 'Well, you'll feel differently when you're back to yourself,' she says, 'and we're now in a position to try to make it all look better.'

She starts scribbling notes and then pauses. 'Unfinished business, isn't it?'

'Yes,' I say. 'The vestiges of seven months ago are still inside me and I want it all out.'

Jo nods, reassuringly. 'You will have that, I promise. Soon. And you will feel differently.'

I ask her why I have to go to a different hospital, with a different surgeon for this next step and she says not to worry, the team is very experienced. And if the consultant sees anything suspicious when he operates, he'll biopsy it. Then she smiles. 'And also, you know how some women look at their friend's shoe collection and go, "Oooh! I envy you all that choice and gorgeousness"? Well, you're going to be under the care of one of the best breast surgeons in the UK, Mr Ash Mosahebi. And I do that same "oooh!" whenever I look into his implants cupboard.' We laugh. 'It'll be great,' she says, 'and there's something rather wonderful about the fact that you were my very first patient of 2015, that you were complicated and messy and your cancer was all over the place, yet we think we've got it all out and here you are now, looking healthy, ready for the last hurdle. The next time I see you will be after the operation in December. I know you're uncertain, I know you're concerned about the cancer returning, but we've done all we can. And I think 2016 will be wonderful.'

Ping-ponging across the hospital, I visit the psychologist to ask what she tells her patients when they're told to live with the uncertainty of disease returning. Her advice is to tell yourself you have done all you can to mitigate it. You've had the surgery and, while you may remain unsure about whether it'll come back, try to think about the proactive steps you have taken. Live with the benefit that the surgery has given you, not the fear of it returning. She brought in some research, knowing that the trainee psychologist in me always needs some hard data. In the first year of a breast cancer diagnosis, 20–30 per cent of patients have clinical depression. Then it diminishes. Time and distance help.

Those I've spoken to and learned from along this curious path say they are all living with uncertainty. Experiencing a major life trauma, especially if it's unexpected, threatens your sense of self and your place in the world. It shatters your previous assumptions and it takes time and distance to rebuild. When you do, you may find you have changed and your perspective has shifted, perhaps for ever. Here's what Andy Puddicombe tells me about how his adversity changed him. He says it's what happens when, 'In those bigger moments you feel like, finally, "OK, I get it, I get what this is about."' For him, it was, he says, 'the sense of being connected and in no way separate from the rest of the world, the shared human experience, not as a concept but as something that felt extremely real. In that moment, life and death aren't separate. It's the ever-changing ebb and flow, this thing called life, because it's death as well, and that's much more scary because of the uncertainty around it.'

RISE

~

> In the midst of winter I found there was, within me, an invincible summer.
>
> Albert Camus, 'Return to Tipasa'

Friday, 30th October

After all the talking and all the reassuring, it's almost here. Just a couple of days before what might be the final surgery this year, to take out what's there, have a look around and put in something else. As it's half-term, I take Seth and Evie to hospital for my pre-assessment and they watch, fascinated, as four vials of blood are taken from my arm. They listen as a nurse asks lots of questions about mastectomies and lymph nodes and they ask their own when she starts issuing instructions about what I have to do the night before the operation. 'Why does Mummy have to swab her body with wipes? Why can't she have breakfast?' Then we're all taken to a small studio with lights and reflectors, and I stand naked to have my photo taken, as a record of what I look like before the next operation. These are torso shots but I still find myself standing and smiling in a particular way – 'my TV face' as Alex and Joss call it. 'This is the strangest photoshoot I've ever been on,' I say, as the photographer clicks away, barking orders: 'Arms up! Arms behind! Stand to the side!' Afterwards, as I'm dressing, Evie looks up at me. 'Do lots of mummies get cancer?' she asks. 'No,' I say, 'but some do and everyone here is doing their very best to get rid of it for them.' Her tiny face is open and interested, quizzical rather than concerned. 'Will I get it?' she asks. What to say to my six-year-old daughter? I can't say no, I won't say maybe. I say that by the time she's grown up, they'll have found a way to make sure that, even if she does get it, which is unlikely, they will get rid of it very quickly.

It doesn't sound like the right answer and I spend all day agonizing about how I could have reframed it. I want them to know that cancer isn't always a death sentence, like it was for their granny. Their last memories of her, this bubbly, active, chatty woman, always bustling in with tea and cakes and fun, were of someone else, someone unable to move, bloated and in pain, who couldn't speak or hold them or smile. I want them to know that you can have cancer and still be you, even when a part of you has been taken away. I want them to understand that hospitals are not full of fear, but packed with people who work their hardest to make you better and you can trust them, sometimes even laugh with them. That it'll be OK.

After the medical necessaries, we meet Liz and her children and walk around Hampstead Heath, chatting. She suggests I bring the kids up to London again tomorrow, so they can stay overnight with her for Halloween. It'll be a good deal more fun 'trick or treating' on her busy street than round our rented home in Kent, where we only have three neighbours and it's so dark, you need torches after 6 p.m. It's a great idea, it'll keep them distracted and allow me and Paul to spend some time together. Not much time though, I'll be busy scripting and researching for this weekend's 'Sunday Morning Live'. The weekend will be crammed and I won't need to think about the operation until the day itself.

Monday, 2nd November

It's the day itself. I feel like a cancer patient again, just as Sue, my fellow breast cancer traveller, told me I would. I haven't slept much. I'm back at Liz's, because I'm being admitted to the Royal Free Hospital at just after seven and couldn't get a train from home to get there on time. We watched 'Strictly Come Dancing' together last night, ate, laughed, hugged and then I went to bed, after some intensive antiseptic swabbing. It's now half past five in the morning and

I've showered and wiped again, also removing make-up, jewellery, individuality. Ready for the anonymity of being just one more disease in a hospital gown. Telling myself that this time it's different, that it's about rebuilding, not destroying, and that it'll be painful but positive. As Sue says, there are trips and triggers that will always take you back, but you have to stop being afraid of it every single day. Cancer returned for her, as it may for me and, like her, I think I'll always be dealing with the impact of it. My skin's being sliced open again today, perhaps along those same scars that have healed to silvery lines, to take out the expanders, the tubes and the ports. I'm finally getting used to how I look, this strange 'otherness'. It's a weird sort of femininity and it'll change again today.

Time to go. Liz's husband Mike offers to drive me to the hospital and we chat about everything, other than what I'm going there for.

7.15 a.m.

I'm told I'm the first on the surgical list but not what time I'll go under and come out again. I'm ready for this, I think. The moment when I wake, maybe with a catheter, drains and a morphine drip attached. Ready for the injections in the stomach, the rasping throat made husky by the tube forcing my airways open. Not quite ready for what follows. Back to being an invalid, 'No, no, I can do it, let me try. Don't tell the kids not to hug me.' (Try not to wince; ouch, ouch ouch.)

I have about ten days to recover before I'm back on air and there's no hiding place on television. There'll be nowhere to put the drain bottles and no excuse for looking pained, or weary. Get on with it, be bright, be breezy, be disease-free.

Because I am, aren't I? Although you are never really sure whether those cancer cells are still floating around, dividing and spreading, I have been told they got what they could when they went in last time and many patients would be grateful to be here. They'll be thinking

'You're lucky. Lucky to be told they got it out. Lucky to replace malignancy with moulded artificiality.' When I sat with my mum in the hospital after she'd been diagnosed with secondary cancer in her liver, the oncologist pointed to the X-ray on a screen, showing how the tumour had engulfed and penetrated so much of her that there was no way any expert could cut it out. She spent the following month with this thing growing, spreading and penetrating. Any healthy tissue turned ugly, very quickly. I am not there, I am here, just over an hour away from something designed to wrap up this year of living with the impact of cancer. Be thankful. My Aunty Sue didn't get here. Alison didn't make it to this stage. Think of all the women going into hospital this morning, or who are there already, like me but with a different prognosis. Be grateful. Look up. Look beyond.

7.30 a.m. Surgical admissions area

I've forgotten my in-patient letter. The nurse sighs, doesn't look at me and passes a slip of paper across the desk. 'Name, date of birth, why you're here,' she mutters, in a rather beleaguered way. I'm not surprised she's weary already. This place is packed. People are sitting on the floor because all the chairs are taken. An elderly man with a stick gestures to his own seat. 'Sit here?' he asks, a glimpse of humanity and kindness in this sea of the sick. 'No thanks,' I reply, 'I'm about to spend a lot of time lying down.' We chuckle. All ages, all races, all manner of ailments crowd this place today, just like every other day. Names are called and acknowledged with worried smiles, 'Yes, that's me, my time to go', staff taking us to our destinations, carrying our overnight bags, all of us swabbed clean and anxious. I ring Paul to say I'm here safely and it goes straight to answer machine. It doesn't matter, we spoke earlier this morning and said our reassurances. 'Can you ask Marianne to send that angel again?' I asked. 'It's already with you,' he replied. 'It's there constantly.'

My name's called. It's my time.

Not quite. Dr Hallam, the anaesthetist, tells me a case has snuck in before mine, and to wait. She explains that once she injects me, it'll be at least an hour and a half of surgery. She asks if I have a responsible adult to take me home tomorrow. Then the registrar, Dariush, comes in and talks through the procedure. I write it all down in my notebook and he's glad, because he wants me to be aware of what's about to happen and 'it can seem bewildering'. I'm told about the operation, the 'exchange of expanders and replacement of bilateral implants to improve shape and symmetry'. Then he explains the risks: 'Less than 1 per cent chance of infection, but you may get a collection of blood by the drain site, or a collection of fluid by the stitches. You may get scarring around the implant. In ten years you'll need rechecking to see if this happens. Are you thinking about nipple replacement?' I say no, not yet. He asks about work. 'I advise you to take a week or two off your job if you can, because you'll be feeling sore, a bit washed out, so just do light duties. Don't drive until the pain is gone. Don't exercise for a few weeks, although walking is OK.'

He's lovely and reassuring. They do five hundred of these breast reconstructions a year, so they know what they're doing.

Thirty minutes to go and Mr Ash Mosahebi comes into the room. He's well used to performing operations on mastectomy patients and gets out his Sharpie pen to start drawing – a dotted line down the centre of my chest, another one across it and lines underneath both breasts. He describes where he'll cut, what he'll do and how long it'll take. I ask all my questions (except the one I really want to know – if the cancer has re-emerged in there, will you see it?) and take lots of notes. I know I will feel washed out and washed up, need to take it easy. Mr Mosahebi asks when I'm back on TV. 'A week on Sunday,' I say. 'Will I be OK by then?' 'Should be,' he says. 'At least I won't have the drains in, will I?' 'No!' he laughs, picturing me striding purposefully across a studio floor, bottles bashing against the sides of my body. In two weeks, there will be nothing to see except bruising, scarring and a more even chest. When he gets up to leave, I shake his hand and say 'Good luck', just like back in January, when it was Jo wielding the knife. He smiles. Another routine operation for him, one of the hundreds he performs annually, on various bodies of all shapes and sizes, recreating something that cancer took away.

Everyone leaves. I get into the hospital gown and put my clothes in a plastic bag. I call Paul again. Damn the Kent mobile phone network, straight to answer machine.

I wonder about the woman who's in theatre before me. What's her story? Wouldn't it be interesting if we were to share experiences and show each other our markings? Chat about how we feel? Meet on the ward and compare fluids? I've only ever spoken to one other person with breast cancer who had a similar diagnosis to me and that was Sue, who makes the bras. She said you had to look at it without being afraid. I take pictures of my scribbled chest using my mobile phone, so I can remember what I lived with for almost a year, to see what difference all this makes, to view it as a curiosity, to look at the full ugliness, without fear.

A nurse comes in, full of smiles. He's from Zimbabwe and we chat about his mum, star signs, anything but the surgery. He takes my blood pressure and it's gone up, as has my heart rate. I'm nervous.

There's a knock on the door. Here we go . . .

11.30 a.m.

Woken by a nurse, groggy, mouth dry, voice hoarse. 'Have they done it?' I ask. She nods and I cry. 'Can I look?' I say, hoarsely. 'If you really want to,' she says, reaching for my hand, giving it a squeeze. I peer down. Wound dressings on top and underneath, not much to see. I'm tired but not enough to sleep. I ask her to ring Paul, who's arrived and waiting downstairs in the café, and then I'm wheeled into a ward with six beds. As the curtains are drawn, Paul appears. As soon as I see him, I weep again, silently. Once I've composed myself, I ask if he wants a look. It's better, apparently, although from my angle, it looks the same. The drains are not those huge plastic bottles I had before, but small packets. I have a saline drip and that's it. No catheter, no intravenous line pumping in drugs, no heated blanket encasing my body. Just one tube going into my hand and a great deal of soreness all over my chest. That's not a bad result, in my view. I tell him to go into work, make himself useful, that it'll be dull here. But perhaps because I cried, or because I have a dry mouth and hesitant speech, or simply because he loves me, he insists on staying. I want to sleep but when I close my eyes, I want to open them again. It's like being exhausted and hyper-vigilant at the same time.

Oww. Once the anaesthetic wears off, you can really feel where the surgeon has been. I ask for the saline drip to be taken out. Then I ring Joss and Alex and say it's gone well, everyone's pleased, sorry I sound so slurred. Joss is bringing in ear-plugs and an eye mask because the ward is bright and noisy. A machine is constantly bleeping. 'Can't they turn that off?' says Paul. 'No,' I say, 'it's probably keeping someone alive.'

Mr Mosahebi has been round. It went well, longer than expected, more like two hours because there was lots of scar tissue to work around, but he's pleased. He tells me 'not to be a martyr' and to take painkillers. Codeine at night, he suggests, although that made me nauseous and a bit bonkers last time. When he leaves, I lie in silence with Paul sitting next to me, until Joss comes in, equipped with all the bits for screening out noise and light, together with some supper. When Paul goes back to Kent to collect the little ones from school, me and my eldest son have the most magical, intense conversations about life and death, childhood memories and muddled parenthood. We hug and cry and tell each other how blessed we are to have one another. That's one of the positives of illness, it forces you to talk about the things you might never have mentioned, were it not for the disease. Everything becomes so heightened, relationships with family become so vital, that words are said that might otherwise have remained unsaid.

8 p.m.

OK, I'm in pain now. It seems to break through the gram of paracetamol every four hours. Everyone has left, the curtains are drawn and I have no energy to speak. Banging headache, exhausted and aching. The lights are on, there are people chatting loudly in the next bed, this is set to be a long night . . .

Tuesday, 3rd November

6.15 a.m.

. . . and it was. The woman in the bed across the way has a hacking cough and keeps shouting 'Oh! Ah! It hurts!' Sounds dreadful. Now the overnight nurse is trying to persuade an elderly man who wants to discharge himself, because he hasn't slept and he's 'frozen', to return to his bed. She comes to take my blood pressure: 85/57, that's low, even for me. Seth will be awake now, getting ready for school. Evie will be asking Paul to plait her hair. I'm draining 50 ml of blood on the right, 30 ml on the left. I've been told I can't have a shower because I won't be able to move my arms and, anyway, it'll soak the dressings.

That poor lady across the ward is doing so much huffing and moaning, I'm surprised she has any voice left. She's talking to her family on the phone a lot and tells them, loudly, 'I'm in agony here.' There's a woman opposite me with a wound infection and we strike up a conversation about our various operations. Another woman in the next bed, much younger than any of us, sleeps all the time. What a curious lot we are.

The moaning, noisy, coughing woman has just ordered meat and potato pie, with mash, gravy and pudding, so she must be feeling better.

We're all trying to be normal, to engage and connect. My surgeon and his registrar are both from Iran and I tell them my husband was declared a 'living martyr' in their country by the 'Tehran Times' after he was mustard-gassed while on assignment covering the first Iran–Iraq war as a journalist. Both their fathers were doctors, called back to Iran to be conscripted for that very same war. They are kind and gentle, these extraordinary men with fascinating pasts, who speak to me about creating 3-D nipples and make me laugh with the incongruity of it all. What would the NHS do without its expertise from abroad? My nurse yesterday was from Zimbabwe, another from the Philippines, my anaesthetist was from Syria, the overnight ward sister from Greece. Just like the first operation, it's the United Nations of healthcare striving to keep us all alive.

Life can throw up such absurdities in serious moments. When the surgical staff have gone, I look at my mobile phone to send messages to family and see an email marked 'urgent'. I'm being asked to sign a contract, help draft a press release and approve a photo, for a job I'm starting in the New Year. Here, now, from my hospital bed. I start writing as the machines bleep and the patients moan, barely able to type and probably not making much sense. I understand the haste to make an announcement. It's taken ages for me to make up my mind and I only said yes to the offer of a new role, recently. I read the email to see how they'd like to announce it. 'Channel 5 today announces Sian Williams as the new face of its flagship evening news programme,' it begins, before going on to use lots of words like 'warmth', 'experience', 'authority', 'hugely respected' and 'charisma'. Not sure I've got much of any of that at the moment. If they could see me now . . .

Why have I been dithering so long about the move? I've been with one employer for thirty years and I don't like change, but perhaps all this has taught me that sometimes, upheaval provides opportunities. ITN runs Channel 5 news and they're relaunching the show, with the broadcaster's new US owners putting some heavy backing behind it. It appeals to the ex-producer in me to be part of a new team with fresh ideas, messing about with running orders. I trust the people behind it, too. The editor is an experienced hand and her boss is someone I've worked with, who told me as she left the BBC that she wanted me to join her sometime. Also, they know what's happened to me. They know because I told them they should really go and find someone else as I had breast cancer and was going in for an operation. They said they wanted to wait. This is a news organization like any other, with deadlines and gossipy journalists, who kept the fact that I have cancer secret and who hung on, without any pressure, in case I felt ready to join them. That shows integrity. I still haven't signed on the dotted line and we've done endless toing and froing, but they've been reassuring about continuing my BBC work, if I want to (although at nearly fifty-one, perhaps it's time to cut the umbilical cord). I've dithered and worried and now I think, sod it. Besides, I fancy a new start for the New Year. If I'm someone different, maybe I can be somewhere different, too. I'm not in a position to do any interviews about the move and I'm not strong enough to look at how people react to it either. I can't tell everyone the myriad reasons for doing this, they're too complex, too personal, would reveal too much about what has gone on this year. Let people say what they say, think what they think. Even if it doesn't work out, how big a deal will that be if it's right for me and our family? It's not cancer. It's not life-threatening. It's a job. With change comes risk, and that's all part of it, all part of the churn and the uncertainty that I need to learn to live with now. Work is a very, very small part of that. It's the unease around cancer that's tough to manage, not this.

I write a few sentences to keep everyone happy, then pack up my hospital things and get ready to go home. I feel weaker yet stronger, tired yet determined, ready to focus on a different future. Before I go, the nurse whips out both my drains with a flourish. 'There,' she says, 'not as bad as you thought, was it?' I smile with relief and explain that I'd imagined this to be far worse, that I'd been caught up in the trips and triggers of the previous experience and this was definitely not like that. 'No,' she replies, 'this is the end of that chapter and the start of a new one.'

Wednesday, 4th November

I'm now at home, putting Evie's hair in plaits and listening to Seth's jokes. Today, after they were taken to school, I walked up the hill to the village to pick up something from the pharmacy for a neighbour and post a present for a godchild. I pop into the doctor's surgery to make an appointment and the nurse asks to see me. She knows what's happened even though we've never met, because she has all my notes. She checks the dressings. 'How did you get here if you can't drive?' she asks. 'I walked,' I say. She shakes her head. 'Too soon. How are you feeling now?' I'm honest with her and say, exhausted, actually. I think back to those early wintry days, when I struggled to get through the field to the reservoir, moving painfully slowly, only to arrive, full of pride and achievement, tears in my eyes, before worrying how on earth I'd ever get home. Gradually, I got my fitness back, incrementally, I was returning to 'normal'. Here I am again, many months later, shuffling, hurting, winded. Yet it's not the same as before because everything's changed. The way I see life, my relationships, my work. The way I see me.

*

After any sort of trauma, there's this constant struggle with the complexity of emotion and the reminders of the original pain. The ups and downs, the positive and negative, the moving ahead and the falling back, the hard-fought growth. Trying, stumbling, getting up again, living with the uncertainty, living with the questions. Sometimes it's just like being back in the snowy field when your boots are leaking and you've only gone a few hundred yards and you don't think you can move much further without breaking down. If you sit to have a rest and a howl, you think you'll never stand, let alone move forward.

But look around. We're all in the field together. Grab a hand and let it pull you up. You may not feel you can do much now, but I promise, if you have the will to survive and the understanding of what works to help you grow, you will thrive. There will be things that will get in your way – a hidden pothole, an unseen snowdrift, a sudden storm – but you will adapt to these. You may stop to reflect on the best way forward, chat to others who've been there before, reach in your backpack for some nourishment to give you energy for the rest of the journey, whatever gets you up again, walking, moving, take it.

When you think you've come to the end of the field and look back, your path won't be a straight one. It'll double-back on itself a few times, take some wrong turns and be slow and winding. But it's your path. And as you mount the stile at the end, you'll go into a new field and guess what? Those snowdrifts and potholes and storms may happen again. But this time, you'll know what works to help get you through them.

Walk, think, talk, eat, rest, love, laugh. Rise. We're all doing it together.

NOTES

CHAPTER 3

1. NHS Choices: PTSD (2013). Retrieved from http://www.nhs.uk/conditions/Post-traumatic-stress-disorder/Pages/Introduction.aspx.
2. M. E. P. Seligman, *Flourish* (New York, Simon & Schuster, 2011), p.159.
3. A. Lieberman, *Shrinks: The Untold Story of Psychiatry* (New York, Little, Brown, 2015).
4. M. Gilbert, *The First World War: A Complete History* (New York, Henry Holt, 1994).
5. W. Sheehan, R. J. Roberts, S. Thurber & M. A. Roberts, 'Shell-shocked and confused: a reconsideration of Captain Charles Myers' case reports of shell-shock in World War One', *Priory Psychiatry Journal Online*, Vol. 2 (2009).
6. E. Jones & S. Wessely, 'Psychiatric battle casualties: an intra- and interwar comparison', *British Journal of Psychiatry* 178 (3), (March 2001), pp.242–7.
7. M. E. P. Seligman, *Flourish*, p.127.
8. M. E. P. Seligman, T. A. Steen, N. Park & C. Peterson, 'Positive psychology progress: empirical validation of interventions', *American Psychologist*, Vol. 60 (2005), pp.410–21.
9. R. A. Emmons & M. E. McCullough, 'Counting blessings versus burdens: an experimental investigation of gratitude and subjective well-being in daily life', *Journal of Personality and Social Psychology*, 84(2), (2003), pp.377–89.
10. M. M. Steenkamp, W. P. Nash & B. T. Litz, 'Post-traumatic stress

disorder: review of the Comprehensive Soldier Fitness Program', *American Journal of Preventive Medicine*, Vol. 44 (2013), pp.507–12.

11. R. Layard & D. M. Clark, *Thrive: The Power of Evidence-Based Psychological Therapies* (London, Allen Lane, 2014).
12. R. G. Tedeschi, C. L. Park & L. G. Calhoun (Eds), *Posttraumatic Growth: Positive changes in the aftermath of crisis* (London, Routledge, 1998).
13. G. A. Bonanno, C. Rennicke & S. Dekel, 'Self-enhancement among high-exposure survivors of the September 11th terrorist attack: Resilience or social maladjustment?' *Journal of Personality and Social Psychology*, Vol. 88 (2005), pp. 984–98.
14. http://www.independent.co.uk/news/world/africa/sousse-beach-massacre-are-we-getting-trauma-treatment-for-victims-right-10451763.html.
15. S. Joseph, *What Doesn't Kill Us: A guide to overcoming adversity and moving forward* (London, Little, Brown, 2011).

CHAPTER 5

1. National Institute for Health and Care Excellence, 'Familial breast cancer costing report (based on the original recommendations)' (June 2013), http://guidance.nice.org.uk/CG164.

CHAPTER 7

1. P. Conrad & J. W. Schneider, *Deviance and Medicalization: From Badness to Sickness* (New York, C. V. Mosby, 1980).
2. D. Hofstadter, 'Changes in default words and images' in *Metamagical Themas: Questing for the essence of mind and pattern* (New York, Bantam Books,1986), pp.136–58.
3. S. T. Fiske & S. E. Taylor, *Social Cognition* (2nd edition), (New York, McGraw Hill, 1991).
4. M. Foucault, *Madness and Civilization: A history of insanity in the age of reason* (New York, Random House, 1965).
5. N. Robinson, *Election Notebook: The Inside Story of the Battle Over Britain's Future and My Personal Battle to Report It* (Bantam Press, 2015).

6. Girls' Attitude Survey, 2014, Girlguiding, http://new.girlguiding.org.uk/girls-attitudes-survey-2014.

CHAPTER 8

1. 'Smile' (Chaplin/Turner/Parsons), Bourne Music Ltd.

CHAPTER 9

1. N. Greenberg, 'TRiM, Trauma Risk Management: An organizational approach to personnel management in the wake of traumatic events', (2009), www.marchonstress.com.

CHAPTER 10

1. S. Nayak, B. L. Wheeler, S. C. Shiflett & S. Agostinelli, 'Effect of music therapy on mood and social interaction among individuals with acute traumatic brain injury and stroke', *Rehabilitation Psychology*, Vol. 45(3), (2000), pp.274–83.

CHAPTER 11

1. H. Soo & K. A. Sherman, 'Rumination, psychological distress and post-traumatic growth in women diagnosed with breast cancer', *Psycho-Oncology* 24(1), (2015), pp.70–79.
2. R. G. Tedeschi & L. G. Calhoun, 'Expert companions: Posttraumatic growth in clinical practice' in L. G. Calhoun & R. G. Tedeschi (eds), *Handbook of Posttraumatic Growth: Research and practice* (Mahwah, NJ, Lawrence Erlbaum, 2006), pp.291–310.
3. C. S. Carver, R. G. Smith, M. H. Antoni, V. M. Petronis, S. Weiss & R. P. Derhagopian, 'Optimistic personality and psychosocial well-being during treatment predict psychosocial well-being among long-term survivors of breast cancer', *Health Psychology* 24 (2005), pp.508–16.

4. K. J. Petrie & A. Corter, 'Illness perceptions and benefit finding among individuals with breast cancer, acoustic neuroma, or heart disease' in C. L. Park, S. C. Lechner, M. H. Antoni & A. L. Stanton (eds), *Medical Illness and Positive Life Change* (Washington, APA Publishers, 2009).
5. N. Bolger, M. Foster, A. D. Vinokur & R. Ng, 'Close relationships and adjustment to a life crisis: The case of breast cancer', *Journal of Personality and Social Psychology*, Vol. 70 (1996) pp.283–94.
6. http://www.nytimes.com/2015/02/19/opinion/oliver-sacks-on-learning-he-has-terminal-cancer.html.
7. S. E. Taylor & J. Brown, 'Illusion and well-being: A social psychological perspective on mental health', *Psychological Bulletin*, Vol. 103 (1998), pp.193–210.
8. G. A. Bonanno, 'Clarifying and extending the construct of adult resilience', *American Psychologist*, 60 (2005), pp.265–7.
9. K. Hefferon & I. Boniwell, *Positive Psychology; Theory, Research and Applications* (New York, McGraw Hill, 2011), p.122–3.
10. A. Stanton, J. E. Bower & C. A. Low, 'Post-traumatic growth after cancer' in L. G. Calhoun & R. G. Tedeschi (eds), *Handbook of post-traumatic growth: Research and Practice*, pp.138–75.
11. C. S. Carver, S. C. Lechner & M. H. Antoni, 'Challenges in studying positive change after adversity' in C. L. Park, S. Lechner, A. Stanton & M. Antoni (eds), *Medical Illness and Positive Life Change*, pp.51–62.
12. Royal Marsden NHS Foundation Trust, 'A Beginner's Guide to BRCA1 and BRCA2' (2013).

CHAPTER 12

1. R. S. Lazarus & S. Folkman, *Stress, Appraisal and Coping* (New York, Springer, 1984).
2. R. S. Lazarus, *Stress and Emotion: A new synthesis* (London, Free Association Books, 1999), p.265.
3. World Health Organization, ICD–10, code number F43.1 (1992), p.147.
4. F. Lanius, S. L. Paulsen & F. M. Corrigan, *Neurobiology and Treatment of Traumatic Dissociation: Towards an Embodied Self* (New York, Springer, 2014).

NOTES

CHAPTER 13

1. R. Layard, *Happiness: Lessons from a New Science* (London, Allen Lane, 2005).
2. M. E. P. Seligman, *Flourish*, p.10.
3. M. E. P. Seligman, *Flourish*, p.26
4. W. James, *On Vital Reserves: The Energies of Men; The Gospel of Relaxation* (New York, Henry Holt and Co., 1911).
5. B. K. Hölzel, J. Carmody, M. Vangel, C. Congleton, S. M. Yerramsetti, T. Gard & S. W. Lazar, 'Mindfulness practice leads to increases in regional brain gray matter density', *Psychiatry Research: Neuroimaging*, 191(1), (2011), pp.36–43.

CHAPTER 14

1. V. E. Frankl, *Man's Search for Meaning: An introduction to logotherapy* (New York, Simon & Schuster, 1984).
2. S. J. Wolin & S. Wolin, *The Resilient Self: How survivors of troubled families rise above adversity* (New York, Villard, 1993).
3. https://www.guernicamag.com/interviews/updike_11_15_10/
4. M. Proust, *Letters to His Mother* (New York, Greenwood, 1971).
5. H. P. Blum, 'The Creative Transformation of Trauma: Marcel Proust's In Search of Lost Time', *Psychoanalytic Review*, 99(5), (2012), pp.677–96.
6. J. Updike, 'From the Journal of a Leper', *New Yorker*, 19 October 1976.
7. F. Kafka & F. Bauer, *Letters to Felice*, 1st English edn (New York, Schocken Books, 1973), pp.544–5.
8. M. de Montaigne, 'Of Experience' in M. de Montaigne, *The Complete Works* (New York, Knopf, 1973) pp.992–1045.
9. G. Wasserstein, 'Lessons in Medical Humanism: The Case of Montaigne', *Annals of Internal Medicine*, 146 (2007), pp.809–13.
10. J. P. Riddle, H. E. Smith & C. J. Jones, 'Does written emotional disclosure improve the psychological and physical health of caregivers? A systematic review and meta-analysis' in *British Psychology Society's Division of Health Psychology Annual Conference 2015.*

11. J. W. Pennebaker & J. D. Seagal, 'Forming a story: the health benefits of narrative', *Journal of Clinical Psychology*, 55 (10), (1999), pp.1243–54.
12. D. M. Sloan & B. P. Marx, 'A closer examination of the structured written disclosure procedure', *Journal of Consulting and Clinical Psychology*, 2004a:72, pp.165–75.
13. S. Terkel, *Working* (New York, Avon, 1972) in Holstein & Gubrium, *The New Language of Qualitative Method* (New York, Oxford University Press, 1997).
14. R. Layard & D. Clark, *Thrive*, p.8.
15. F. Shapiro, 'The Role of Eye Movement Desensitization and Reprocessing (EMDR) Therapy in Medicine: Addressing the Psychological and Physical Symptoms Stemming from Adverse Life Experiences', *Permanente Journal*, 18(1), (2014), pp.71–7.
16. R. Layard & D. Clark, *Thrive*, p.251.
17. Health and Social Care Information Centre, Office for National Statistics, 'Prescriptions Dispensed in the Community, Statistics for England – 2004–2014' (July 2015).
18. B. McGuinness (ed), *Wittgenstein in Cambridge: Letters and Documents 1911–1951* (London, Blackwell, 2014), p.320.

CHAPTER 15

1. Y. Harrison, J. A. Horne & A. Rothwell, 'Prefrontal neuropsychological effects of sleep deprivation in young adults: A model for healthy aging?' *Sleep*, 23 (2000), pp.1067–71.
2. M. J. Sateia, K. Doghramji, P. J. Hauri & C. M. Morin, 'Evaluation of chronic insomnia', *Sleep*, 23 (2000), pp.243–308.
3. D. F. Kripke, L. Garfinkel, D. L. Wingard, M. R. Klauber & M. R. Marler, 'Mortality associated with sleep duration and insomnia', *Archives of General Psychiatry*, 59(2), (2002), pp.131–6.
4. APA, revised *DSM-IV* (1994), 4th edition.
5. G. De Palma, P. Blennerhassett, J. Lu, Y. Deng, A. J. Park, W. Green, E. Denou, M. A. Silva, A. Santacruz, Y. Sanz, M. G. Surette, E. F. Verdu, S. M. Collins & P. Bercik, 'Microbiota and host determinants of behavioural phenotype in maternally separated mice', *Nature Communications*, 6: 6. Article No. 7735.

6. K. Schmidt, P. J. Cowen, C. J. Harmer, G. Tzortzis, S. Errington & P. W. J. Burnet, 'Prebiotic intake reduces the waking cortisol response and alters emotional bias in healthy volunteers', *Psychopharmacology* (2014), DOI: 10.1007/s00213-014-3810-0.
7. G. A. Eby & K. L. Eby, 'Rapid recovery from major depression using magnesium treatment'. *Medical Hypothesis* 67(2) (2006), pp.362–70.

CHAPTER 16

1. S. N. Young, 'How to increase serotonin in the human brain without drugs', *Journal of Psychiatry & Neuroscience*, 32(6), (2007), pp.394–9.
2. R. S. Duman, 'Pathophysiology of depression: the concept of synaptic plasticity', *European Psychiatry*, 17 Suppl 3 (2002), pp.306–10.
3. E. W. Griffin, S. Mullaly, C. Foley, S. A. Warmington, S. M. O'Mara & A. M. Kelly, 'Aerobic exercise improves hippocampal function and increases BDNF in the serum of young adult males.' *Physiology and Behaviour*, 104(5), (24 October 2011), pp.934–41.
4. http://well.blogs.nytimes.com/2011/11/30/how-exercise-benefits-the-brain/.
5. J. C. Lauterborn, E. Pineda, L. Y. Chen, E. A. Ramirez, G. Lynch & C. M. Gall. 'Ampakines cause sustained increases in brain-derived neurotrphic factor signaling at excitatory synapses without changes in AMPA receptor subunit expression', *Neuroscience*, 159(1) (2009): pp.283–95.
6. http://news.sciencemag.org/biology/2013/10/how-exercise-beefs-brain.
7. M. Richards, R. Hardy & M. E. J. Wadsworth, 'Does active leisure protect cognition? Evidence from a national birth cohort', *Social Science & Medicine*, 56 (4), (2003), pp.785–92.
8. K. C. Heesch, Y. R. Van Gellecum, N. W. Burton, J. G. Van Uffelen & W. J. Brown, 'Physical Activity, Walking, and Quality of Life in Women with Depressive Symptoms', *American Journal of Preventive Medicine*, 48(3), (2015), pp.281–9.
9. NICE guidelines 2009, 1.4.4.

RESOURCES

Macmillan Cancer Support
Professionals, volunteers and campaigners, supporting those with cancer with practical help, information and more.
http://www.macmillan.org.uk

Breast Cancer Care
A UK-wide charity providing care, information and support to people affected by breast cancer.
www.breastcancercare.org.uk

Breast Cancer Now
The UK's largest breast cancer charity, created by the merger of Breast Cancer Campaign and Breakthrough Breast Cancer.
www.breastcancernow.org

Coppafeel!
A breast cancer charity creating awareness of the disease in young people.
www.coppafeel.org

Mind
Providing advice and support for anyone going through a mental health problem. Campaigning to raise awareness and improve services.
www.mind.org.uk

RESOURCES

Time to Change
A Mind and Rethink Mental Illness campaign to reduce stigma and discrimination in mental health.
www.time-to-change.org.uk

Samaritans
A confidential, volunteer-run service allowing anyone going through tough times to talk to someone.
www.samaritans.org

Combat Stress
Treating veterans suffering from PTSD, depression and anxiety.
www.combatstress.org.uk

March On Stress
Providing courses for TRIM (Trauma Risk Management) and PTSD prevention.
www.marchonstress.com

NHS Choices
Comprehensive health information with resources, information and research.
www.nhs.uk

Action for Happiness
A movement for positive change, which tries to create a happier, more caring society.
www.actionforhappiness.org

Dart Center for Journalism and Trauma
A global network of journalists, educators and health professionals improving media coverage of trauma, conflict and tragedy.
www.dartcenter.org

RESOURCES

USEFUL AND INSPIRING BOOKS:

Arden, J. B. *Rewire Your Brain: Think Your Way to a Better Life* (2010)

Hamilton, C. *How to Deal with Adversity (School of Life)* (2014)

Joseph, S. *What Doesn't Kill Us: The New Psychology of Posttraumatic Growth* (2012)

Layard, R. and Clark, D. M. *Thrive, the Power of Psychological Therapy* (2015)

Seligman, M. E. P. *Flourish: A New Understanding of Happiness and Well-Being – and How To Achieve Them* (2011)

Servan-Schreiber, D. *Healing Without Freud or Prozac* (2012)

Siegel, D. J. *Mindsight: The New Science of Personal Transformation* (2010)

Webb, L. *Resilience: How to cope when everything around you keeps changing* (2013)

EXPLORING THE SUBJECT AND THE SCIENCE FURTHER:

Calhoun, L. G. & Tedeschi, R. G. *Facilitating posttraumatic growth: A clinician's guide* (1999)

Calhoun, L. G. & Tedeschi, R. G. *Posttraumatic growth in clinical practice* (2013)

Clegg, B. *The Universe Inside You: The Extreme Science of the Human Body* (2013)

Hefferon, K. & Boniwell, I. *Positive Psychology. Theory, Research and Applications* (2011)

Janoff-Bulman, R. *Shattered assumptions: Towards a new psychology of trauma* (1992)

Jarrett, C. *Great Myths of the Brain (Great Myths of Psychology)* (2014)

Lazarus, R.S. & Folkman, S. *Stress, Appraisal and Coping* (1984).

Swaab, D. *We Are Our Brains: From the Womb to Alzheimer's* (2015)

Tedeschi, R. G. & Calhoun, L. G. *Trauma and transformation: Growing in the aftermath of suffering (1995)*

ACKNOWLEDGEMENTS

Thank you to the amazing medical teams at University College Hospital, The Royal Free Hospital and the Royal Marsden Hospital for reminding me of just how brilliant, caring and efficient NHS staff are, despite working under tremendous pressures. A personal thanks to Shirley Day, Joanna Franks, Rob Carpenter, Dr Glen Blackman, Dr Gill Ross and Ash Mosahebi, for their expertise, their candour and their compassion. Thanks too, to Dr Mary Burgess, Dr Sarah Heke and Dr Andrew Sikorsky, for helping me see the journey differently.

Thank you to the academics, researchers and scientists who gave me their wisdom or checked my words. Professor Neil Greenberg, Professor Stephen Joseph, Dr Catherine Loveday, Dr Alan Gow, Dr Angela Clow, Dr Hannah Critchlow, Dr Annette Bruhl, Professor Barbara Sahakian, Stephanie Ridley and Dr Chloe Paidoussis-Mitchell.

Heartfelt thanks to those who shared their remarkable stories with me in the knowledge that it would help others: Stuart Hughes, Patrick Howse, Julie Nicholson, Baroness Floella Benjamin, Trude, Scilla White, Dr Catherine Loveday, Andy Puddicombe and Sue Pringle.

I could not have got through this year without all the outstretched hands that helped me up. Thank you to my incredible friends, Lizzy,

Brett, Dixi, Jude, Zoë, Sam, Sophie, Jane and Alice. You put up with me at my lowest, making me laugh and keeping me sane. To Alison, your approach to cancer influenced mine – we all miss you. I'm blessed with brilliant neighbours, so thank you Sarah, Caroline, Josie and Sue for your flowers, fish pie and friendship. Thanks too, to my agent Sue Ayton and everyone at Knight Ayton for carefully managing and navigating a very difficult time and for never pushing me before I was ready. To Alan Samson and Lucinda McNeile at Orion for their passionate belief in this book from the very beginning, for convincing me I could write it, and for their expert advice and guidance throughout. And to Annabel Merullo, my literary agent, who first inspired me to put pen to paper and who saw the potential to help others through my story.

Thank you to my family. To my father John who read the manuscript as a journalist, even though it hurt to read as a dad. To my mum, who thankfully never knew that the disease which killed her sister would hit her daughter too. But whose compassion and courage, both in life and while facing death, gave me the strength to deal with it all without her. To my brothers, Dave and Pete, and their wives Louisa and Katy for their understanding, love and support. To Paul's family; Michaele, Jeremy and Cherine for their acceptance and encouragement, to Marianne, who sent me an angel, and to Martin – wise, funny and insightful, whose own experience of cancer gave me hope and made me look at mine, anew. I am also grateful to my ex-husband and lifelong friend, Neale.

To my incredible children, Joss and Alex, who hugged and loved and nurtured me when I became the frightened child. To Emily, my step-daughter, for her endless warmth and concern. And to Seth and Evie for constantly reminding me that there was a wonderful life still to be had, with or without cancer. I am immensely proud of you all.

And finally, to Paul. For your unconditional love, even when I was not my best self. For your patience and your courage. And for being the man who stands next to me, fearless and protective, ready to face whatever our next future holds. You are extraordinary.

Sian Williams,
Kent,
March 2016.

INDEX

INDEX

INDEX

INDEX

INDEX

INDEX

INDEX

INDEX